EXPERT SYSTEMS IN PRODUCTION AND SERVICES II

From Assessment to Action?

International Workshop on
Expert Systems in Production and Services
Chicago, USA, September 13–15, 1988

organized by The Green Meadow Foundation (GMF)/
Gottlieb Duttweiler Institute (GDI)

in collaboration with
the International Labour Office (ILO)
Arthur Andersen and Co.
and
The Office of Technology Assessment of the US Congress (OTA)

EXPERT SYSTEMS IN PRODUCTION AND SERVICES II

From Assessment to Action?

Proceedings of the International Workshop on
Expert Systems in Production and Services
Chicago, USA, September 13–15, 1988

edited by

Thomas BERNOLD
Coordinator Technology Transfer
Istituto Dalle Molle di Studi Sull'Intelligenza Artificiale
Lugano, Switzerland

Ulrich HILLENKAMP
Head Expert Systems Project
International Labour Office
Geneva, Switzerland

ELSEVIER

Amsterdam – Oxford – New York – Tokyo 1989

ELSEVIER SCIENCE PUBLISHERS B.V.
Sara Burgerhartstraat 25
P.O. Box 211, 1000 AE Amsterdam, The Netherlands

Distributors for the U.S.A. and Canada:

ELSEVIER SCIENCE PUBLISHING COMPANY, INC.
655 Avenue of the Americas
New York, N.Y. 10010, U.S.A.

ISBN: 0 444 88471 8

Printed in The Netherlands

Preface

George Kanawaty
Director, Training Department
International Labour Office
Geneva, Switzerland

The use of expert systems and artificial intelligence is spreading at an exponential rate in many areas of economic activity but particularly so in manufacturing and services. New skills will be needed by both blue and white collar workers to enable them to use this rapidly evolving technology intelligently and develop further the scope of its application. An early start in identifying the implications expert systems can have on present and future qualification requirements can be a valuable tool for educators and trainers.

With this in mind, the Federal Ministry of Education and Science of the Federal Republic of Germany took the initiative of launching and financing a three-year research project on the impact of expert systems in manufacturing and services, on job qualifications and working life. The International Labour Office has been entrusted with executing this project within its series of major studies devoted to advanced technology and human resources issues in industrialised countries. The research is restricted to the five countries: Federal Republic of Germany, France, Japan, United Kingdom, and the United States of America. Preliminary findings point out to the fact that despite earlier forecasts, the introduction of expert systems in manufacturing and services has not yet reached the scale which would result in verifiable and significant across the board changes in employment patterns, job qualifications and conditions of work, all the more so since the introduction of expert systems in many enterprises has been fairly recent. Thus speculation has replaced hard facts in many instances when projections are being made.

Apart from desk studies, interviews and field visits, the research encompasses the organisation of international roundtables among high-level specialists and users of expert systems with a view to exchanging information and views on developments for such a rapidly changing technology. The first roundtable took place in Rüschlikon/Zürich in November 1987 and its proceedings were published by North Holland (Bernold/Hillenkamp), 1988, Expert Systems in Production and Services – Impact on Qualifications and Working Life, Elsevier Science Publishers). The present publication sets in perspective the proceedings of the second roundtable which was held 13 - 15 September 1988 in Chicago, Illinois, USA, as a joint undertaking of the Gottlieb Duttweiler Institute, Arthur Andersen and Co., the Office of Technology Assessment of the US Congress and the International Labour Office. Participating in this roundtable were practitioners, researchers, managers, consultants, concerned staff from private enterprises, representatives of government, trade unions and international organisations. The result has been a stimulating, fruitful and wide-ranging discussion of the trends, issues and implications of expert system introduction and the workplace, which should be of interest to many readers.

Geneva, January 1989

Acknowledgement

The papers are the result of the 2nd international Workshop, held 13 - 15 September 1988 in Chicago, Illinois, USA, jointly organised by the Gottlieb Duttweiler Institute, Zürich, Arthur Andersen and Co., Chicago, the Office of Technology Assessment of the US Congress, Washington DC and the International Labour Office, Geneva. The organizers thank particularly Carla Paonessa and her staff of Arthur Andersen and Co. who provided an excellent working environment over the three days. The Workshop was part of a three-year ILO project on the impact of expert systems on qualifications and working life, initiated and financed by the Federal Ministry of Education and Science, Bonn, Federal Republic of Germany.

Authors

Bernold Thomas, CH
Dr., Coordinator Technology Transfer,
Istituto Dalle Molle di Studi Sull'Intelligenza Artficiale
CH-6900, Lugano

Buckingham Joanna, UK
Center for Business Research
Brighton Polytechnic, Brighton

Chamot Dennis, USA
Dr., Associate Director, Department for Prof. Employees, AFL/CIO,
Washington DC, 20036

Daniel Manfred, FRG
IBEK, Postfach 3405
D-7500 Karlsruhe 1

Dateki Sei, J
National Institute of Employment and Vocational Research
Tokyo

Drinkuth Andreas, FRG
Dr., IG-Metall, PF 11 10 31
D-6000 Frankfurt am Main

Ebel Karl, CH
Dr., ILO, Manufacturing Industries Branch
CH-1211 Geneva 22

Fujihara Kinuko, J
National Institute of Employment and Vocational Research
Tokyo

Herron Orly, USA
Dr., President, National College of Education
Evanston, Illinois 60201/USA

Hillenkamp Ulrich, CH
Dr., ILO, Head of Expert Systems Project, Training Department
CH-1211 Geneva 22

Hilton, Courtland M.,USA
Dr. INTEL Corporation
Chandler, Arizona 85226

Hirai Yoshimitsu, J
Artificial Intelligence Promotion Center
Minato-Ku, Tokio 105

Hirashi Junko, J
National Institute of Employment and Vocational Research
Tokyo

Igogeit Albrecht, FRG
Volkswagen AG, Postfach
D-3180 Wolfsburg 1

Karatsu Hajime, J
Professor, R&D Institute
Tokai University, Tokyo

Kempf Karl, USA
Dr., Intel Corporation
Components Technology and Manufacturing Group
Knowledge Applications Laboratory
Chandler, Arizona 85226

Kishi Norimasa, J
Dr., Research Engineer, Electronics Research Laboratory,
Central Engineering Laboratories, NISSAN MOTOR CO., LTD
Yokosuka 237

Koster Henk, F
Dr., Councellor, OECD
F-75016 Paris

Molldaschl, Manfred FRG
Dr., Institut für sozialwissenschaftliche Forschung München
D-8000 München 40

Mulvey David, UK
Logica UK Limited
London W1A 4SE

Oakley Brian, UK
Chairman, Logica Cambridge Limited
London W1A 4SE

Schefe Peter, FRG
Prof., Dr., Fachbereich Informatik, Universität Hamburg
D-2000 Hamburg 13

Scheifele Manfred, FRG
Department «Computer Aided Engineering Systems»
Fraunhofer-Institut für Arbeitswissenschaft und Organisation
D-7000 Stuttgart 80

Senker Peter, UK
Science Policy Research Unit, University of Sussex
Brighton, Sussex BN1 9RF

Skingle Barry, UK
Logica UK Limited
London W1A 4SE, U.K.

Stafford Sue, USA
Dr., Manager Coopers & Lybrand
Boston Mass. 02110

Townsend Joe, UK
Science Policy Research Unit
University of Sussex

John B. Wallace, CH
ILO, Management Development Branch
Geneva

Wiig Karl, USA
The Wiig Group
Arlington, Texas, USA

Table of Contents

Summing Up

Introduction

EXPERT SYSTEMS IN PRODUCTION AND SERVICES II
Th. Bernold and U. Hillenkamp (Editors)
Elsevier Science Publishers B.V., Amsterdam – Printed in The Netherlands

Expert Systems in Production and Services – From Assessment to Action?

Thomas Bernold
Istituto Dalle Molle di Studi sull'Intelligenza Artificiale
Lugano, Switzerland

Ulrich Hillenkamp
International Labour Office
Geneva, Switzerland

Knowledge, expertise and know-how become increasingly recognized as strategic factors in securing long-term competitiveness of commercial companies. As products and services grow rapidly more sophisticated and complex, aids to improve problem-solving and decision making gain importance. Obviously traditional data processing techniques with their highly structured, algorithmic approach will not suffice. They reach about 10% of the total information processing of a firm. An additional 20% are covered by what is loosely called office automation. This leaves 70% to traditional methods of pencil and paper, memos, established procedures and experience of personnel (Brott, 1989). Expert systems, a product of applied research of Artificial Intelligence, offer a new opportunity to approach this area of the working world.

Expert systems (ES) represent a first generation of computer techniques which aim to encode and mediate factual and heuristic knowledge within well defined domains. The commercial applications are developed with the intention to support decision making by delivering expert reasoning to the individual user or to preserve expertise beyond the employment period of a specialist. The tasks which have to be supported are characteristically ill defined and have usually multiple solutions. People answer them by referring to previous experience or intuition. «Knowledge based systems for knowledge workers in a knowledge oriented industry» summarizes content and context as seen from the perspective of AI specialists.

A brief excursion into the technology shows clearly that in the past ten years of business applications, these systems are still far from maturity. There is even disagreement about the basic methodology. Nevertheless most of the Fortune 500 companies recognize the strategic potential and employ at least small groups to explore the technology. Potential applications range from medicine to manufacturing. Particularly in the services sector where rationalization is still low, the introduction could revolutionize the industry by opening new areas to automation (Fellman, Bernold, 1986). But even if fully operational systems are yet beyond the horizon of business requirements or just not realizable, the combination of man and machine might fulfil today's expectations for the mere fact that man makes up for the deficiencies of the specific technology.

This should not reduce the issue of the potential of these advanced systems to a mere question of perception regarding the (imagined) characteristics of a new technology. A review of the press of the early 80's indicates both fears and unjustified enthusiasm of the potential of AI. The actual development of technology and applications show to the expert rather quickly that the initial promises could not be met at the expected schedule. It took, however, almost half a decade till more realistic expectations took hold even that early on simple prototypes proved to be of help. But were they really AI?

The conflict between a pragmatic approach and the ideal of a machine that can do everything indicates a much deeper antagonism about the fundamental relation between man and machine. There is no doubt that a majority of companies base their decision to introduce new technologies on the expectation of gaining higher productivity and efficiency by a mere reduction of the workforce. It has yet to be proved that such a solution is the road to long-term success. There is evidence that competition will enforce higher quality of products and particularly services (Quality Management in Insurance, 1989). In this context creativity and innovation are decisive factors to increase the potential of the employee. Such a development, however, calls for a more symbiotic approach of the supporting information and communication technologies.

Considering the present state of technology and application the discussion about the commercial use of expert systems and particularly their impact might seem premature. Recent history, however, proves again and again that the rate of technological developments soon exceed the rate of change of social and public institutions. If this gap grows too large the social and later even the economic benefit of a new technology might become jeopardized. Besides early information about its characteristics, education and training play a key role in the successful adaptation of a technology. The assessment of potential changes of work and corresponding qualifications are the basis to develop new curricula or to renew traditional vocational training.

Technology is but one factor causing the fundamental change professional training is presently undergoing. In the past, company training programs were principally based on the adaptation of an individual employee's abilities to the demands of a specific job. In an era of slow change this approach was appropriate and met the needs of most companies. For the future – and even for today – internationalization of the markets, office automation, the introduction of a whole spectrum of new communication intensive services and products are changing both industrial and service corporations beyond recognition. Company training, also in the context of this new business environment, must be reassessed.

Many companies have already begun to adapt. In the first wave, technology supported teaching aids supported traditional learning models. What was essentially a quantitative change didn't achieve the high expectations of the time. Today, we realize that a qualitative change of the structure, methodology and supporting technology is necessary. Thus the technology we were talking about is not only cause but also means of the forthcoming education environment.

In context of assessing some of these factors of change in the workers' daily world, the Federal Ministry of Education and Science of the Federal Republic of Germany offered the International Labour Office (ILO) in Geneva to set up a three-year project on expert systems and qualification changes related to skilled workers and clerks. The project started officially on June 1, 1986. It was set within the Training Department. The study is one of the major ILO studies on human resource issues in the highly industrialized nations.

The main topics of the project were set as follows:

- Review of the diffusion of expert systems and the economic strategies adopted by the business community to take advantage of the technology.
- Documentation and analysis of the impact of expert systems in manufacturing and services industry on employment, qualification, training needs and management. Special emphasis should be given to stimulate political action.

The study should refer primarily to developments in France, Japan, the United Kingdom, the United States of America and the Federal Republic of Germany.

As practical experience gained in routine use is still rare, a critical assessment of expert system technology has to rely, to some extent, on the extrapolation of case studies, the experiences made in comparable fields of computer technology and scenario techniques. A comprehensive quantitative analysis seems under these circumstances nearly impossible yet not a precondition for the current discussion. A qualitative approach was therefore chosen. Complementary sources of information such as evaluation of the literature, attendance to conferences, tutorials and workshops, interviews, experts opinion and a survey of selected case studies provided both the broad view as well as indepth studies of prototypical cases.

During the course of the project a series of three workshops were organized in collaboration with the Gottlieb Duttweiler Institute in Rüschlikon/Zürich. The discussion among scientists, practitioners and representatives from industry, trade unions and governments allowed to assess the project and to synthesize the individual results to a more coherent view.

The first workshop was held in Zürich, November 21-23 1987. It reviewed the State-of-the-art of commercial applications of expert systems in production and services as well as the national and transnational supporting programs for their further development. The climate for the future demand of expert systems in industry, commerce and administration was analyzed under the assessment of promoting and impeding factors as well as expected benefits and limitations. It revealed that business recognizes ES today as a valuable tool to enhance productivity and efficiency. Industry regards the technology as stable enough to be used at a larger scale. It was expected that it will become an integral part of advanced software environments. The results are summarized in Bernold and Hillenkamp (1988).

Little was provable, however, regarding the impact on work, organization of work, decision making, management structure, skills, skill transfer, qualification, training and retraining needs. The emphasis of the second workshop was therefore to analyze the changes the application of ES caused on the basis of case studies. Particular focus was given to the management of change and how to prepare workforce and management accordingly.

The second workshop was hosted by Arthur Andersen in Chicago, September 13-15, 1988. By and large it confirmed earlier findings. The individual contributions compiled in this book highlight the current assessment from the viewpoint of industry, unions, education and science. ES as seen today are part of the general trend of the informatization of the working environment. As such they seem not to require drastically different strategies to cope with. Nevertheless it is foreseeable that they accentuate developments such as e.g. dequalification on the work place if they are introduced on traditional Tayloristic principles.

ES and related technologies have not yet matured to the extend that they drive secondary consequences like the organisation of work. The rate of diffusion of expert systems particularly the installation of large systems is lower than predicted providing the chance of social innovation in the context of their use. Many of the limiting factors are rooted in the technology itself particularly in the context of identification and handling of relevant knowledge. Other problems, however, are caused by the structure and management of the companies. A number of failures can be traced directly to wrong expectations by the clients and correspondingly wrong decisions.

The technology is still young in comparison to traditional EDP. The money spent for its development is small compared to the billions and man-years invested in today's mainframes and application software. The fast rise of AI has to do with a specific constellation in the early 80's (Bernold Hillenkamp, 1988). In the light of the latter parts of the decade the hype has given way to a more sober evaluation.

This recognition lies in the general trend of a critical assessment of past computer installations. Generally speaking EDP was often under a weaker cost control than other projects of comparable size and importance within a given company. Today they cannot easily be justified by the previously envisaged productivity gains. With the almost explosively accelerating innovation rate investment strategies have to be rethought. At the same time computers reach finally the management who feels in turn now better qualified to analyze use and spending on the technical infrastructure of their company.

What they often find, is a lack of clear goals and assessment criteria to review current and past EDP strategies. In addition many of the assessment programs cover only a narrow range of indicators centered around economic performance. The examples of a comprehensive analysis are still rare and there is growing evidence indicating the absence of a general accepted methodology.

The present disenchantment with AI and expert systems doesn't mean that this technology has become a non-issue. The general trend for rationalization will continue and not stop at functions which today seem reserved for human beings. If there is one conclusion to be drawn from this project then it is that the underlying motivation of use is the crucial issue and that more then ever the challenge to meet is the shaping of technological developments. AI is a forerunner of a new generation of technologies which aim at cognitive tasks. Even if its development is not as fast as predicted it is a excellent case to develop appropriate assessment methodologies and corresponding strategies of action.

Reference

Bernold T., Hillenkamp U.(Editors), 1988, *Expert Systems in Production and Services – Impact on Qualifications and Working Life*, Elsevier Science Publishers B.V. (North Holland).

Bernold T., Hillenkamp U., 1988, "Perspectives on the Assessment of Commercial Expert Systems" in *Expert Systems in Production and Services* (see above).

Brott K., "Commercial Expert Systems – Key to Competitiveness" in *Commercial Expert Systems in Banking and Insurance 89*, Bernold T. editor, in preparation.

Fellmann U., Bernold T., "Information Technologies – Multiple Interface in Service Production" in *User Interface – Gateway or Bottleneck?*, Bernold. T., editor, 1988, Elsevier Science Publishers B.V. (North Holland).

Quality Management in Insurance, International Conference of the European Center for Education in Insurance, Lugano April 17-18, 1989, Information : European Center for Insurance Education, Kirchlistrasse 2, CH-9010 St. Gallen.

Impact

EXPERT SYSTEMS IN PRODUCTION AND SERVICES II
Th. Bernold and U. Hillenkamp (Editors)
Elsevier Science Publishers B.V., Amsterdam – Printed in The Netherlands

Changes in Tasks and Functions – The Services Sector

Sue P. Stafford
Manager, Decision Support Group, Boston
Coopers & Lybrand
Boston, USA

1. Introduction

The development of expert systems for the services sector offers opportunities for improved operations and profitability. These opportunities have been widely acclaimed and magnified by both the press and vendors of expert system software. The changes in tasks and functions which accompany the introduction of expert systems into the workplace have been less widely publicized, undoubtedly because they are less well understood. But these changes are of equal, if not greater, importance to the success of expert system technology. If we look across the services sector in general, we see an environment in which work is done in a context filled with paper files, forms, procedure manuals of various kinds, and numerous self-styled prompts and memory aids. Professionals either interact face-to-face with each other or contact one other by telephone. The networks of communication are vast and vital to getting the job done. Computers may be used routinely to review information or perform various analytical functions. In the midst of all of this seemingly outward activity, ideas are conceived, strategies are tested, and decisions are made.

The introduction of expert systems in an environment as rich as that just described will necessitate changes in the physics of the work environment, in the tasks and functions performed, in the skills of professionals, and in the role of those who would guide the process of change and the work environment that results. These changes may be looked at from three perspectives: that of the **user** of an expert system, that of the **management** of an organization wishing to deploy an expert system, and that of the **developer** of an expert system.

2. The User's Perspective

Seen from the **user's perspective**, expert systems promise to eliminate some tasks entirely, and to provide automated assistance for others. But relying on automated assistance is itself a new task, one for which workers are ill-prepared. Currently, advice in the workplace is given by humans, and is understood and judged in the context of its human source. The advice of our mentors is interpreted in light of our understanding of their strengths, shortcomings, and the time pressures under which their advice is given. Automated advice is comparatively context free; we don't know how to react, when to trust it, nor what its limitations are. With the introduction of an expert system, a new task has been introduced as old tasks have been eliminated; the new task is that of understanding what the expert system can, and cannot do, and learning to work intelligently with it.

Consider the world of a life insurance underwriter. Currently, work is centered around one or more paper files which contain an application for insurance, letters from brokers, medical records, medical test results, and perhaps other documents. Each underwriter develops an individualized style of structuring the information available to him, spreading out the papers in the file, glancing from one to the next and back again. Certain pieces of information "jump out" as significant, and other information is significant in its absence. As one underwriter told me, "I write all of that down in my mind." Occasionally, he will also write notes to himself on paper. With this loosely structured set of information, the underwriter's job is to assess the risk of the applicant and make a decision concerning policy features and premium. This judgment and decision are to be made with as little additional information as possible; requesting more information takes time (and the applicant may lose interest in purchasing the policy) and costs money (which may cut into the profits of the company). The underwriter's task is analogous to trying to identify the subject of a jigsaw puzzle picture by looking at as few pieces as possible.

In the case of the underwriter, however, outside sources of help are available. There is always one's supervisor, the underwriter in the next cubicle, the broker who can be reached by phone, underwriting guidelines published by the company, medical reference manuals, on-line databases, and actuarial statistics which may be consulted. Experienced underwriters know how to judge the advice and information received form each of these sources. Information and advice are interpreted in the context in which they are given. Company guidelines are conservative; the supervisor tends to always think the worst, and besides, he has the flu today; these actuarial statistics don't tell me much; the Attending

Physician's Statement suggests a family history of diabetes; there's important family history information missing on the application.

Expert systems promise to reduce or eliminate the need for reliance on all of the pieces of paper and the multiple sources of information and advice. Expert advice is now available in the form of a computer system which one can consult when advice is needed; or perhaps the expert system is one module of an underwriters' workstation, and interactively works with the underwriter as he underwrites the case. How is the underwriter to interpret the advice of such a system? Should he accept its suggestion that a blood sugar test be ordered? How much does the system know about a family history of disease? Has it taken into account the age of the applicant? How important does it think that age is? A new form of judgment is being required of the underwriter with the introduction of automated advice. He must now judge the value of the system's suggestions, and the value of its reasons for its suggestions. The suggestions and reasons are relatively context free. **They don't belong to anyone!** Why not ask the supervisor for help? But part of the reason for developing the expert system was to eliminate the need for asking the supervisor. With the introduction of the expert system, old tasks are being eliminated, and new tasks are being introduced. The existence of automated advice requires that users learn to act intelligently with a machine. The fact that the advice is relatively context free means that users must understand the limits of that advice.

Working intelligently with an expert system which provides automated advice often requires new cognitive functions on the part of users. The life insurance underwriter, whose job once required frequent discussions and picking out important pieces of information from an array of papers spread before him on his desk, must now find the important information on a computer screen, or on a series of screens. There is a risk involved in replacing an individualized style of working with information spread upon the desk top with a structured series of computer screens. Freedom to glance "randomly" at two pieces of information "at once" has been removed; the information may be on different screens. The same style must be adopted by all. A new structure of information must be mastered, and the skills required to master that structure are quite different from those required to cull that information from paper files and conversations. As one underwriter put it, if you take away the paper and my notes, "I lose the context of my thoughts."

The change in skills required for the performance of tasks in an environment populated by expert systems suggests the need to rethink job descriptions in terms of both tasks and functions. It is likely that the skills which were adequate for entry level underwriters in a non-automated, paper-filled people-populated work environment are not adequate in an environment in which a major part of the job function is intensive interaction with an expert system. Indeed, the very aptitudes which suit an individual for successful work in one type of environment may preclude success in the other. In addition, thought must be given to the sorts of support which must be given to the new cognitive functions required for task performance. If the job of the underwriting is not amenable to procedural serialization, if competent judgment requires the ability to jump from one piece of information or one idea to another at will, automated support must respect those requirements and allow them to occur. Finally, care must be taken in hiring and on-the-job training to insure that these functions are performed recognizing the new cognitive requirements introduced by automated advice.

3. The Perspective of Management

The new demands placed on workers as they perform their jobs assisted by expert systems suggest that the role of **management** must change. The unit to be managed is the human/computer team; to develop and manage that team successfully requires a new breadth and depth of understanding. The current decision-making processes of both company experts and potential expert system users must be understood if expert system technology is to be employed to its best advantage in the development of systems. This requires a microscopic look at how work is done and how knowledge and expertise are applied as work is done. It requires a recognition that knowledge exists in multifarious places - in procedure manuals, in the minds of experienced workers, in the various prompts and memory aids that competent workers create for themselves, in the relationships that exist among workers, and in the very flow of work itself. Management is not accustomed to commissioning analyses at this level of detail. Experience has shown, however, that unless competent decision-making and the environment within which it occurs are understood at this fine-grained level of detail, expert system technology is likely to fail altogether or be trivial in its application. It is up to management to see that the technology is applied appropriately and successfully.

Successful expert system development efforts offer management a unique opportunity. When business is understood at a fine-grained level of detail, management has an opportunity to evaluate just how business is done, and to rethink how it ought to be done. Numerous expert system development projects have resulted in significant changes for the better in the very conduct of business. Once there is an articulation of what is being done and how it is being done, changes can be initiated and automation can be introduced in appropriate ways. Indeed, managers have remarked that the task environment analysis performed as part of an expert system development project was of such value, that the expert system project was judged to be a success even before the completion of the system!

Once management becomes aware of the knowledge that is applied in the daily conduct of business, and once the role that knowledge plays is articulated, the challenge and opportunity of knowledge management arises. Managers are well aware of the value of information to their business; indeed, the whole industry of information systems has evolved to meet the informational needs of business organizations, and MIS is a reflection of the need to manage that information. Knowledge-based and expert systems have begun to illuminate the value of knowledge to an organization. Just as information can be viewed as a corporate asset, so knowledge itself, once it is identified and understood, can be viewed as a corporate asset.

Knowledge of the knowledge that allows a business to function successfully affords management the power to capture, codify, and leverage that knowledge through the development of systems that either embody or support it. This is a new task for management, and one for which many managers are ill prepared. It requires a deeper look at tasks and functions than has been taken in the past. It requires recognition and respect for sophisticated decision making as well as for the simple knowledge of "how to get things done around here." And it requires commitment to hiring and training systems developers who share that recognition and respect.

4. The Perspective of Expert System Developers

All of this points to changes in the tasks and functions performed by expert system **developers**. Proficiency in the computer-science aspects of the technology is not sufficient to develop expert systems which can function effectively in a support mode with humans. New skills are required of system developers, skills imported from the fields of cognitive science, anthropology, philosophy, and management. Expert system developers must be able to understand operating and business environments, just as conventional systems developers must. In addition, however, they must be able to understand how knowledge is used in that environment, what role it plays, what difference it makes, and how work suffers in its absence. This requires the elicitation of knowledge from those who hold it. Knowledge elicitation requires skillful interviewing approaches and techniques; if an "expert" is simply asked how he does his job, he will likely be unable to articulate it, or will tell a story which is plausible at first glance but will be shown to be inadequate upon further analysis. Skills in knowledge analysis and the rational reconstruction of that analyzed knowledge must also be developed.

All of this is in addition to the more easily taught knowledge of AI architectures, AI programming languages, man/machine interfaces, MIS integration, and conventional computer science methodologies. This new combination of skills will ensure the development of expert systems which meet business objectives, contain a breadth and depth of knowledge appropriate to computer assistants, and can interact with their users in ways which enhance their intelligent behavior.

5. Conclusion

The introduction of expert system technology could be viewed as a destructive force which extracts knowledge from those who hold it and delivers it in a dehumanizing, mechanized way to those who lack it. But this need not be the case. There are new cognitive functions required of users and developers of expert systems, and new tasks facing the managers of those users and developers. These demand either the re-training of the current workforce or the hiring of a new workforce with a different set of skills. In addition, as with the introduction of any new computer system, the flow of work must be changed to reflect the new realities of the workplace. If these changes in tasks and functions are recognized, positive steps can be taken to insure a harmony between man, machine and the workplace. Indifference to these changes renders the potential of the technology unfulfilled, a mere overblown, unfulfilled promise. Critics will argue that the new technology is indistinguishable from conventional technology.

Expert systems technology, then, offers us both a challenge and a new responsibility. The challenge is to harness personal knowledge and deliver it to users in the form of automated advice, complementing their skills and enabling the intelligent performance of tasks. The responsibility is to meet that challenge with an appropriate division of labor between human and machine.

EXPERT SYSTEMS IN PRODUCTION AND SERVICES II
Th. Bernold and U. Hillenkamp (Editors)
Elsevier Science Publishers B.V., Amsterdam – Printed in The Netherlands

Expert Systems in Industry – Changes in Tasks and Functions

Manfred Scheifele
Fraunhofer-Institut für Arbeitswirtschaft und Organisation (IAO), D–7000 Stuttgart 80

1. Introduction

The boom of conferences and seminars and the flood of papers on expert systems, expert systems on test, expert systems and the factory of the future etc. seem to indicate the existence of an enormous number of applied expert systems. The commercial benefits of expert systems are seen in the following:

- They save the knowledge of the experts ("the expert may leave, his knowledge remains");
- they multiply rare expert knowledge;
- they have greater flexibility compared with conventional algorithmic programs;
- they meet the problem of rapid growth and obsolescence of facts;
- there is a great need for better advisory capacity as is offered by expert systems;
- expert systems are able to manage ill-structured problems;
- in an (increasingly) complicated economic environment, there is need of support in decision-making;
- expert systems may contribute to greater flexibility of the production process by applying more expert knowledge to planning systems;
- expert systems are able to manage tasks which require high-valued knowledge with less skilled persons;
- expert systems offer a further potential for rationalization;
- finally, expert systems contribute to improving services.

In trying to answer the question of changes in tasks and functions a brief survey of the distribution of expert systems over different areas in a production plant can give us first hints. At present it is difficult to gather profound information about successful applications of expert systems. Their evaluation and their integration in other systems have often hardly been accomplished. A study of Fähnrich, Thines, Groh (1988) which is based on a sample of 218 recent systems in USA, the UK and West Germany shows the following distribution: 33% of the expert systems are applied in construction and design followed by maintenance with 20%, production planning (15%), production process control (12%), and quality control (7%). Systems to support marketing, assembly and part-manufacturing play a minor part.

Classifying this sample with respect to various types of expert systems, diagnosis and selection systems (for classification purposes) dominate with a share of 25% each. They are followed by planning systems (13%), interpretation systems (11%), configuration systems (10%), monitoring systems (9%), and decision support systems (6%).

When attempting to acquire more information or to conduct real case studies, it becomes clear that often only singular solutions or prototypes are in application and many projects have been stopped at an early stage. But this might give a false impression. Probably management decision makers withhold an investment until a strategic placement of various expert systems and their integration becomes feasible. At least at that time the impacts will be more clear.

In the following paper, I will briefly present four "case studies" which show some aspects of the application range of expert systems and their organizational embedding. Looking at previous experiences in introducing new technologies, we can currently detect some tendencies regarding the impacts on the different kinds of users, on qualifications and on possible feedback effects.

Furthermore I will attempt to give a brief sketch of the characteristic of expert systems, without neglecting the ways in which expert systems and other electronic data processing technologies effect each other. In addition, I think it is necessary to deal with some technical aspects of expert systems, because this will also influence the organizational embedding and qualification concepts, too. The final section of this paper deals with the question of how expert systems may be socially shaped for the benefit of the employees.

2. Range of Applications

2.1. Case 1: XCON

DEC's famous XCON for configuring VAX computers is dealt with as case 1. There are a lot of articles describing this system and the extended strategy of integrating expert systems in the "order cycle". In order to discuss some special aspects of XCON, there follows a summary of its objectives and some of its characteristic features:

DIGITAL'S marketing strategy has been to provide customers with the freedom to choose precisely what they need from the wide variety of hardware, software, communication products and application offers. The consequences of offering customers this flexibility is that DEC receives many highly specific system orders. XCON, developed by Intelligent Systems Technology Group of DEC in cooperation with the Carnegie Mellon University (CMU), decides whether an order is complete or what additional equipment would be required to configure the line items, and why. XCON defines spatial relationships among the components on the order and how the line items could be built, including additional software configuration. "Used daily in production, XCON assembles virtually all major DEC systems. A typical orders deals with 50-250 components, 25-125 pieces of information about each components, and typically takes 1000 steps to configure a system. It accounts for such things as cable length constraints, sizes and layout of cabinets, and power requirements" (Lynch et al. ; 1986). It takes about two minutes for XCON to configure a system order, saving an enormous amount of time in the order processing cycle.

Sviokla reports that the correctness range of 65% to 90% (pre XCON) moved to a correctness of 95% - 98% (Sviokla ; 1986, p 258). Therefore final tests could be reduced. "Over 7 years, XCON has grown to 6'200 rules, of which approximately 50% change every year" (Soloway at al. ; 1987, p. 824).

It was possible to achieve an enormous increase in productivity which is mainly based on the employment of the expert system. According to Sviokla, p. 225, before the introduction of XCON 23 persons (technical editors) produced configurations of 19'000 units, and after the introduction of XCON the corresponding figures were 17 and 60'000. The work of these 17 technical editors, however, has become more monotonous: "Post-XCON, all technical editors found a routinization of their work. Those technical editors who were active in feeding back information and corrections to the knowledge-engineering teams, found a shift in their roles as checkpoints in the order flow to roles as expert consultants to the XCON user design and knowledge engineering. The technical editors who were interviewed expressed a desire to return to the old way doing configurations where the challenge of figuring out new and creative solutions was greater and there was less technical "nitpicking" work. To the expert technical editors, some of the challenging aspects of their jobs were removed by XCON. Furthermore, the more expert XCON became, the more expert the reviewer needed to be to discover any bugs or problems in the output. Yet, for the most part, reviewing output was less interesting than creating configurations from scratch." (Sviocla; 1986, p. 229 f.).

One of the challenging aspects in the jobs of technical editors could be the updating of the knowledge base; due to the complexity of the expert system, updating now lies in the domain of software specialists.

2.2. Case 2: AGV - Maintenance

In a production plant an expert system has been developed for the purpose of fault diagnosis in a specific type of automated guided vehicles (AGV. The main objective of this project has been to gain experience in the operation of a new programming style and software development process, and also in the solution of organizational problems.

An advanced prototype is now installed in the AGV maintenance section. The system is eventually intended to train persons previously unfamiliar with the maintenance of the electronic components in the AGV.

A semi-skilled worker in this plant, for instance, neither had any experience in the maintenance of electronically controlled systems, nor did he have any basic knowledge in this field. He has been transferred to the AGV maintenance section and is to carry out his new maintenance tasks with the aid of the expert system. If the expert system fails to identify certain faults, specialists must be called in. In this case the user must store the data concerning these faults in a database. This information will later be used to update the expert system.

2.3. Case 3: Fault Diagnosis and Maintenance of Advanced CNC-Machines

The development of CNC machines has resulted in a rise in complexity and automation. The efficiency of such systems strongly depends on their availability and reliability in the production process. Therefore a user should be able to detect breakdowns in a machine, and to repair most of them immediately by himself. With the help of a diagnosis system integrated in the computer control system of the machine, the user is able to interact with a dialogue component which leads him through the process of fault deduction and usually gives him instructions for repair (cf. Puetz, Eichhorn, Fähnrich ; 1987, p. 101). The knowledge was acquired by several means: experts were interviewed, and the knowledge they were able to articulate was restructured, covering the following aspects:

a) pure facts;
b) variations in machine conditions;
c) actions subsequently required of the user;
d) rules for combining the steps outlined above into one consistent procedure.

The inference engine encompasses heuristics which are applied to the knowledge base and which decide on the next question or action to be taken. The inferences are made dependent on uncertainty values. An object knowledge editor in combination with an explanatory component facilitates the implementation of the expert system.

2.4. Case 4: Intelligent Assistant

Different program systems compute characteristic physical or chemical parameters to describe the performance of chemical substances. These parameters are used for planning chemical processes. It has to be checked whether a certain method is applicable in the context of the assumptions made. A rule based system has been constructed to select the appropriate methods according to the given assumptions and the availability of base values stored in a database. As in case 2), a main purpose lies in gaining experience in the development of an expert system as a better interface between various methods. The expert system assists specialists in applying methods for computing physical values of chemical components. The updating of the knowledge base is done by domain expert(s). In this case the expert system is a better medium for applying methods. So far no implications specific to expert systems have been identified.

3. Expert Systems as a Further Step of Formalizing and Structuring Human Work

In order to discuss the impacts of expert systems, a survey of their technical potentials is required. Here, the term of technical potentials refers to the fields of application of expert systems and the contribution of expert systems and AI respectively to the EDP.

There is an increasing importance of expert systems as a medium to gain better access to information or to select different methods according to their range of application more easily.

Expert systems as "method handlers" are under investigation and have so far been partially realized. The following example may serve to illustrate the use of expert systems as a tool which can contribute to computer integrated manufacturing. Expert systems enable the user to extract features at 'higher' levels from data at 'lower' levels. So the required feature information may be obtained for subsequent use in other systems by interpreting the geometry which has been created by normal procedures on a CAD-system. Knowledge based systems can be used as development tools for the design of complex software systems or for programming interfaces between different systems.

The ideas of representing knowledge in "frames" and the implementation of knowledge representation languages are closely related to the object-oriented programming methodology which is based on objects, messages and classes. The object-oriented approach is seen to have the following advantages:

- it can reduce the development time by facilitating concurrent work;
- the software becomes more flexible;
- the software is more comprehensible for programmers and users;
- correctness proofs are facilitated by the modularity.

In applying these concepts to databases, the resulting systems allow a better information retrieval. "Another important advantage of object-oriented semantic data models is the availability of organizational principles, which are important for (1) application domains with highly structured components, and (2) application domains in which different levels of abstraction are desired" (Ramamoorthy, Sheu ; 1988). On the one hand, object-oriented programming has extended some traditional AI systems; on the other hand, AI is expected to contribute to resolving the present shortcomings of object-oriented systems which so far have prevented their use on a larger scale.

Together with some other elements of AI, expert systems stimulate the development of EDP.

Finally some 'spin-off' effects should not be neglected: Expert systems encourage the programmers to become acquainted with new programming styles which can lead to a higher productivity in software development. We must also concede that expert system projects can lead to more insights and a better understanding of the process in ill-structured domains, but on the other hand the reliability of expert systems in treating structured domains should not be over-estimated.

Expert systems and AI will penetrate existing technology and will therefore increase the 'informatization' of work. Computer science is not only the development of hard- and software, but also the science of the reorganization of work by means of information technology. Expert systems as a new discipline of information technology are therefore an instrument for the reorganization of work as well. Problem areas are the impacts of rationalization, of the stabilization of management control over the human work, of processes of qualification and dequalification and new structures in the division of labour. Because of the nature of the actual development there are hardly any empirical studies analyzing these topics. Problems specific to expert systems will be discussed in the next section.

4. New Problems Emerging from Expert Systems

Let me sum up my position as follows: The AI community does not posses a profound theory concerning the understanding of mental processes or the formal logic underlying the expert system technology. "AI is not based on concepts, but only short-term solutions" (Coy; 1988), or in the German original, "Die KI hat keine Begriffe sondern nur Schlagworte" (Coy ; 1988).

4.1. How Much Expertise is an Expert System Capable of?

The euphoric promises to be found in papers concerning fifth generation computing or the daring visions of prominent AI-researchers may be illustrated by Feigenbaum, McCorduck: "Such methods are already in use. Modest pilot projects, with the name of expert systems, have demonstrated that a computer is capable of the same kinds of intelligent behavior as a physician making a diagnosis, or a geologist deciding where to seek minerals. And these expert systems do this in much the same way human experts do by combining textbook knowledge with the rules of thumb that experience teaches, and then making informated guesses about the situation at hand, whether it concernes sick human being or range and basin. We call such expertise in humans intelligence, intuition, inspiration, and professionalism. When a machine demonstrates the same kind of behavior, there is no compelling reason not to call it intelligence then, too." (Feigenbaum, McCorduck ; 1983, p. 16).

In contrast to these assertions Dreyfus'/Dreyfus' characterization of an expert in their exposition of the five stages of skill acquisition is quite different: "An expert generally knows what to do based on mature and practiced understanding. When deeply involved in coping with his environment, he does not see problems in some detached way and work at solving them, nor does he worry about the future and devise plans. We usually don't make conscious deliberative decisions when we walk, talk, drive, or carry on most social activities. An expert's skill has become so much a part of him that he needs be no more aware of it than he is of his own body." (Dreyfus/Dreyfus ; 1988, p. 30).

Discussing the possibility of a machine representation of an expert's skill, they conclude: "Human beings, however, exhibit a flexibility, judgment, and intuition that resist decomposition into specification and inferences and have proved equally difficult to instill into logic machines (p. 63). The practical significance of this statement has been demonstrated in many projects for developing expert systems: Up to now they have been developed in rather limited domains. But one should not forget plans to employ expert systems in military applications (the strategic computing initiative SCI) or attempts to achieve 'distributed' or cooperative expert systems, some of them even in realtime applications.

4.2. Technical Problems

But there are also technical problems to be considered when dealing with expert systems. These technical problems may be manifested in recommendations or instructions which may lead to wrong decisions by the user. This depends, however, on the level of qualifications and insight on behalf of the user and on his disposable time.

The increasing density of labour, which is caused by the development of technology in general, leads to additional stress and then to new conditions of making decisions when using expert systems. Someone who has become dependent on an expert system has also become incapable of deciding freely and independently as a situation may require.

The following line of argument was inspired by W. Coy (1988), who works in a research project on technical problems of expert systems.

4.2.1. Problems of Formal Logic

- Consistency of the knowledge base with respect to syntactic consistency and semantic consistency: The risk of inconsistencies increases with the size of the knowledge base.The 'Frame problem': What happens for example, when the knowledge base changes or when rules are time dependent? This problem of truth-maintenance is according to F. M. Brown (1987), "One of the most fundamental problems in AI". Dreyfus/Dreyfus outline the frame problem as follows, "The attempt to capture human, temporal, situated, continuously changing knowhow in a computer as static, desituated, discrete, knowing that has become known as the frame problem. It has been defined as the problem of finding a representational form permitting a changing complex world to be efficiently and adequately represented. More specifically, it is the problem of representing in some systematic way that as time passes and/or actions are performed, some but not all facts change and only a few of the changes are relevant to current action" (Dreyfus/Dreyfus; 1988, p. 82).

- complex modelling: There is no satisfactory probability theory based on mathematics: "It must be understood, however, that we are concerned not with modes of inductive reasoning but with something that might be called physical or statistical probability. In a rough way we may characterize this concept by saying that our probabilities do not refer to judgments but to possible outcomes of a conceptual experiment. Before we speak of probabilities, we must agree on an idealized model of a particular conceptual experiment such as tossing a coin, sampling kangaroos on the moon, observing a particle under diffusion, counting the number of telephone calls. At the outset we must agree on the possible outcomes of this experiment (our sample space) and the probabilities associated with them" (Feller, 1968, p. 4, italics in the original). The "uncertainty logic", being ill-grounded itself, is not acceptable as a substitute. Therefore expert systems which include uncertainty values are unpredictable in their performance, providing considerable problems for the user.

4.2.2. Software problems and "the escalation of the software crisis" (Partridge 1986).

- The linear phase models of software-engineering are no longer applicable. They have been replaced by a circular development of specification -implementation - test - maintenance. The tasks within this spiral are neither precisely defined nor precisely based on theory: "In AI we loose even the prerequisites of proof and verification." (Partridge ; 1986, p. 38).

Today many expert system projects do not exceed the prototype stage. The few which are developed further may be confronted with "scaling problems": How to upgrade prototypes without losing quality? XCON of DEC is a lucid example.

"In software-engineering terms what happens to a large rule base as it changes over time is a 'degradation in integrity': What may once have been a coherent rule base, turns into a rat's nest of special rules, tightly coupled rules etc. While software engineers have been able to label this problem, (...) they have not presented a general solution (..)" (Soloway, Bachant, Jensen ; 1987, p. 824).

But the problem is even more serious than that: Soloway et al. conclude their discussion on the issue of reimplementation in another language as follows: "Moreover, we should not expect that all the maintenance problems will be alleviated by XCON-in-RIME; after all, there are many problems yet to be discovered (e. g., what happens when the rule base hits 18'000 rules? 27'000 rules?)."

5. Remarks on Responsibility and the Scope of Application

Taking the existing technical shortcomings of expert systems seriously, we must conclude that they must not be applied in risky or complex environments. Automatic deciding systems in all fields of implementation have to be forbidden by law.

Assertions like the following that a certain system "is the generation of repair advisers for any complex device and plant e. g. computers, copy-machines, chemical plants, power plants" should catch our attention, because a wrong decision has implications of quite a different range. The question of responsibility has to be discussed.

I think it is necessary to discuss this topic within a broader context in order to make the challenges of expert systems more evident. The main argument put forward by David Parnas when he resigned from the SDIO panel was that the intended computerized battle management system including a lot of expert systems would not be trustworthy. Again, it should be noted that trustworthiness denotes a relation between humans and technology, and is not itself an attribute of the computer. It is based on our previous experience in the development and use of complex data processing systems and thus cannot be replaced by "In principle ...." - arguments based on certain newly developed technologies or tools. (cf. Parnas ; 1987).

"It is a dangerous illusion if we expect expert systems to replace the responsibility of man for the evaluation of the results. For expert systems are designed to tolerate uncertain results without always making these recognizable as such" (Ethik ; 1988). Expert systems, just as other technical devices, cannot assume responsibility, but they can indeed conceal responsibility.

6. Changes of Tasks and Functions

The following section deals with the question of how an expert system implemented in an operational procedure affects the work of those employees who are either in direct contact with the expert system or are indirectly influenced by it.

First it should be noted that there is no organizational standard underlying the implementation of expert systems. On the one hand, expert systems operated in isolation permit a range of alternative organizational options. On the other hand, expert systems which are linked together to form a compound information processing system limit the range of organizational options. In both cases, business objectives specify the organizational structures to a certain degree.

With the exception of Case 4 in which the expert system is no more than an additional aid for the user in fulfilling his task, the range of qualifications required to perform operational functions has changed.

In Case 1, a segmentation process among the technical editors results in two unequal groups. The first group needs, and eventually will have, less configuration knowledge. The second group, maintaining a higher status, must have the qualifications necessary to deal with difficult cases not covered by the expert system. This group of technical editors must also be able to detect faults in configuration proposals of the expert system.

Case 2 clearly shows that the expert system substitutes a maintenance specialist. The specialist who had provided the knowledge to create the expert system was later transferred to another department. The semi-skilled worker mentioned in this context may be able to detect certain faults behind specific symptoms, but he still depends on the expert system. The qualifications he has so far accumulated as a user of the expert system do not enable him to evaluate the instructions given by the expert system. Case 3, on the other hand, demonstrates that it is possible to increase the range of tasks performed by CNC machine operators. They are able to carry out uncomplicated repairs themselves; in more difficult cases, they can communicate more efficiently with the repair service of the CNC machine manufacturer. As a result, the importance of the maintenance section on plant level decreases.

In his investigation of three large-scales expert systems in use, Sviokla comes to the conclusion "that these systems seem to create a phenomenon referred to as 'progressive structuring'. This process alters the nature of the underlying task and the organizational mechanisms which support it. This phenomenon is dynamic and evolves over time." (Sviokla ; 1986, p. VIII).

6.1. The Level of Expertise

The more qualified work of the "winners" of rationalization also tends to be affected by expert systems. Carefully designed systems in clearly defined domains can support specialists, but they can also multiply their knowledge for the benefit of others, thus improving the quality of their work. Even in the most favorable scenario, expert systems, designed to the support, and not to substitute, the specialists, as shown in case 4, may eventually restrict individual capabilities of action and cognition. The dangers outlined here will become visible in the medium term. Dreyfus/Dreyfus conclude, "The most that can be expected is that expert systems may someday take their place alongside planning charts, management information systems, and professional training programs as useful tools for improving overall performance. A genuine danger, however, faces the company or government going that route. To the extent that junior employees using expert systems come to see expertise as a function of large knowledge bases and masses of inferential rules, they will fail to progress beyond the competent level of their machines. With the leap beyond competence to proficiency and expertise thus inhibited, investors in expert systems may ultimately discover that their wells of true human expertise and wisdom have gone dry." (Dreyfus/Dreyfus, p. 121).

6.2. Knowledge Engineers

In the design process of expert systems, a new type of model building has engendered a new profession - the knowledge engineer. His task is to "elicit" the knowledge from the domain expert(s) and to adapt it to computer use. This "elicitation" requires a variety of techniques, including psychological ones. The difficulties in knowledge acquisition prevent a more rapid spread of expert systems. The main problem is generally regarded to be the shortage of qualified knowledge engineers, or more seriously, the lack of support by appropriate software tools. But there are also obstacles against knowledge "elicitation". Berry considers it essential for knowledge engineers to be aware of the problem of "implicit" or "tacit" knowledge (Berry, p. 101) which cannot be fixed by rules. Strictly speaking, it seems that knowledge engineers are expected to possess superhuman qualities, worthy of a hero in Feigenbaum's "Second computing revolution". On the one hand, they must be familiar with the techniques of representing knowledge; on the other hand, they must possess the "social competence" required of a sensitive interviewer or a person capable of stimulating the social interaction process which will yield the knowledge of the experts.

I am in doubt whether a few courses in psychology or engineering will enable a computer specialist to master such a combination of ambitious tasks; the same applies, in my opinion, vice versa to an engineer who has been given a briefing in AI.

7. Some Remarks on the Social Shaping of Expert Systems

Phrases like "expert support" sound tempting, but often express little more then wishful thinking, i. e. they are mere palliatives. The employment of expert systems in a situation fit for humans to work in depends on specific social and organizational conditions. The expert system technology must be open to dispute both in public and on plant level, taking technological and organizational alternatives to expert systems into account. The following remarks focus on the most urgent problems; the connection between expert systems and conventional EDP should be constantly kept in mind.

The process of developing and integrating an expert system on plant level should be accompanied by an authentic participation of the affected (white collar) workers in all phases. Thereby it is possible to achieve a broad consensus on legitimate, socially adequate domains and to emphasize the issue of responsibility. Otherwise the feedbacks can cause serious dangers for the development of the company, as the standardization of knowledge can become counterproductive. Rather, innovation needs diverging opinions. There are tasks which are better carried out by humans than by an expert system, no matter how "intelligent" it may be.

While there is no disagreement on the necessity of qualification programs, it is far from clear which basic qualifications are required, and how this are to be taught. The few example presented here are sufficient to show that there are qualification deficits both in the operation of expert systems and in the command of specific knowledge required in a certain field of application. This includes the "competence of action" which is required of a user whenever the control of the expert system requires an active adjustment. Human potentials, however, should be promoted in any case; these include; in addition to those outlined above, abilities of organization and communication. The latter are also required by the designers of expert systems on plant level. In the last section we have already warned not to overestimate the abilities of knowledge engineers. Nevertheless the critical reflection by an knowledge engineer on his function should become part of his university training. Finally, trade unions and works councils must pay more attention to problems of modelling and of coherence in their policies on plant level.

7.1. Restriction of the Potential for Control

Expert systems are intended as tools of support in production; this should be done in a manner that new forms of monitoring the employees are avoided. Monitoring systems tend to enforce the structure of a "Big Brother" from whom no individual privacy may be concealed. If the value of human dignity, which in West Germany has led to the individual's right of "informational self-determination" (as the new term was coined by Federal Constitutional Court) is taken seriously, this will influence the basic design of an expert system.

7.2. Tool Perspective

The development of an "expert critiquing system" could give room for individual by drawing the user's attention to neglected facts:. "The machine can convey a kind of 'coaching' in which new possibilities for interpretation and action emerge." (Miller; 1986, p. 179). According to Miller critiquing systems differ from the usual recommendation-oriented programs in that they require and respond to a proposed solution by the user. Although taken from medicine, another interesting example is RECONSIDER which works "by encouraging the doctor to consider alternatives and not jumps to conclusions" (Dreyfus/Dreyfus ; 1986, p 118).

Experience suggests that employees need more rights to influence technological development. Most of the current information systems are introduced without involving the people affected. In Germany works councils have a lot of difficulties in representing the interests of the employees because their instruments of collective bargaining as they are provided by law are insufficiently adapted to changes in technology. It is crucial to negotiate agreements concerning technological developments in general, and expert systems in particular.

References

Berry, D. C. (1988): The Problem of Implicit Knowledge. In: Göranzon, B. (ed.): Culture, Language and Artificial Intelligence. Preparing papers for an international conference, Stockholm, May, 30-June, 3, 1988.

Brown, F. M. (1987): The Frame Problem. Proceedings: Los Altos: Morgan Kaufmann.

Coy, W. (; 1988): Personal communication about a research project concerning technical problems of expert systems. University of Bremen.

Dreyfus, H. L.; Dreyfus, St. E. (1986): Mind Over machine - The Power of Human Intuition and Expertise in the Era of Computer. New York: Free Press Paperback Edition 1988.

Ethik der Informatik: Positionspapier zur Jahrestagung 1988 der Gesellschaft für Informatik. Frankfurter Rundschau 28.12.1988.

Fähnrich, K.-P.; Thines, M.; Groh, G. (1988): Einsatz von wissensbasierten Systemen in der Produktion. In: Fähnrich, K.-P. (ed.): Kommtech'88 - Expertensysteme in Planung und Produktion. Velbert, Online GmbH.

Feller, W. (1968): An Introduction to Probability Theory and its Applications. New York: Wiley International Edition, 3rd ed.

Feigenbaum, McCordruck (1983): The fifth Generation: Artifical Intelligence and Japan's Challenge to the World. 2. Aufl. New York: NAL Penguin, 1984.

Miller, P. L. (1986): Expert Critiquing Systems: Practice-Based Medical Consultation by Computer. New York: Springer.

Parnas, D.L (1987): Warum ich nicht an SDI mitarbeite: Eine Auffassung beruflicher Verantwortung. Informatik Spektrum (1987) 10: 3-10.

Puetz, R. D.; Eichhorn, R.; Fähnrich, K.-P. (1987): Fault Diagnosis on CNC Machines. In: A. Mital (ed.): Proceedings of the IXth International Conference on Production Research. Cincinnati, University.

Ramamoorthy, C. V.; Sheu, P. C.: Object-Oriented Systems. IEEE Expert (1988), Fall, 9-15.

Sviokla, J. J.: (1986) PLANPOWER, XCON and MUDMAN: An in-depth Analysis into Three Commercial Expert Systems in Use. Harvard 1986.

EXPERT SYSTEMS IN PRODUCTION AND SERVICES II
Th. Bernold and U. Hillenkamp (Editors)

Elsevier Science Publishers B.V., Amsterdam – Printed in The Netherlands

Acceptance and Social Aspects of the Introduction of Expert Systems

Albrecht Igogeit
Volkswagen AG
Wolfsburg, FRG

1. Introduction

The continuously tightened competition forces any enterprise to permanently use all opportunities to increase the productivity. The maximum effect is gained, if the introduction of new technologies and equipment is in accord with the internal company organization and the motivation of the employees. If the interrelation is unbalanced, the results necessarily suffer (fig. 1). Therefore it is an important management task to control all factors relevant to the success in agreement with the goal.

When steps to increase productivity are taken, the goals of the company frequently collide with the individual and social interests of employees. In particular this is true for the introduction of expert systems. The range of contrasting points of view concerning this matter reaches from exaggerated expectation to irrational rejection. Figure 2 shows the area of conflict between acceptance and rejection of expert systems as well as between motivation and demotivation of experts and users.

2. New Wave of Rationalization due to Expert Systems?

The increase of productivity to ensure the interpose to stay competitive lies in the interest of both, the management and the employees. Nevertheless the term "rationalization" is frequently equated to job killing, and therefore decreases the willingness to cooperation concerning the introduction of new technologies.

The principal question is, wether the jobs of specialists and managers are threatened, which have been considered to be safe against rationalization up to now (fig. 3). Do experts make themselves superfluous by participating in Artificial Intelligence (AI) projects (fig. 4)?

Up to now we do not know any example of an human expert made superfluous by an expert system. To the contrary, the following can be observed: The system takes some of the routine work off the expert and gives freedom to gain new insight. In addition, the experience gathered so far shows, that expert systems need to be permanently maintained and extended by the experts.

The situation may look different, if an employee of low qualification is to be supported by an expert system, and thereby has to work with the expert's competence transferred to a machine, without having gathered the specialist's knowledge himself. In this case a dependence from the computer could arise. By too fast response time behavior, the system can trigger the human work and create pressure. On the other hand, too slow response time behavior may cause stress symptoms. Both decrease the acceptance.

A positive aspect with economic and social results is the increased self-determination of office hours by the expert. Stand-by duties outside of office hours can be reduced, and holidays can be organized more flexible (fig. 5).

3. The "Transparent" Expert

An essential point concerning the acceptance of expert systems is the preparedness and courage of the expert to make his knowledge and reasoning transparent.

The preparedness to uncover and to put to discussion one's own competence needs real superiority in the special field and personal qualities (fig. 6).

The expert system may become an "X-ray screen for competence" (fig. 7).

To uncover the own competence, possibly "demystifies" the special field and the expert's image (fig. 8).

In many fields there is not the "one and only" expertise but certain "camps" and trends in the opinions of specialists. Then first of all a common basis needs to be found. In more than one case, under the cover of an objective discussion, positional fights to back the own expert status are carried out (fig. 9).

By means of the declaration component of an expert system, the solution path can be made comprehensible. This way also errors in the knowledge base can be located. Necessary alterations and additions to the knowledge base lead to the fact that an expert system can never really be called "complete". Additionally, by the use of vague knowledge the conclusions are only "probable" but not necessarily "definite".

4. New Dependencies

Expert systems are often used in the expectation to reduce the dependence on a few high qualified experts. By doing this, however, new dependences on systems as well as on specialists in hardware and AI may be created (fig. 10, 11). The management has to take care that there do not arise any new "ivory towers" for software fans.

By transferring the expert's competence to a computer system, today's belief in experts is projected to the computer. As a result, the dependence on experts is transferred to computers. Enlightenment has to prevent a new belief in machines. Above all, people must be prevented from delegating their responsibility to a computer.

5. Chances for Qualification and Job Enrichment

As any new technology, expert systems offer a chance for qualification and job enrichment to the employees. This is a motivation factor to work on AI subjects.

Experts are often overtaxed by routine tasks, and they do not have enough time to be creative within their domain. Expert systems can assist the human expert and can help to blow up the labyrinth of routine and open up the field of creativity and innovation (fig. 12). So the expert is given a chance to extend his knowledge to subsidiaries and to develop an interdisciplinary way of looking at problems (fig. 13).

A systematically and methodically prepared knowledge base is a prerequisite to transfer a knowledge domain. Because of that, an expert system can be used for teaching and learning. The experts mostly take on the teacher's job. This also improves their qualification.

Over and above that, the involvement in developing an expert system promotes the image of the expert. By creating an expert system he is able to build a "memorial" for acceptance and acknowledgement of his authority (fig. 14).

Together with the commercial use of expert systems the new job outline of a "knowledge engineer" arouse. The knowledge engineer operates as a link between the expert and the developer of AI software.

6. Impoverishment of Working Contents and Dequalification through the Introduction of Expert Systems

Apart from the chance for job enrichment and development of higher qualification, expert systems bear the risk of impoverishment of working contents. This is especially true for system users in line functions. It is necessary to make out this tendency, in order to take appropriate steps to avoid negative consequences on the motivation and thereby on the working success.

For users without an expert's knowledge, there is a strong trend towards taylorism. E. g., a diagnosis system can restrict the search space for results and delivers the most likely result in a smaller amount of time. This reduces the requirement of time needed for a diagnosis and, by a higher frequency of examinees, increases the frequency of repetition. If, in addition, examination data are provided automatically by the machine, this leads to an impoverishment of working contents. A narrowing down of the free structuring of working contents can also be the result of the menu guidance of the user interface of an expert system (fig. 15).

The effects of the tayloristic separation of tasks on motivation and acceptance are worst, if the understanding of goal, reason and effect connections of the task to be carried out is lost. Therefore, anything that contributes to the understanding of interrelations, has to be supported. For this reason an eminent importance falls to the declaration part and the user interface of an expert system.

Experts do not need to fear an increase of taylorism. The chances for job enrichment are predominant. Just because of this, the danger of a "two class society" with increasingly competent experts and users being degraded to "slaves" of the system, has to be prevented.

If the user receives the expert knowledge he needs from an expert system, the immediate contact between him and the expert is reduced. So the expert might disappear from the scene of the user in his function as mentor, discussion partner, teacher, problem solver, motivator and also as social person to whom to relate. He is substituted by a screen (fig. 16). On the other hand, the user is possibly freed from the role of a permanent petitioner and layman. The resentment against repeated questions is diminished, the self-esteem is strengthened.

7. Ethical Aspects of the Introduction of Expert Systems

Expert systems provide a way to preserve the expert's knowledge. They also make it available and usable at any place and time and at a constant quality level.

Also if an open information society is basically assumed, there are borderline cases, where there is a scope of responsibility for the presentation of facts and especially for the way of information transport.

In many cases the responsibility may not be transferred to a machine. The decision about the application of knowledge must remain with the expert.

Acknowledgement

This paper is based on the results of a German working group, and on the part documented by W. Weber (ref). The group consisted of 15 people from 13 companies and institutes. Their results were first presented on a workshop in March, 1988.

Reference

(1) Weber, W., Akzeptanz und soziale Aspekte beim Einsatz von Expertensystemen - Arbeitsumfeld im Wandel, in: AWF and VDI-ADB, (eds.), Expertensysteme in der betrieblichen Praxis (AWF, Eschborn, 1988), pp. 240-270

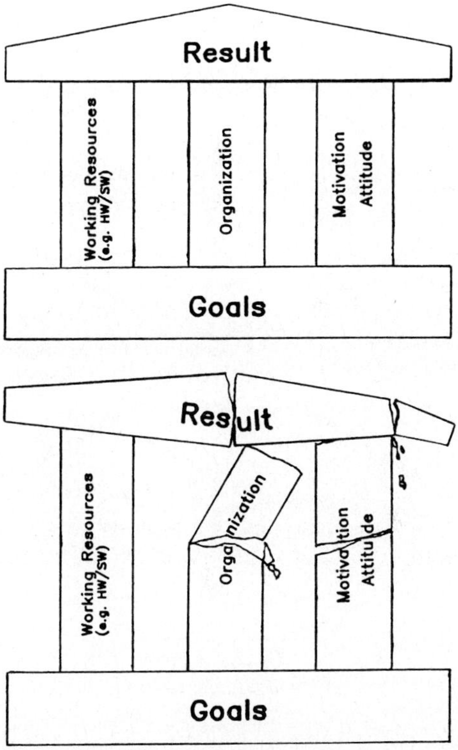

Figure 1: Motivation of employees as a medium to reach the company's goals

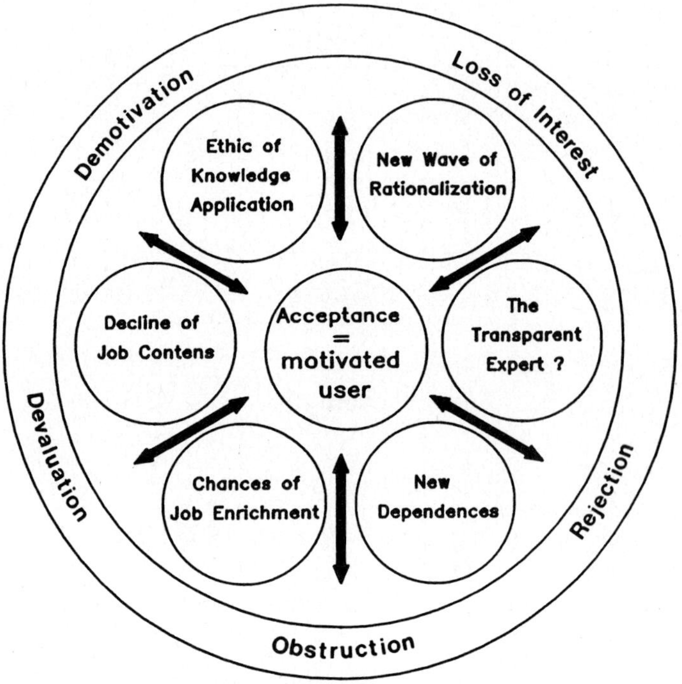

Figure 2: Area of conflict between acceptance and rejection of expert systems

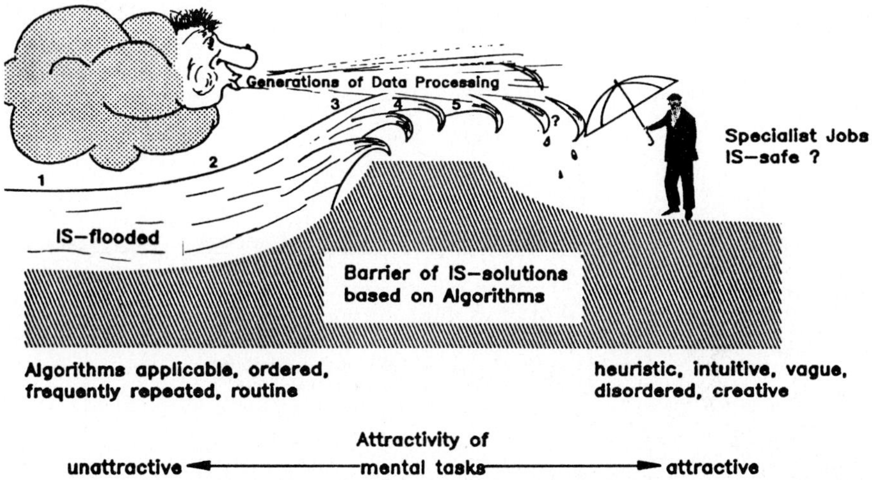

Figure 3: Does AI threaten the attractive jobs of specialists?

Figure 4: Does the expert make himself superfluous by participating in AI projects?

Figure 5: **More flexibility in working hours for experts**

Figure 6: The courage of the expert to prove his competence

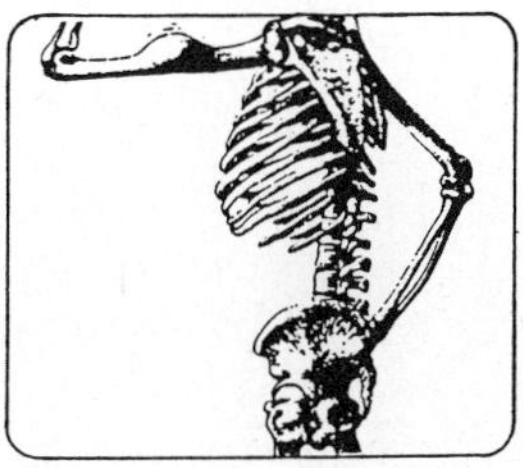

Expertsystem:
X – ray screen
for competence

- What do I know ?
- How do I work ?
- How do I decide ?
- What mistakes am I doing ?
- What knowledge am I lacking ?
- When do I act intuitively ?

Figure 7: Expert system: "X-ray screen for competence"?

Figure 8: The demystification of the expert

Figure 9: Expert discussion about the "valid" solution

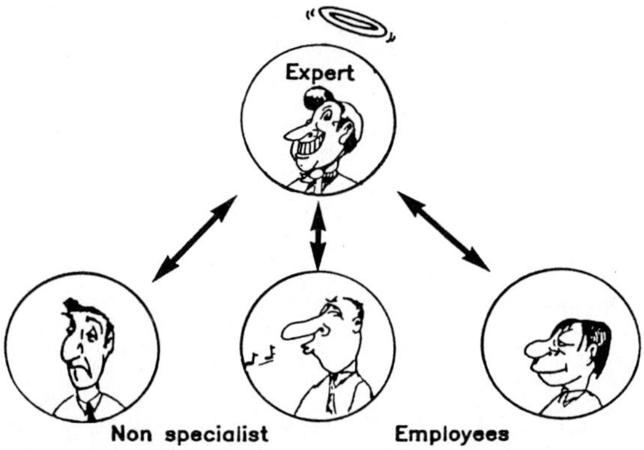

Figure 10: Dependence on an expert

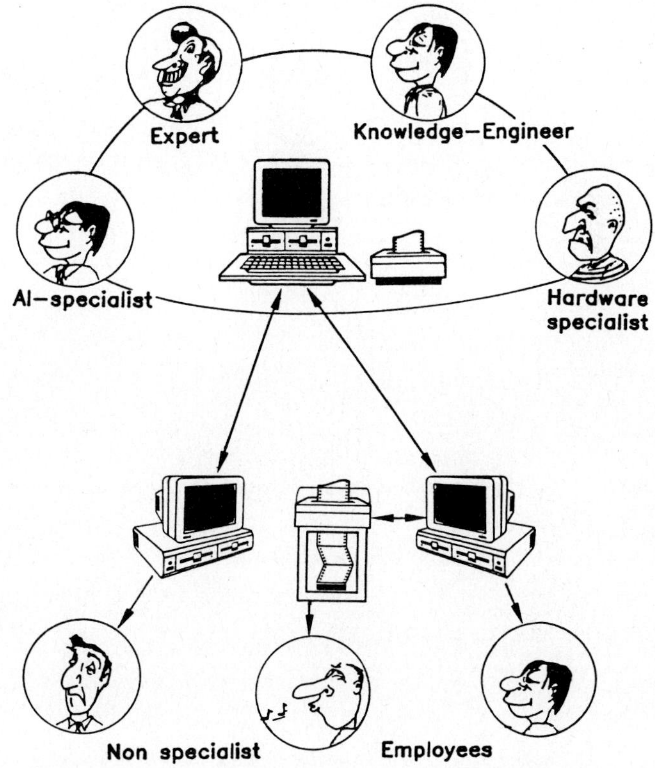

Figure 11: Dependences using an expert system

Figure 12: Expert systems blow up the labyrinth of routine and open up the field of creativity

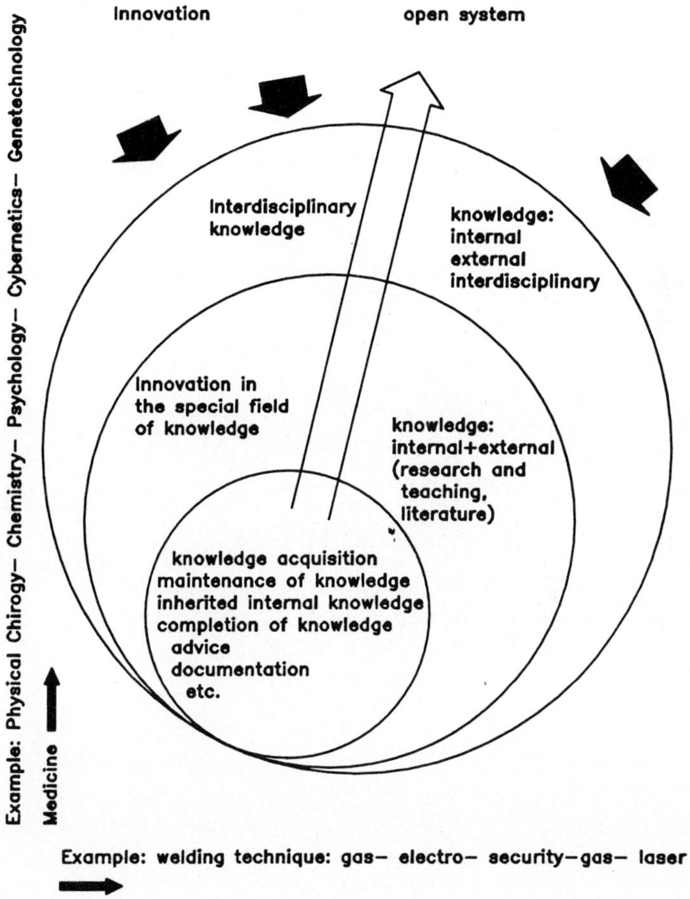

Figure 13: Chances for development of knowledge in relief from and automation of routine processes

Figure 14: Expert system as memorial for acceptance and acknowledgement of the expert's authority

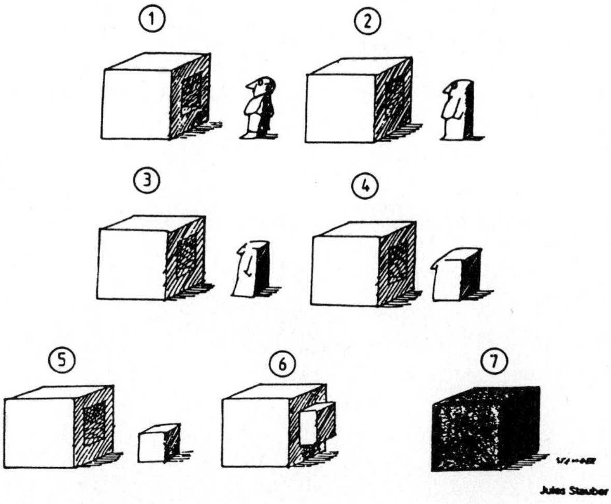

Figure 15: The expert system reduces the degree of freedom in the user's task design

Figure 16: Impoverishment of communication caused by the introduction of expert systems

EXPERT SYSTEMS IN PRODUCTION AND SERVICES II
Th. Bernold and U. Hillenkamp (Editors)
Elsevier Science Publishers B.V., Amsterdam – Printed in The Netherlands
GDI, 1989

Work in the Factory of the Future: Is Computer-Integrated Manufacturing a Mirage?*

Karl-H. Ebel
Manufacturing Industries Branch
International Labor Office
Geneva, Switzerland

1. Introduction

There is a widening circle of opinion supported by case studies and research suggesting that industry is at the threshold of a new era in manufacturing. It is often believed that computer-integrated manufacturing (CIM) will transform the world of work beyond recognition. However, there are also many voices and evidence which tell a cautionary tale of failures in the wake of the introduction of this new technology, although failures are seldom advertised because they affect the image of companies. Has the CIM concept really the potential for far-reaching qualitative changes in manufacturing and what can we reasonably expect to happen to the men and women employed in manufacturing? What will be the role of the human factor in the "factory of the future"?

There is no generally accepted definition of CIM. It usually denotes the computer control of the entire production process from design and manufacturing to product delivery. It comprises computer-aided design (CAD), computer-aided planning (CAP), computer-aided manufacturing (CAM) and computer-aided quality assurance (CAQ). These functions and the subfunctions in each area are parts of a system and are fully integrated through computer networks and have access to a unified data base. CIM is thus essentially about organising and controlling manufacturing of components and assemblies as logically and flexibly as possible and mastering and co-ordinating the corresponding flow of data and information. It aims at optimising the use of equipment, decreasing lead time and inventories, high product quality and lower unit costs. The synergies created through integration are expected to lead to cost reductions, higher productivity, and rapid adjustment of product quantity and product variations, as well

* This paper was initially prepared for a seminar on CIM organised by the United Nations Economic Commision for Europe

as delivery times to demand in competitive national and international markets. It appears to offer an opportunity to keep up with shorter product life cycles and to eliminate much waste.

The concept seems rational, sensible and appeals to the tidy mind. It satisfies the quest of the engineer to create order out of chaos. It assures and comforts the manager looking for efficient means to control the production process. Why is it then that the realisation of projects runs into much difficulty in practice? Are expectations too high? Even if allowance is made for the fact that CIM can only be introduced step by step, that it requires much computing power and the mastering of complex system architectures and software developments, that different production processes need varying CIM systems (i.e. they must be tailor-made) and that "Rome was not built in a day", it is by now obvious that optimism of many automation equipment and system suppliers, engineering researchers and management strategists is not matched by the practical results achieved so far. The "factory and the future" as described by CIM advocates of the engineering profession remains largely a figment of the imagination despite some science-fiction type realisations. And even staunch technocrats readily admit that industry is far removed from realising the full potential of CIM, although partial solutions such as flexible manufacturing systems, automatic materials handling, computer-aided design, computer-numerical control of machine tools (CNC) have made much promising headway. "islands of automation" have thus been created in many plants, but linking them is clearly not an easy task. Some CIM systems have been set up as demonstration or pilot projects and serve to learn about this new approach to manufacturing, but they are usually very costly and isolated experiments outside the real world of production. The installation of operational CIM systems in industry is in inverse proportion to the talk about it. Should we, therefore, regard CIM as an impasse, fading fad or a technocrat's pipe-dream of the manufacturing paradise?

As experience in this field accumulates through trial and error as well as failures and successes, and as different schools of thought try to impose their particular vision of the "factory of the future" it becomes increasingly clear that there are various dimensions to the problem. They are of a socio-economic, technical, managerial and human nature and they are partly rooted in industrial history.

2. The Socio-Economic Perspective

The CIM concept has evolved in the highly industrialised countries characterised by significant capital accumulation and high labour cost as well as a solid and wide scientific and technological base, and a developed social and economic infrastructure. It owes its birth to rapid advances in computer and information technology. Pilot projects and accompanying research to put the concept into practice in manufacturing are concentrated in Japan and the United States and some industrial advanced European countries. However, there are considerable differences in the approaches chosen which tend to be a response to the specific socio-economic situation, the industrial traditions and the factor endowment of the various countries and individual enterprises.

These varying approaches may be typified as the "technocentric" and the "human-centered" approaches. No industrial society has the monopoly of one or the other and they co-exist, although one or the other tendency may prevail. The analysis below which only points out the main features of these approaches and neglects the historic roots needs to be seen in this perspective.

In the United States the so-called "technocentric" approach tends to dominate in its purest form. It has often served as a model in other countries [1]. It denotes an attempt to gradually reduce human intervention in the production process to a minimum and to conceive systems flexible enough to react rapidly to changing market demand for high quality products. Workers and technicians on the shop-floor are sometimes seen as unpredictable, troublesome and unreliable elements, potentially disturbing the production and information flow which is best centrally controlled through computers. The "unmanned factory" is the ultimate goal. It is the extreme division of labour reaching its paroxysm as subdivided and simplified tasks executed by amass of low-skilled labour are progressively taken over by increasingly flexible intelligent and versatile industrial robots and machine systems communicating among each other via networks and com-puters.

Only a residual role is assigned to workers as their skills are supposed to be gradually and progressively embodied in the machines. It is hoped that this approach will stop the ongoing erosion of production know-how and regain lost superiority of US-style manufacturing and competitivity in the global market-place. Much capital and sophisticated technology are expected to overcome a deep-seated structural problem: the decreasing competitivity of American manufacturing in its home market and abroad. It has been called the "moonshot" approach. Since US manufacturers produce for a large and homogeneous home market, they can concentrate on high volume products and relatively large batches in component manufacturing. The ensuing production process is relatively inflexible even though flexible manufacturing systems and machining

---

1 W. Wobbe: "Technology, work and employment - New trends in the structural change of society", in Vocational Training Bulletin, CEDEFOP, No., 1, 1987, pp. 3-6; P. Brödner: "Towards an anthropocentric approach in European manufacturing", in Vocational Training Bulletin, CEDEFOP, No. 1, 1987, pp. 30-39.

cells are used. The central engineering challenge is thought to be arriving at continuous flow production of large varieties of products and components without much work-in-process, i.e. without idling capital. This would ensure high productivity and adequate returns. The human factor plays a minor role in this equation. This is a late vindication of Taylorism or Fordism which was baed on the principles and management of using vast pools of unskilled and semi-skilled labour. The increasingly sophisticated machinery is thought to make most labour dispensable. Traditionally adversarial industrial relations and little commitment and loyalty of the workforce reinforce this attitude. The technical office manned by professional engineers and technicians becomes increasingly the repository of production know-how to the detriment of production workers.

This approach carried to its extreme has proven not to work very well or only at excessively high cost. It has, for instance, been found that flexible manufacturing systems installed in the United States often performed worse than conventional technology. The relevance of the technocentric approach for the future of manufacturing seems, therefore, questionable [2]. It may be a dead-end because of an essential flaw: there is mounting evidence that the type of flexible automation which forms the core of CIM systems will only work and remain operational when manned by high qualified and motivated workers who can cope with relatively frequent breakdowns of such complex and sophisticated equipment and with software problems. In fact, there are persistent complaints that the specific skills needed for high-tech manufacturing are scarce or simply not available. If there is a lack or shortage of committed skilled and thoroughly trained staff, systems tend to perform far below their potential capacity. Inadequate performance of such sophisticated installations appear to be the rule rather than the exception. At any rate, their is generally a long learning and running-in period with uncertain future returns as a result of excessive reliance on unproven technology.

The Japanese approach to CIM is driven by a different rationale. Companies introducing advanced and flexible automation systems can rely on a highly qualified, versatile and loyal workforce, and do so. Instead of progressing in the technological field by giant leaps they prefer incremental improvements of the production process and of quality, often enough initiated by motivated engineers, technicians and workers on the shop-floor. The wide adoption of the quality circle movement is only one manifestation. Emphasis is on product quality and production scheduling (i.e. just-in-time production and electronic ordering of materials and components). Compared with the outstanding manu-

---

2 St. S. Cohen and Y. Zysman: "US competitiveness suffers - The emergence of a manufacturing gap", in Transatlantic Perspectives, No. 18, Autumn 1988, pp. 6-9.

facturing skills manifesting themselves in the wide application of industrial robots, the integration of the information flow through computers is relatively less developed due to gaps and difficulties in software development. The most flexible element in the system is, in fact, the people who make it work. Moreover, most companies operating such systems tend to serve large local and export markets and therefore produce relatively large series, although the flexibility of the equipment is utilised to a greater extend than in American manufacturing thanks to the higher qualified workforce. The strength of this approach shows in diversified high-quality mass production. It is facilitated by a co-operative industrial relations system.

Manufacturers catering for relatively small, heterogeneous or specialised internal or export markets demanding high-quality components and customised products, as is largely the case in Europe, have been inclined to rely on another strategy in the introduction of CIM. In view of the high investments required and the often limited capital base they usually opt for a cautious, pragmatic and gradual approach. The panoply of CIM is adopted with restraint. The skilled and highly skilled craftsman and technician has mostly remained the centerpiece of manufacturing. While Taylorism had made some inroads in European manufacturing, particularly in the automobile and consumer durables industries, it never replaced skill-based production in medium- and small-scale enterprises in the capital goods sector where division of labour is only applicable to a limited extent. Such enterprises competing in narrow markets or occupying market niches always had to be flexible and innovative to survive. The new computerised flexible and integrated automation equipment is primarily seen as a more perfected tool in the hands of a skilled and versatile workforce serving to enhance existing know-how, to obtain greater flexibility, higher productivity, better quality and shorter delivery time. It is not regarded as a panacea to all production problems, but as helpful in gaining a market share. Such enterprises also tend to make a sustained effort to retrain their staff. Also, a lesser division of work allows the allocation of greater and wider responsibility to workers according to their qualifications and consequently more flexible forms of managerial control and organisation, including teamwork and imaginative applications of CIM using available skills [3].

There are only vague estimates of the potential economic benefits of CIM. They are usually based on a few cases and stem from equipment vendors or research into limited applications. They are suspect in so far as business accounting methods in use do not permit - or at the best approximately so - to calculate the real returns of such investment. The following indications are therefore given with due reservation and should only serve as a basic orientation.

---

[3] H.-J. Warnecke: "CIM in Europe", Stuttgart, unpublished paper, 1987.

Thus, CIM is expected to lead to a per cent rise in output, 5 to 20% reduction in personnel costs and 10 to 15% lower production costs. Inventories could be reduced by 20%, scrap by 10% and order lead times by 50% [4]. Another estimate assumes the potential overall cost reduction to be 5 to 10%, i.e. more than the profit margin of most companies; and points out that CIM mainly gets rid of "hidden" costs and overheads, e.g. accumulation of work-in-process, idle machine time [5]. There are also more indirect benefits such as shorter product development cycles and accelerated production of prototypes which help to maintain or improve market position. The time-span in which such economic benefits could materialise is not specified.

All investigations tend to concur that the actual saving in labour cost is marginal when considering that the latter normally ranges between 5 and 15% of total product cost. CIM just signifies that there will be less but better remunerated highly skilled labour. Such savings do not offset the higher capital cost. It has been suggested that the reduction of excess stocks and work-in-process could potentially finance all reasonable investment in CIM [6].

There is encouraging evidence that in general the aggregate level of employment in industrial societies is relatively little affected by the introduction of new technologies. The long-term trend of a fall in manufacturing employment observed in industrialised countries certainly continues and technological innovation is a contributing factor primarily eliminating unskilled work. However, on the whole, job displacement and redeployment of workers in the innovation and rationalisation process appear to balance, and where technological change goes along with strong economic growth, expansion of markets and investment, it even tends to induce positive employment effects through the revitalisation of the economy. Japan´s technology drive and growth pattern a a case in point. However, it would certainly be vain to pin exaggerated hopes on the introduction of CIM and other high technology and their spin-offs as an employment creation device. "Reindustrialisation through high technology" is certainly a misleading concept [7]. Only a very small proportion of the labour force of the highly industrialised countries - some 2 or 5% - are engaged in this advanced sector, and this proportion will rise only slowly, if a tall, if past trends and experience are any guide.

---

4 G. Garner: "Potentials of CIM", in Chemical Engineering, 28 Mar. 1988

5 H.-J. Warnecke, op. cit.

6 ---, "Factory in the Future - A survey", in The Economist, 30 May 1987, pp. 17-18.

7 W. Wobbe, op. cit.; K.-H. Ebel and E. Ulrich: "The computer in design and manufacturing - Servant or master?" Social ans labour effects of computer-aided design/computer-aided manufacturing, Working paper, SAP 6.1/WP9, Geneva, p. 19 ff.

3. The Technical Perspective

CIM is many things to many people. Enterprises have to seek their own solutions to the multitude of technical problems in response to their specific requirements. Depending on the complexities of the manufacturing process and the existing organisation pattern they may well be formidable. Existing model solutions are not generally applicable and only show that integration is feasible to a large extent and under specific circumstances - though often at a high price.

It is, therefore, useful to keep in mind what can be gleaned from various studies of CIM introduction about the state of the art.

There are first of all a number of technical shortcomings. A great deal of research and development effort goes into eliminating such technical bottlenecks hindering a wider application of CIM. Considerable progress is being made on a large front and, a priori, one cannot say that remaining problems are insoluble. However, there is still many a hard nut to crack and it is not sure when and at what cost effective solutions will be found.

The linking of a wide variety of numerically controlled machine tools and industrial robots, process control computers, automatic transport and storage facilities, quality assurance, design and production planning functions and management information systems through networks is the technical rationale of CIM. So far, the different subsystems of CIM as CAD, CAM, CAP, etc., have been treated as isolated functions with their own requirements, logic and software. There are many partial solutions to bridging these functions. They have helped to bring about "islands of automation" in factories. Truly integrated large systems, comprising all functions of designing, manufacturing and assembling products with a great number of components do not exist yet.

Networking of systems is mostly in its initial stages. The development of computer software for such tasks is painstaking. The general adoption of standards which are vital for linking computer hardware and automation equipment of various makes is lagging behind. As a matter of fact, there are constant complaints about the proliferation of proprietary operating systems, communication options and control programmes. The existing chaos holds back networking as manufacturers hesitate to commit themselves. It also increases costs. Vendors and users of flexible automation equipment are painfully aware of this situation. General Motors, as one of the large clients, has therefore pioneered an industry-wide standard – the manufacturing automation protocol (MAP) – for the linking of inventory control, robotics, CNC machinery and quality control and will only buy equipment conforming to these standards. The company has recently agreed with the aircraft manufacturer BOEING which uses the technical office protocol (TOP) to make the two systems compatible. TOP is largely complementary to MAP. These plans have aroused some controversy. These systems have been criticised for being too slow and exclusive, and for not tying in with industrial robotics. They are tinged with the image of company proprietary standards. The International Standards Organisation has fixed a more ambitious objective; it promotes the Open-Systems Interconnection (OSI) which is to enable all computer systems to communicate with each other. However, OSI also encounters delays and acceptance problems [8]. It appears that a great deal of research is still needed to arrive at satisfactory world-wide standards.

Compatibility of equipment and systems is certainly a crucial problem, but there are still others. Much information required in the production process is not suitable for coding, computer processing and transmission. This means that available data are not always complete or reliable. However, full integration of the production process means that it must be predictable. Stringent procedures are required which have to be formalised and cover process planning, tool supply, production planning and logistics. Such strict procedures are, of course, the antithesis of flexibility, but they are necessary because robots can neither think nor anticipate.

Further problems are unreliable software and automation equipment, rudimentary sensory abilities of industrial robots, poor data quality and accessibility. The need for constant updating of data bases is another drawback. The result of such combined difficulties is that systems are vulnerable and break down frequently, often more than one-third of the available time.

It might be added that optimal CIM requires real time data processing. However, current computer-aided manufacturing (CAM) systems process about 85 to 95% of data by batches which is considered insufficient [9]

CIM is praised for its flexibility which is true up to a point, in particular when it comes to machining of families of parts. On the other hand, it is relatively inflexible with respect to alteration of batches and when process innovation is contemplated. In fact, every change of a customer's order or equipment, tools or materials has first to be modelled in the computer system.

---

[8] A. Cane: "Computers in manufacturing", in Financial Times Survey, 2 June 1987, pp I and II.

[9] G.G. Axelson: "Computer-integrated manufacturing: How to get there", International Management Institute, Report No. 002, Geneva, Oct. 1985, p. 48.

There are some technical remedies on their way. The development of fault-tolerant computer systems is making progress. The sensory abilities of robots are constantly improving. Greater data storage density and processing speed of computers will help to build more "intelligent" systems. Moreover, some promising developments in "artificial intelligence" and expert systems may well help to make systems more tolerant and responsive to faults. Expert systems are already being used in standardised procedures and routine checking, and are beginning to play a role in maintenance, fault diagnostics, production control, quality assurance, planning, scheduling, design, notably computer-aided design (CAD), and support software development and training. Nevertheless, such systems have their limitations. They embody knowledge extracted from experts and reason according to rules, but there are limitations to formalising human abilities, sensorial experiences as well as open and complex industrial processes. Also common-sense knowledge is not programmable, nor do expert systems have intuition or practise associative thinking. They can therefore support, but not replace, human decision-making.

Another way minimising technical problems is the initial design of products in such a way that they can be processed and assembled with the available flexible automated equipment. This means simplification and reducing the number of components, streamlining assembly operations and generally taking into account the ability of machines and robots at the design stage.

4. The Managerial and Organisational Perspectives

There are different management attitudes on how to cope with CIM. In part they are a mirror image of the national idiosyncracies and different industrial histories evoked above. Thus the technocentric approach results in management strategies which neglect or underrate the human factor in production. It is frequently aggravated by short-term profit maximisation considerations which are the curse of technology planning and management. The introduction of CIM requires long-term strategic thinking. From the managerial point of view it is fundamentally an organisational quandary. It is about creating order out of chaos. Equipment needs to be carefully selected and compatibility ensured. However, the essential question is how to reshape existing production processes, how to alter organisational boundaries and to make them permeable. This requires redesigning the information and data flow. The difficulties of actually doing this in existing organisations, to make them more effective and efficient should not be underestimated.

CIM introduction may well act as an antidote to poor management practices. This is when the human factor comes in. Industrial case studies and experience accumulated so far clearly indicate that a pragmatic management approach advancing step by step, building up the skill, responsibility and motivation of the workforce, investing in people operating the systems and relying on the human factor in making them flexible, has consistently paid off best.

The conviction that this is really so seems to be lacking in many management circles, otherwise the revalorisation of the human factor would be pursued more systematically and consistently. At any rate, it has been found that in general CIM is not primarily introduced "to humanise work". The motives and expectations of management mostly relate to inventory reduction, more transparency of the organisation, reduction of lead time, greater adherence to deadlines, saving of personnel, greater marketing flexibility, increased capacity use, higher product quality or keeping up with technological developments, all leading to higher productivity. Better working conditions tend to be a low priority and a rather accidental by-product [10]. In fact, working conditions may even be neglected or worsen, particularly when automated machinery is used to enforce an accelerated pace of work, where only residual tasks are entrusted to workers or when stressful situations are engendered by computerisation.

A management style allowing more autonomy of production personnel may well mean a break with entrenched principles and thus be conceived as a threat to vested interests and the power structure in an organisation. It is hardly surprising that such clashes are avoided almost at any price. It is, in fact, possible to switch to a new technology without making fundamental organisational changes, and to keep compartmentalisation and established hierarchies in place. Information technologies may serve to institutionalise and even reinforce ineffective and counterproductive management practices such as excessive centralisation of decision-making or abusive monitoring of individuals if the powers that be manage to fend off restructuring. This is, of course, costly and leads to mediocre results while it prolongs the life of organisational dinosaurs. It signifies the defeat of the primary purpose of CIM, i.e. the integration of all functions. Such integration requires "vertical and horizontal synchronisation of departments, people, machinery and processes in the flow of information and material" [11]. In such a system the necessary flexibility can be achieved through decentralisation of information and responsibility within a given framework to achieve small and fast control loops. This enables the production system to respond rapidly to market demand, particularly in the case of many product options.

---

10 K.-H. Ebel and E. Ulrich, op. cit., pp. 53-57.

11 H.-J. Warnecke, op. cit.

If progress is to be made in the effective introduction of CIM a clear strategy is needed endorsed by senior management and promoted by the rank and file. Nothing much can be done without the consistent backing of top management but the stumbling block can be middle-management which stands to lose influence when hierarchies tumble and all required information is available "on-line" without intermediary to all participants in the production process. This emphasises the need for top-level management, a function frequently neglected as legal, financial and marketing aspects tend to dominate decision-making at the top. It is not enough to let middle-management acquire technology and then to do crisis management at the top when bottlenecks occur in the organisation or qualifications are lacking.

Some have traced existing problems to the lack of managerial competence [12]. Managers' knowledge of advanced manufacturing systems is frequently limited even when they have had a technical education or are professional engineers. Manufacturing technology and, more in particular, information technology, is moving fast. Professional knowledge and experience once acquired becomes rapidly obsolete without continuing exposure to shop-floor experience. Thus, potential users of automation equipment fear that they cannot muster and constantly update the necessary know-how. They often depend on outside consultants and equipment suppliers. They naturally tread carefully in unknown territory and avoid incalculable risks.

As capital requirements for the implementation of CIM are high, managers are under pressure to justify such expenditures. By the standards of a short-term return-on-investment (ROI) approach the financial feasibility of CIM projects is mostly doubtful despite the hypothetical economic advantages outlined above. In fact, there are no generally agreed methods for doing reliable cost-benefit analyses of CIM. As a matter of fact, the cost of full CIM implementation is often considered to be prohibitive despite the fact that most equipment to build such plants may be available. It is also feared that the systems are inefficient to use and expensive to maintain because technical change would constantly require the replacement of parts of the system, by definition not an easy job in an integrated system.

To this should be added that in present flexible manufacturing systems fixed costs constitute about 70% of the total outlay. This is an indication of the high risks which management takes when installing CIM.

---

[12] R. Hodson and J. Hagan: "Skills and job commitment in high technology industries in the US", in New Technology, Work and Employment, pp. 113-124

There is, of course, also the more positive side of the coin: risks are balanced by opportunities if the predicted economic benefits of CIM materialise. Moreover, in the coming years capital requirements are bound to descend because cheaper systems are being put on the market. It has also been estimated that CIM plants could break even at 30 to 35% of capacity use as against 65 to 70% in the case of conventional plants. Also the planning of CIM and at least a partial implementation could help management to improve the organisation of the production process and the flow of communication.

But costs are not the only element to be considered in making strategic decisions about the introduction of CIM. A responsible and forward-looking management may well conclude that it cannot afford to be left behind in the technology race and that research and development expenditures for process technology must be met and that investment in CIM is required to remain competitive in the long run. Clearly, much depends on the specific situation of the enterprise.

If the strategic decision to implement CIM is made, management's essential task in implementing CIM is overcoming organisational resistance to change starting from shop-floor through all layers of the organisation. The streamlining of an organisation and making it fit for CIM may be a considerable challenge but may be well worth it. The finding of a variety of surveys concur, in so far as those manufacturers who have introduced advanced manufacturing systems attribute between 40 and 70% of the total improvement achieved to organisational changes. In other words, the main benefit does not necessarily stem from sophisticated and integrated technology but from the reform of management and production practices and from a more transparent and efficient organisation [13].

5. The Human and Social Perspective

5.1. The Indispensable Human Factor

If we admit that a technocentric approach to CIM would be inefficient and counterproductive it follows that the key role of the human factor must be recognised. The art is to assign a really effective function to it and to give people an opportunity to make full use of their knowledge, capabilities and skills, and to help them master the production process. This means putting them in appropriately designed jobs and workplaces, having adequate man/machine

---

13 B. Haywood and Y. Bessant: "The integration of production processes at firm level", Research paper, Brighton Polytechnic, Jan. 1987.

interfaces, making the production process transparent, setting up a suitable work organisation as well as providing the necessary training.

It is important to look at the potential weaknesses and strengths of the human factor in a CIM environment. Human beings involved in the production process are error-prone, particularly under physical or psychic stress. Noise or bad lightning may lead to fatigue. The error rate also grows with information overload. Survey findings show that 70 to 90% of the failures of technical systems are due to faulty human intervention or system design. Human beings do not always work with full concentration, come to wrong conclusions, make mistakes or do not act when they should. Their operating behaviour is relatively unpredictable. Is this sufficient reason to try to banish people from the production process?

There is clearly a wide range of tasks and functions which are best done by machines, industrial robots and computers. This range is widening constantly and more and more manual operations are taken over by machines. The improvement of sensors and actors makes robots and other production equipment more versatile, rapid and exact. Some jobs can actually be done infinitely more efficiently and reliably by information systems and computers than by human beings. This is particularly true for routine functions such as data collection and their statistical analysis as well many surveying and control functions which are the basis for automatic process and quality control in production. It can be envisaged that the executing of increasing numbers of specialised functions can be transferred to machines and computers. We are therefore faced with a growing complexity of such technical systems.

However, as such systems become more complex they also tend to be less fail safe. In fact, they break down frequently, causing high cost. They can be repaired and perfected but this requires skilled human intervention. In such an event workers responsible for the operation have to make choices and decisions which no technical system can make for them. Often quick intervention is required which is based on knowledge and experience and takes into account the limits of the system. The human being despite its weaknesses is, thus, indispensable for an optimal and efficient use of automated equipment. The qualified, motivated and experienced worker familiar with the system can cope with uncertainty and is able to assess situations, to find and interpret faults rapidly and correct them. Judgement supported by technical knowledge and experience, understanding of systems and common sense are qualities which cannot be replaced by computers or artificial intelligence in the foreseeable future. In CIM systems machines and computers may well take over most routine and physical tasks but they do not dispense the people involved from thinking, critical decision-making and responsibility.

5.2. The Design of CIM Systems

As the human factor cannot be replaced it is crucial that the CIM systems are designed and planned in such a way that people involved can do their job in optimal conditions and can really apply their empirical knowledge. In the first place this means that they must not be made totally and helplessly dependent on the system. This might have serious consequences when system errors cannot be corrected in good time. Also, such dependence limits initiative, improvisation and creativity. It fosters submission to routine which makes the systems, and consequently the enterprise, vulnerable. Overdependence on systems and machines has not only provoked disasters in nuclear and chemical industries, it is also cause of perhaps less spectacular, but none the less very costly failures in automated production. Workers in CIM systems designed to make use of the human factor should be able to intervene in the production process to optimise it. This signifies that the system must allow shop-floor programming of CNC equipment on the basis of indications provided and discussed with the design office. The implementation of such organisational presupposes the availability of appropriate man/machine interfaces and software. An example of what can be done is the use of portable electronic sketch pad which could help to overcome the notorious divorce of designers from the realities and constraints of the production process which has been accentuated by computer-aided design. Such a device will help them to discuss design ideas with shop-floor personnel [14].

A further problem to be considered is that the physical distance between the personnel operating or supervising the equipment and the process tends to widen. Much visual and manual control is replaced by sensors which transmit data to screens and data bases. The worker is faced with control data at his workstation, but loses direct touch with the process. Often it can only be monitored from a control room. It has been found that such distance from the process may make quick reaction and the correction or compensation of system faults more difficult because warnings emitted by the system can be misinterpreted and workers lose the "feelings" for the process. This means that the process must be designed transparently, be comprehensible and sufficiently accessible without hazards in order to allow the required or desirable intervention. Some research has been done on the significance and role of empirical knowledge and materials which experienced skilled workers possess. It appears that

---

[14] M. Cooley: "Technologischer Wandel - Probleme und Möglichkeiten", in BFZ Info. Essen. No. 3. 1988. pp. 4-5.

they develop a feeling, almost a sixth sense, telling them what is wrong with a machine and how it works best. This capability is precious and should not be underestimated for the smooth running of advanced manufacturing systems [15].

In the technocentric approach to CIM there is clearly a danger that most production knowledge will be incorporated in the computer and expert systems without giving workers sufficient opportunity to exercise their skills which would waste away because they are no longer used. However, this would make production systems very unwieldly and vulnerable and their formalism would cause considerable constraints. Moreover, the human knowledge base of enterprises could be eroded to such an extend that their future is put in jeopardy. This is too high a price to pay for enterprises which depend on the qualification, skill and adaptability of their workforce.

Moreover there are signs that the technocentric approach may cause the disaffection of the workforce. Research findings in the United States suggest that workers in high technology industries are less satisfied than other manufacturing workers due to more rigid rules, stricter discipline and closer supervision and monitoring [16]. Apparently such disaffection has been noted particularly in the case where production workers felt threatened by deskilling. This may well be related to the fact that management has a tendency to leave the troubleshooting and maintenance and repair of advanced systems to specialised services without involving the operators of the equipment. It is probably significant that this neglect of shop-floor skills has led to a great increase in production down-time [17]. The way out is obviously to entrust as much responsibility for maintenance as possible to suitable qualified workers on the shop-floor.

The practical problem of taking all these aspects into account in designing CIM systems and of making optimal use of the human factor must not be underrated even when such human-centered systems are recognised as superior. A multidisciplinary approach is required which is by no means easy to organise. Managers and engineers designing the system will have to be committed to such an approach and should associate ergonomists, training specialists and social scientists. There are few tried methods since the technocentric approach neglecting ergonomics and social concerns prevails up to now. Often engineers and er-

---

[15] F. Böhle and B. Milkan: "Vom Handrad zum Bildschirm - Eine Untersuchung zur sinnlichen Erfahrung im Arbeitsprozess", München, Campus Verlag, 210 pp.

[16] R. Hodson and J. Hagan, op. cit.

[17] P. Chabert and P. Laperousaz: "Modernisation - Attention aux idées reçues!", in L'Usine nouvelle, No. 3, 21 Jan. 1988, pp. 4-8.

gonomists tend to be at cross purposes. This is a field which needs further exploration [18].

5.3. Skill Requirements for CIM

The above observations imply that the skill level of shop-floor workers is going to increase despite some skills becoming obsolete and that division of labour will regress. CIM requires versatile craftsmen and technicians, computer and software experts, mechanical and communications engineers and, in general, people who understand production methods and -systems. They should be capable of coping a great deal of technical information and able to take decision on the spot. There is little room for unskilled workers such as assemblers, labourers, machine loaders, transport workers, etc. CIM also makes clerical workers redundant, that is those who are occupied with ordering parts and materials and scheduling the workload of machines.

Also managerial jobs at the middle level are bound to be changed or diminished in CIM systems which entail a general dissemination and free flow of information. There tend to be fewer hierarchical levels and demarcation lines lines, and there are less co-ordinating tasks. Emphasis is on planning, anticipating problems, less formal communications, team-work and interaction and much less on giving instructions. Excessive monitoring of workers which is technically possible is best avoided because it can antagonise the very people needed to man the systems. It is a new world for team leadership in CIM which requires a combination of human, conceptual and technical skills in managers [19].

5.4. New Types of Work Organisation

As many specialised jobs are abolished due to a lesser division of labour, work organisation tends towards group work. In such relatively autonomous groups members execute complementary tasks and must be versatile as varying tasks are allocated with the objective of keeping the system functioning smoothly. Group members must be able to communicate beyond narrow technical boundaries and to co-operate. They also have a certain autonomy in the choice of tasks and detailed planning. Thus existing qualifications are better used and mutual coaching takes place. If properly organised, greater job satisfaction is the result.

---

[18] J. M. Corbett: "Human-centred advanced manufacturing systems: From rhetoric to reality", in INFO Pack No. 4, Committee on Social Effects of Automation, International Federation of Automatic Control, Mar. 1989, pp. 1-12.

[19] O.L. Crocker and R. Guelker.: "The effects of robotics on the workplace", in Personnel, Sep. 1988, pp. 26-36.

However, such participative work organisation is by no means an automatic outcome of the introduction of CIM. Management must consciously seek to overcome outdated, demotivating and unsuitable hierarchical forms of organisation which means the shedding of old power relationships - often a painful process fraught with pitfalls. Vested interests in the status quo are usually very strong. However, it should be some comfort to management deciding to base CIM on group technology that production is usually less capital-intensive since it is less computerised and requires less expensive software because many decisions are taken on the shop-floor which also helps to make it flexible. Moreover, existing qualifications of the workforce can normally be used and few new ones are required. There is also a reduction of through-put-time [20].

Some concern has been expressed that CIM will lead to the social isolation of the relatively few workers left on the shop-floor who remain there to mind the system. In fact, much communication takes place via computer terminals and opportunities for social contacts are diminished. This may well affect individuals and the working atmosphere in plants negatively. In the end such dissatisfaction would have negative consequences for the overall result of the production process. At any rate, system designers need to keep this aspect in mind and provide opportunities for social contact as a contribution to quality of working life.

5.5. Hazards in the New Working Environment

While the new job requirements in CIM systems are becoming better known, there is much uncertainty about new occupational safety and health hazards. It stands to reason that physical risks are diminished because less workers are in direct contact with production equipment and most production takes place without direct human intervention. On the other hand, there is usually a higher pace of work as well as much shift work which tends to increase fatigue and the accident rate. It has been found that work at computer terminals can be very stressful indeed, particularly in the case of computer-aided design.

A potentially very serious problem is that apparently an increasing number of psychosomatic illnesses may be caused by the new automated systems. Workers confronted with the new expensive and complex equipment often do not feel up to it and feel powerless. They cannot intervene in the process while being responsible for running it. The combination of high responsibility and insufficient qualifications to master the job at hand or to intervene is extremely stressful. This may be aggravated by frequent breakdowns which have to be repaired under time pressure. The resulting permanent stress can lead to ner-

---

20 P. Brödner, op. cit.

vous and physical disorders and is said to affect a disproportionate number of workers in advanced manufacturing systems. Training and ergonomically designed workplaces may help. However, it is probably more important that system designers do not place excessive demands on system users and maintenance staff nor do the opposite and make jobs undemanding and monotonous which also causes stress.

Another cause for concern is the fact that work becomes more static and jobs need more brainpower than muscle. Physical activity is much reduced as machines and robots take over materials and components handling. Such reduced physical activity has been identified as a significant threat to health. Countermeasures may well be needed.

A further cause of fatigue and stress is the ineptness of much computer software. Much of it is not user-friendly and remote from actual workplace requirements. This can make man/machine interaction very cumbersome. "Cognitive" ergonomics addresses these problems. However, this is a relatively new science and improvements in software design taking into account research findings are only slowly forthcoming.

System designers who usually have an exclusively technical or scientific background tend to overlook such considerations in the planning stage of installations. However, this is the time when preventive measures have to be taken. Planning and investment costs are usually only slightly increased. It is much more costly to rectify ergonomic mistakes once a system is installed and is therefore mostly not done [21].

The principle objective should be the creation of humane working conditions, for only workers treated primarily as responsible human beings will commit themselves to company goals. A definition of humane work which deserves attention in this context is the following:

> *Work is called humane if it does not damage the psycho-physical health of the worker, does not, or only temporarily, impair his psycho-social well being, meets his requirements and qualifications, allows him to exercise individual and/or collective control over working conditions and systems of work, and is able to contribute to the development of his personality in activating his potentials and furthering his competence* [22].

---

21 W. Wobbe, op. cit.

22 T. Martin, E. Ulrich and H.-J. Warnecke: "Appropiate automation for flexible manufacture", in Preprints, 10th World Congress on Automatic Control, Munich, July 1987, International Federation of Automatic Control, Laxenburg, Austria, Vol. 5, pp. 291-305.

5.6. The Preparation of the Workforce for CIM

If people are the key to successful CIM, much hinges on their preparation for the new systems. In all industrial countries there is a shortage of professional, technical and managerial personnel able and qualified to mastermind the implementation of CIM. The major constraint is not only the lack of adequate computer hardware or software. At the shop-floor level also the necessary skills are mostly in short supply. The recruitment difficulties of enterprises and the high initial salaries paid to capable young engineers and technicians in this field are case in point. This skill shortage may well explain many of the failures of systems reported hitherto. Often management appears to have only a hazy idea where they are going. Also, workers´ representatives are seldom aware of the intricacies and possible social consequences of CIM.

There is no easy way out. One of the answers is systematic training and further training of the workforce based on a specifically designed training strategy endorsed by management and workers' representatives. Such training is required before the new equipment is installed and will have to emphasise not only specialised technical competence, including computer literacy but, above all, system knowledge, planning, organisational and communication skills and group dynamics. It needs to be done mainly by the enterprises themselves in co-operation with system suppliers because CIM systems are tailor-made for the specific requirements of enterprises and training institutes rarely have the expertise in leading edge technology.

Another answer may well be the widest possible use of expert advice in the planning stage of CIM and an open discussion of alternatives among all concerned. This includes the workers' representatives who far too often are faced with a fait accompli. A thorough discussion of the economic, technical, organisational, and manpower parameters and of the objectives of an innovation subsequently facilitates an informed assessment of the social consequences and the negotiation of working conditions. Both management and the workforce usually move into unchartered territory and might as well recognise this.

5.7. The Impact of CIM on Industrial Relations

In the real world the transition to CIM systems even when well planned and prepared will rarely proceed without tension and potential, if not open, conflict in organisations. The workforce has good reason to worry since there is plenty of evidence showing that its interests might not be taken sufficiently into account or simply neglected. Far too often technology is put before people who then have to cope with it somehow without being properly trained or involved in its choice. Small wonder that systems fail. Workers fear pay losses through less overtime, redundancy, the erosion of promotion prospects and lower manning levels, expropriation of know-how through data bases and expert systems, higher stress through responsibility for expensive capital goods, more strenuous shift work patterns, individual performance monitoring through the computer system, deskilling and generally the unknown, and the stress of the adjustment to new working patterns. This can be, but must not be, the outcome.

With a strategy that puts people first and seeks genuine consultation at all levels, such fears may be overcome and do not have to materialise. The positive aspects of change to the advanced systems and the new opportunities will more easily impose themselves such as safer and less physically taxing jobs, learning and training opportunities, greater responsibility and more interesting assignments, better remuneration, generally better working conditions or greater job security in a more competitive enterprise. It can also bring down the rate of absenteeism. Innovations have, in fact, the potential of influencing industrial relations to the good, if more emphasis is put on consultation at all levels and less on "the arrogant expertise of technologists".

The positive aspects can only prevail in an atmosphere of social dialogue and good will at the enterprise level. Adversarial industrial relations could easily spell the failure of CIM projects. CIM presupposes a reconciliation of interests of management and workers. The dialogue between social partners is thus essential for product and process innovation, higher productivity and flexibility in manufacturing.

There is indeed evidence that in an adversarial industrial relations atmosphere management resorts to excessive division of labour as a means of restricting the influence of unions. In such circumstances management tends not to entrust blue-collar workers with more autonomy and control (e.g. the the programming of NC tools) thus avoiding rules and constraints imposed by collective bargaining agreements. This has the perverse effect that unionisation inhibits skill acquisition by blue-collar workers and their upgrading [23].

The greatest menace to workers' autonomy and to job satisfaction stems from centralised control which also introduces much demotivating rigidity and formal procedures into the production process. Decentralised systems coupled with a maximum of decision-making at the shop-floor are well suited to small batch or customised production, tend to enrich jobs and qualifications, cut down machine-down-time through better scheduling and maintenance and,

---

23 M. R. Kelley: "Unionisation and job design under programmable automation", in Industrial Relations, Spring, 1989.

therefore, enhance productivity. They often prove to be economically superior to rigidly centralised systems with excessive division of labour [24]

A high degree of consensus and co-operation is indeed required if CIM systems are to work smoothly, which does not exclude a resolute defence of workers' rights and interests. It cannot be overlooked that highly skilled workers and technicians and their representatives in integrated manufacturing are in a strong position and cannot easily be replaced. In fact, enterprises installing such systems depend on the quality and commitment of their workforce. Qualified personnel is needed to maintain the complex and costly equipment and keep the systems working. Advanced systems are vulnerable to strikes by a small proportion of their workforce. Responsible management is therefore well advised to seek the social dialogue and collective agreements providing a framework for the operation of the systems. An unorganised workforce kept in check by management prerogatives and arbitrariness, subdued by authoritarian supervision and anti-union policies could easily be resistant and harmful to CIM. Industrial relations based on mutual confidence and respect would appear to be more conductive to success [25].

However, it should not be overlooked that as hierarchical structures change and as middle management is threatened by CIM the role of unions and workers' representatives in enterprises might also be weakened. Autonomous groups of highly qualified staff may feel less in need of union representation and intermediaries vis-a-vis management and may have a more direct influence on the determination of their working conditions.

It should be obvious that in enterprises wishing to operate CIM systems the social dialogue cannot be limited to questions of remuneration and benefits. At any rate, exclusively achievement oriented wage systems may well have to be redesigned as system success or failure and higher productivity generally cannot be attributed to individual machine operators but depends essentially on reduction of down-time of automated equipment. The social dialogue will have to embrace questions and problems related to the implementation of the new technology, such as more flexible working time arrangements, adjusting working conditions to team work, redeployment, etc.

---

[24] F. Manske: "Social and economic aspects of alternative computer-aided production systems in small and medium batch runs", in Design of work in automated manufacturing systems, Proceedings of IFAC Workshop, Karlsruhe, Federal Republic of Germany, 7.,9. Nov. 1983, Pergamon Press, Oxford......, 1984, pp.51-55.

[25] F. J. Kador: "Das Soziale in High-tech-Unternehmen", in Der Arbeitgeber, No. 3/40, 1988, pp. 94-95.

5.8. Employment Consequences of CIM

It has already been pointed out that a relatively small percentage of the total manufacturing labour force is working in advanced manufacturing systems and that in this respect not much change is foreseen. The great majority of manufacturing workers will not experience radical change caused by CIM systems in the near future. Nevertheless, it must be expected that CIM will accentuate the already existing labour market segmentation. A core highly qualified craftsmen, technicians, engineers and professional workers manage and operate such systems and are increasingly indispensable. They are generally well paid and their working conditions are stable thanks to their position as knowledgeable workers and experts, but access to this core is more and more difficult to achieve. Ancillary workers have little opportunity for upward mobility unless they possess or acquire the necessary skills. Their conditions of work are also more precarious. This situation may eventually lead to social conflicts.

5.9. Research on the Promotion of the Human Factor in CIM Systems

It is one thing to identify the features which a CIM system, taking into account the human factor, should and could have, but it is quite another to design and make such systems acceptable to management and work in practice with an adequate rate of return. In most manufacturing the division of work is still well entrenched and tends to be used as a means of social control. The Taylorist mentality in production management is widespread and resistant and will not disappear from one day to the next, particularly in mass production. A conscious effort is needed to promote the human-centered approach to CIM. As the movement is gaining ground a great variety of research projects have been launched throughout the industrialised world with the objective of development models and defining the technical, ergonomic, organisational, social and training criteria for such systems [26]. This research is sponsored under several national and some international programmes of the European Community [27] (e.g. FAST, ESPRIT, EUREKA, RACE, COMETT, BRITE), involving a wide range of technical, social science and training research institutes, enterprises and employers' and workers' organisations. Partial results have been reported - some of them encouraging, other less so. Also, contradictory findings are not rare. It is clearly not easy for work science, ergonomics, design and system engineering to grips with the manifold aspects and the complexity of the problems at hand. Interpretations, recommendations and proposed remedies also depend considerable on the point of view and the ideological leanings or ethical

---

[26] The present state of research is reflected in: "CIM oder die Zukunft der Arbeit in rechnerintegrierten Fabrikstrukturen, Ergebnisse einer Fachtagung der IG-Metall", Frankfurt a. M:, Union-Druckerei und Verlagsanstalt, 1987, 198 pp.

[27] European Communities: Europe and the new technologies, Brussels, Mar. 1988.

principles of researchers as there are few certainties but much wishful thinking. It is obviously too early to assess the impact of such research on industrial practice. However, as the technocentric approach to CIM runs into growing difficulties the opportunities for alternative models necessarily brighten as enterprises may be more willing to give them a try.

There are some hopeful signs. In the United States the Work in America Institute – a tripartite body – co-operates with a series of large enterprises in the effort to enhance the role of the human factor, recognising its decisive influence on productivity. Only a small minority of enterprises are involved, but it is a beginning [28].

The development of design criteria and methods under the ESPRIT project "Human-centered CIM systems", in which representatives of various disciplines of engineering, ergonomics and social sconce co-operate, looks particularly promising. Eight industrial and academic partners based in Denmark, the Federal Republic of Germany and the United Kingdom are involved. Results are expected in 1989 [29].

Mention should also be made of the promotional activities in this field of the Industrial Federation of Automatic Control (IFAC) whose Committee on Social Effects of Automation makes a considerable effort to assess the social impact of control and automation and gathers concerned scientists, control engineers, managers, system designers, social scientists, industrial psychologists and specialists of other disciplines from research institutes and industry of a wide range of countries. The committee emphasis the social responsibility of control engineering and aims at the establishment of socially desirable requirements for the development of automated systems, demonstrations of alternatives of design of such systems, the strengthening of links between technologists and social scientists, and the dissemination of knowledge of these topics among the scientific and technical community. It has encouraged a considerable number of projects in which industry has co-operated. It has contributed in no small measure to the germination of the idea of the human-centered approach to CIM, and that slowly but surely it makes its way [30].

---

28 ---: "Réseau de 20 enterprise appliquant des systèmes socio-technique", in UIMN Social International, Feb. 1989, p. 11.

29 J.M. Corbett, op. cit.

30 International Federation of Automatic Control: "Aims-Structures-Activities", in IFAC Informations, ed., 1988.

6. Outlook

At present there is hardly a change of reconciling divergent views on CIM. Many of its advantages or faults are in the eye of the beholder. However, it is definitely not a panacea for all problems encountered in production as some seem to see it. At any rate, the promised land of total manufacturing integration is still far away, although an increasing number of enterprises appear to be engaged on an evolutionary path towards integration.

By any standard, the introduction of CIM is a risky undertaking. If it is to be successful the manufacturing organisation and product range have to be reviewed and rationalised. The pace of transition would depend on the knowledge, qualifications and abilities of the planning and operating staff.

CIM is a leading edge technology and its introduction requires long-term strategies and possibly forgoing immediate financial benefits. The most essential element in such a strategy is the preparation of the workforce for the impending changes. This means consultation at all levels and a systematic training effort. The neglect of further training of staff is inevitable very costly in terms of machine down-time and scrap production.

All experience accumulated so far speaks for a cautious and incremental approach as the absorptive and learning of the workforce might be overstretched with negative results. However, the trend towards more manufacturing integration is bound to continue and scientific advances will continue to propose solutions to pending technical problems. However, CIM is most likely to fail where it tries to supplant essential human qualities. The subjugation of people to machines and technical systems is proving more and more counterproductive. Instead, work organisation is needed which enables and motivates people to use their theoretical and empirical knowledge and skills in mastering advanced means of production and operating them efficiently. CIM will only be as good as the people in charge.

Are we heading in the wrong direction? Evidence suggests that the difficulties and complexities of introducing CIM on a large scale were initially underestimated. The technocentric approach aiming at the "manless factory" is now questioned for a very good reason: it has not produced the expected results so far. This is having a sobering effect on the unconditional technocrats. There is probably not just one type of "factory of the future" but many alternative solutions to manufacturing problems.

Will CIM really spell the end of Taylorism? It is definitely too soon to consider its methods dead and buried. It will continue to subsist in mass production alongside with dedicated automation and machinery and so will the corresponding hierarchical management structures. However, mass production and market dominance of mass-produced goods are declining in many manufacturing activities. The markets demand differentiated, diversified and customised products. This means small-batch production. CIM, i.e. flexible automation, could do the job if properly conceived.

Integrated manufacturing systems are very vulnerable to disruption. Running them efficiently and to the extent possible round the clock presupposes harmonious industrial relations, for work stoppages, go-slow or other types of resistance stemming from demotivating working conditions can cause major losses. Success of CIM, therefore, presupposes a good understanding and co-operation between management and workforce and its representatives. While it is certain that the introduction even of well-designed CIM systems will cause tensions, it also offers new opportunities to intensify and improve the social dialogue and to break down barriers - a chance not to be missed.

EXPERT SYSTEMS IN PRODUCTION AND SERVICES II
Th. Bernold and U. Hillenkamp (Editors)
Elsevier Science Publishers B.V., Amsterdam – Printed in The Netherlands

Impacts of Commercial Applications – Emerging Trends

Manfred Daniel
ibek
Ingenieur– und Beratungsgesellschaft für Organisation und Technik mbH
Karlsruhe, FRG

Abstract

The following paper presents interim results of a project assessing the possible impacts of expert systems applications. One of the project's central goals is to develop propositions for the design of human-centered technology.

We will discuss the social impacts of expert systems applications for those employees whose jobs are established in industry, banks and insurances. Considering the commercial goals for the development and implementation of expert systems we then look at the fundamental impacts concerning the following aspects:

- employment
- work quality
  - employer-employee relations
  - workload, working conditions
  - work content, qualifications, personality
  - power, control, communication
  - participation and interest

It turns out that there are especially risks for skilled workers and office employees which can be avoided by involving them in the design of this technology by active participation based on the right to take part in the decision process too.

---

1. The Background – Brief Outline

The following presentation consists of the interim results of a project which is investigating the social impacts of expert systems applications:

Artificial Intelligence, Expert Systems – Applications, New Services, Social Impacts

The project is being sponsored by the Minister of Labour, Health and Social Services of North Rhine Westphalia as part of their Socially Acceptable Technology Program ("Sozialvertraegliche Technikgestaltung"). We have been working on the project for a year and will be publishing our final report at the end of this year.

The consideration of applications refers to expert systems in the production sector and in the fields of banking and insurance. Four central questions are being addressed:

1. Past developments and the present status of expert systems technology
2. The further development of expert systems technology and its application up to the year 2000
3. Probable social impacts
4. Options in the design of human-centered technology

Owing to the special orientation of the above-mentioned research program the project has been based on a retention of values the which apply primarily social criteria in the evaluation of technologies and their applications. This results in five problem areas which we will be concentrating on in our identification and evaluation of the possible impacts of expert systems technology:

1. Employment
2. Work quality
3. Products and services on offer
4. Knowledge in culture and society
5. Corporate competitiveness

In accordance with the subject of this conference, I will be limiting this presentation to the problems of the employment and work quality of skilled workers and office employees.

Our results so far are based on an extensive literature analysis as well as a series of interviews, one in West Germany, the other in the USA and Japan. Before turning to the following expert systems applications in production and services, I would like to give a brief basic evaluation of expert systems technology.

2. The Technology – a Basic Evaluation

Expert systems technology was the most practical trend to develop out of AI research as it was limited to a) specific types of problems and b) to specific domains of knowledge. Expert systems can be applied only in very restricted specialist areas and are far away from an emulation of general human intelligence. They are suitable only for those problems which can be solved by a manipulation of symbols. We are basing this assertion on the arguments of the Dreyfus brothers (1) who have proved that expert systems cannot reach the stage of true expertise as this is tied to human-specific qualities such as intuition, association, analogous deduction and the holistic apprehension of given situations.

In spite of the limits imposed on this technology, it nevertheless offers a new rationalization potential in the world of work and is thus attractive to numerous companies. In respect of its rationalization and control properties, expert systems technology is always considered in combination with, and as one of a team of several information and communications technologies. Insofar as it produces a computer simulation of certain human cognitive capabilities, however, it has an especially important role to play in the expanding industrialization of non-material work processes.

3. Applications – an Overview

Expert systems are applied in those task areas which were previously either not affected at all or affected only to a limited extent by technological rationalization. Today's system developments and applications are concerned primarily with pre- or post-production functions or with those that accompany actual material production. As to the question of the impacts of the use of expert systems on the world of work, the first step must be to identify those who will most probably be affected. First, we should consider those who are directly affected, i.e. those employees whose jobs will be fundamentally changed as a result of the introduction of technology. The number of those indirectly affected is usually far greater.

Even today, we can identify certain occupational categories which will be the first to come into contact with expert systems technology and, in future, will be those affected to the greatest extent by its introduction. The following list of these groups is based on the worldwide distribution of expert systems in commercial task areas (2) and on information obtained in the course of our interviews.

The occupational categories potentially affected industry:

- research, development, and product design
  - technical draughtsmen
  - designing engineers
  - laboratory assistants
  - software engineers
  - electronics

- sales
  - sales clerks

- manufacturing
  - machine operators
  - maintenance technicians
  - monitoring operators
  - work preparation personnel
  - production planning & control
  - quality control personnel

- administration
  - computer center personnel
  - office personnel

Banks:

- customer consultation
- credit clerks

Insurance:

- customer consultation
- insurance settlements
- clerks
- financial management
- risk management
- Tax consultants

Auditors

Lawyers

To summarize, we can say that expert systems technology is oriented primarily towards qualified specialists, engineers and clerks. Computer backup of the tasks of top management is something for the distant future.

At present, diagnostic and configuration systems for use in objective technical domains predominate in terms of sheer numbers. Thus the main groups to be affected at present are maintenance technicians and sales clerks. A sector-specific consideration of the diffusion accomplished thus far shows that the development of expert systems technology is being promoted primarily by the key industries data processing and electronics, the automobile industry, machine building and chemicals as well as banking and insurance.

4. The Identification of Trends – a Problem of Methodology

Experience in the application of expert systems from the point of view of those employees who are to replace or back up are practically non-existent. This may be attributed to the fact that, on the one hand, there have not yet been enough systems applied in practice over a long period of time and, on the other, that so far, there have been no known empirical projects which study work-oriented problems systematically. An identification of trends in this field therefore has to rely on what little concrete experience we have at our disposal, on analogous deductions from the application of known information and communications technologies and, in addition, on the use of a little reasonable imagination.

In estimating the possible impacts of the application of technologies, it can be assumed that the fundamental impacts will be determined by the goals connected with the use of technology. The way in which the technology in question is applied, however, must also be taken into consideration. Besides the specific features of technological systems, both their embedding in the structural and organizational environment of the work system and the division of labour among people and machines will also play an important role in the identification of possible effects.

5. Commercial Goals – an Attempt to Structure

The starting point in our identification of trends has been those commercial goals gleaned from our study of the literature and our interviews. In the following list, we have arranged the individual subgoals under the headings of the three main goals: rationalization, improvement of controls and quality improvement. One should, however, note that in some cases, these subgoals could have been allocated to more than one main goal.

Commercial goals in the application of expert systems rationalization

- An increase in productivity in expert domains
- A reduction in personnel costs owing to the hiring of fewer qualified staff
- Savings in training costs
- The realization of shorter turnover times

Improvements in the quality and safety of production processes, products and decisions

- Improvements in the safety of production processes
- A more secure, more complete and faultless assessment of given situations
- Improved quality control
- Consideration of more alternatives in decision-making
- Consideration of greater complexity
- Improvements in preparation of service mission
- Attainment of a uniform level of expertise through the distribution of knowledge
- Individualization of products, customizing
- Attainment of competitive advantages through added-value products

- Extension of consultants' and sales clerks' scope of consultation
- Improved and cheaper products as a result of the optimum selection of construction principles and materials

Improvement of controls and management

- Increased acceptance of technological systems
- Standardization
- Attainment of knowledge accessibility, for example on night shifts or after certain experts have left the company
- Improvement in production planning and management
- Standardization of work principles and the principles of decision-making
- Social impacts – a problem of design

In the following, we have assumed that the trend in the application of expert systems will be influenced essentially by these goals. It should be emphasized that, in addition to the general comments made here, a differentiated consideration of specific domains of applications and types of usage is also necessary as the impacts will vary considerably depending on these factors and the specific management objectives. Such a consideration, however, is way beyond the scope of this presentation. Only a few general risks and design problems can be mentioned here.

This is the central idea of our Technology Assessment Study: If we think of the future social implications of a technology we should not only passively look what is coming up and at best ask how to achieve acceptance. The question we have to put is: How should the socio-technical work systems be designed, so that the risks can be avoided and instead of this optimal working conditions will be realized?

6. Impacts

6.1. Impacts on Employment

Those companies which have specialized in AI applications, whether in the manufacture of specific hardware, systems development, training or consultation, have experienced positive effects in regard to employment over the past few years. It is worth noting, however, that measured against present market demands, they have already achieved an overcapacity which, in the last few months, has led to large scale lay-offs among those U.S. companies who have specialized in AI. In West Germany, on the other hand, there appears to be a lack of of AI-oriented workers.

Now, the talk is of a totally new profession and course of training: that of knowledge engineering, although this term has still not been clearly defined. Furthermore, if one considers the argument so often propounded that expert systems are only economical if the knowledge acquisition components have been so far developed that it is the experts themselves who compile the knowledge basis, we may justifiably doubt the actual employment potential for newcomers in the field of knowledge engineering. We thus consider it more probable that the most suitable experts already available will receive further training in the field of knowledge acquisition.

Should the increase in productivity envisaged through the use of expert systems actually be realized, we must expect negative developments on the employment market. On the other hand, as these systems are being applied primarily in growth sectors and in expanding task areas, it is unlikely that those directly affected will in fact be laid off. Systems which are capable of replacing all the tasks performed by a given expert are hardly being developed at present. The curve of new employment in the above-mentioned domains will simply flatten out when expert systems are applied.

From a quantitative point of view, the indirect impact of expert systems on employment will be much more serious in that their application will result in an intensification of those negative trends already brought about by conventional information and communications technologies. This intensification may be attributed to the fact that expert systems are applied mainly in order to accelerate the diffusion of other rationalization technologies.

Thus expert systems are applied, for example, in all phases from design to production, marketing and the introduction of new information and communications technologies. Expert systems are now regarded as an essential tool in dealing with the increasing complexity of advanced rationalization technologies such as network systems, computer integrated manufacturing and office communications.

6.2. Impacts on Work Quality

The following identification of trends has been organized according to the main criteria drawn up by the German Confederation of Trade Unions' institute "Arbeitswissenschaft fuer Arbeitnehmer" (Manpower Studies for Employees) for the evaluation of work situations from the point of view of the employee. (3).

6.3. Employer-Employee Relations

If subjective knowledge is expropriated and put under the control of management, obviously, the general tendency will be towards a weakening of the employee's position in relation to his/her employer. Even in those domains in which companies have so far been relatively dependent on their employees' knowledge, it will be easier, in future, to withdraw from employment contracts. On the other hand, it will also be easier to enter into new contracts as the knowledge of those who have left the company will be stored in the company system thus making the training time for new employees much shorter.

Should the dreaded tendency towards a segmentation of staff into core staff and peripheral staff become a reality, there may be an important role in store for expert systems.

6.4. Workload, Working Conditions

In general, the purpose of expert systems is to back up the work of experts. At the same time, they are also intended to bring about an increase in productivity. This could lead to an increase in workload, especially if, for example, the system deals with all the routine cases and leaves only the problem cases to the human worker. This would result in the removal of the beneficial effects so often associated with the processing of routine cases.

It is well-known that technological systems which appear inscrutable to the user and which he/she has difficulty in mastering, are an additional source of stress in a work situation. Many fear that expert systems are particularly difficult to comprehend in their possibilities and limitations on account of their unstructured functioning. An incorrect estimation of the limitations of the system may lead to serious errors in the decision-making process.

There have already been reports of some systems which have become a burden to their users as a result of their unsuitability for the task in hand. The user is obliged to spend time and effort on the operation of the system and in conducting dialogues – and this in addition to other tasks – without having the benefit of a real reduction of his/her workload.

6.5. Work Content, Qualifications, Personality

In this respect, the effects of the application of expert systems are most dependent on the division of labor among men and machines, as also among the employees themselves.

Some of the expert's knowledge is objectified in the knowledge base. For him, this results in a depreciation of his subjective qualifications. As one's own and others' estimation of personality is generally, or frequently reliant on the value attributed to subjective knowledge, the apprehension of personality will probably be negatively influenced. One should also remember that direct work experience plays an important part in the development of the personality and that this effect will be suppressed in future. The possession of knowledge based on experience is to be rendered superfluous and rather this knowledge, second hand and in the form of knowledge bases, will be made available to inexperienced employees.

There is also a risk of the employee's feeling of accountability for the results of his/her own work being reduced if essential tasks, right up to the decision-making process are assigned to the system. If an employee no longer has an influence on the decisions reached and if, under certain circumstances, he/she is unable to comprehend the machine's decision finding process there could be a tendency towards a transfer of responsibility the system. A work system so unfavorably designed would result in a sense of futility and alienation from the tasks remaining to the employee.

Before each application, we should ask whether an optimum division of labor among men and machines can be found, i.e. whether the machine is to be assigned only those tasks which lend themselves to mechanization and the human worker left those tasks in which his performance will be superior. It should also be decided whether, besides the division of labor, a division of knowledge is acceptable. We speak of a division of knowledge if the user works with a knowledge base the contents of which he does not normally have at his disposal and which for him are inscrutable (4).

If a knowledge base is maintained as a result of the experience of only certain selected experts within a central maintenance team and this knowledge is then disseminated to the entirety of users by means of an updating of the knowledge base, we can describe such a dissemination as unfavorable.

Generally, the application of expert systems stipulates a change in the range of tasks assigned to certain positions. The most probable change would be in an organizational restructuring involving job enlargement. We encountered various examples of this in the course of our interviews.

With the aid of a diagnostic expert system integrated into a CNC lathe, the operator is to be enabled to undertake fault analyses and, possibly, repairs himself. An investment consultant in a bank who previously specialized only in low-risk investments should be able to offer advice on securities and investments in home loan associations. A technical draughtsman previously limited to the constructive details of steel constructions should, in future, be able to consider static conditions as well.

Each of these changes in the division of labor should be considered individually. Investigations would have to be made as to whether job enlargement would mean an upgrading of the work situation of those concerned or rather an additional workload.

At present, our experience with expert systems is so rudimentary that we cannot yet say whether or not the use of expert systems in certain domains of knowledge and applications will become sufficiently stable and standardized for new professions with respecting courses to arise as a result.

6.6. Power, Control, Communication

As already mentioned in the section "Employer/employee relations", the in-company balance of power will tip in favour of the employer as a consequence of the objective availability of knowledge and attempts on the part of management to free themselves from their dependence on the subjective knowledge of their employees. If new regulations are transferred in the same form by means of an updating of knowledge bases for all users within the company, central directives will be more efficiently disseminated and thus more effectively applied throughout the company.

The application of expert systems will most probably result in a further reduction in interpersonal communications. Discussions with experienced colleagues who could perhaps help in certain complex situations are to be replaced by interactions with expert systems.

7. Participation and Interest

One conclusion which must be drawn from the above-mentioned developments is that the employee's possibilities to discuss and represent their own interests in the company will decline. In the acquisition of knowledge and the further development of the knowledge base, organizational structures ranging from participation-oriented procedures with the involvement of as many experts as possible to extremely centralized structures, are conceivable. In the first case, that of participative structures, many of the negative effects so far described could be avoided.

From what has been said so far, it is probably clear that in principle, general statements on the effects of the application of expert systems – especially in view of the fact that this technology is still in its teething stage – are extremely precarious. Thus the identification of trends just presented either consists primarily of questions, or it shows merely the design decisions with which we are dealing.

Clearly, the present trends in the application of expert systems technology must be more critically than positively evaluated from the employees' point of view. In order to avoid the potentially negative impacts for the employee, it is very important that in the introduction of these systems, as also in the case of other technologies, the employees and their representatives are given a right to full co-determination and the principles of human-centered systems design are realized.

Employees should not be forced to experience the consequences of the introduction of technology as accomplished facts. Rather, these impacts should be the subject of negotiations in which those concerned are not only concerned, but also well informed, active participants enjoying equal rights in the determination of their future working environment.

Bibliography:

(1) Hubert L. Dreyfus, Stuart E. Dreyfus: Künstliche Intelligenz: Von den Grenzen der Denkmaschinen und dem Wert der Intuition, Reinbek 1987

(2) Peter Mertens, Volker Borkowski, Wolfgang Geis: Betriebliche Expertensystemanwendungen , Berlin, Heidelberg 1988

(3) L. P. Schardt: Qualifizierte Mischarbeit , Düsseldorf 1987, AWA Arbeitspapier 121

(4) O. Oestberg: Applying Expert Systems Technology: Division of Labour and Division of Knowledge in: Bo Göranzon, Ingela Josefson (Eds.) Knowledge, Skill and Artificial Intelligence Berlin, Heidelberg 1988

EXPERT SYSTEMS IN PRODUCTION AND SERVICES II
Th. Bernold and U. Hillenkamp (Editors)
Elsevier Science Publishers B.V., Amsterdam – Printed in The Netherlands
GDI, 1989

Trends in the Development and Application of Expert Systems in Japan: April 1986 to February 1988

Yoshimitsu Hirai
ICOT-JIPDEC AI Center
World Trade Center 7th Floor
Tokyo, Japan

1. Introduction

In 1986 the ICOT-JIPDEC AI Center conducted a survey of trends in the development of expert systems (ES). In order to ascertain subsequent developments, a second survey was conducted in February 1988 and its results were analyzed. This second survey focused on the various approaches to ESs taken by a wide range of businesses.

In the first survey, questionnaires were sent to about 600 organizations, of which 203 responded. In the second survey, questionnaires went to about 1000 organizations, of which 323 responded. Summarizing the results, organizations developing ESs (including under investigation) accounted for 53.6% (173 organizations) of those responses, in contrast to 48.3% (98 organizations) in the first survey, indicating a gradual increase in the ES developments. In particular, 36.2% of the organizations reported 114 systems which had reached the stage of practical use (including field test), a significant increase over the 19.1% (74 systems) reported in the first survey. Looking at a breakdown by category of business, in addition to the types of businesses most frequently reporting the development of ESs in the first survey, such as steel, electrical machinery, and others, ESs development had increased in the finance industry, as well as in the electricity industry. With the increase in efforts to develop ESs in service industries, the general trend of ESs development has expanded from manufacturing industries, comprised mainly of blue collar workers, to industries chiefly employing white collar workers, where ESs are being developed to support decision making and to be incorporated in intelligent office information systems. In short, ESs are finding applications in an ever-widening range of fields.

2. State of expert system developments

As cited above, organizations already engaged in the development of ESs accounted for 53.6% (173 organizations) of those responding to the second survey, in contrast to 48.3% (98 organizations) in the first survey (see Figure 1). Of the remaining 150 organizations, 63 (19.5% of the total) are about to begin ES development by next year. Projecting on the basis of these results, by 1990, over 75% of the organizations in Japan will be engaged in ES development.

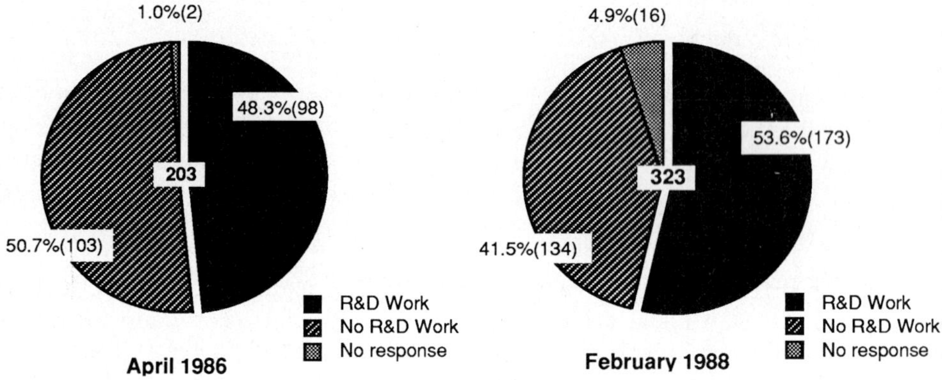

Figure 1 State of Expert System Developments

Turning to the number of ESs under development, in the first survey, 98 organizations accounted for a total of 388 systems, for an average of 4.0 systems per organization. The corresponding figure in the second study is 1.8 systems vis-a-vis 315 systems being developed by 173 organizations, representing a decline in the average number of systems being developed per organization. On the other hand, figures for in-use ESs present the opposite picture. The second survey found that 114 (36.2%) out of 315 systems, were in practical use, a large increase over the 74 systems (19.1%) reported in the first survey (see

Figure 2). This indicated that in only two years, a large number of organizations have made great progress in more clearly and specifically expanding their ES applications. Factors responsible for this advance include the narrowing down of the possible systems under investigation and the fact that the development of demonstration systems for understanding AI technology are just about a thing of the past.

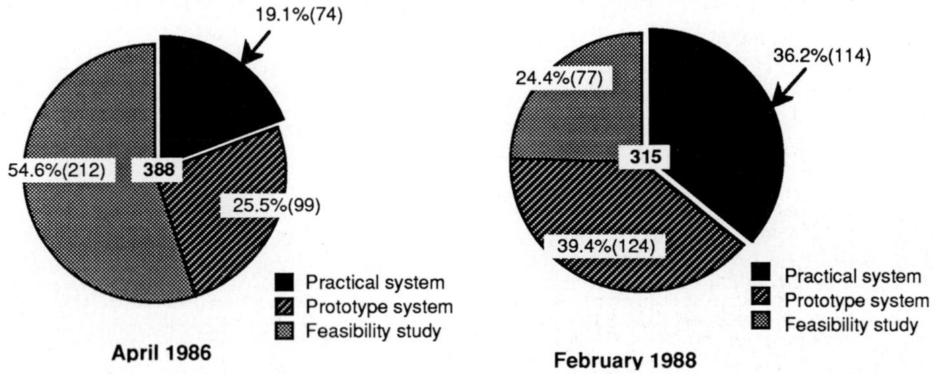

Figure 2 Stages of Expert System Development

3. Expert System Applications in Industry

The second survey found that ESs were already in use in 19 different industries, more than double the nine industries reported in the first survey. The implication is that ES applications are no longer limited to just certain fields but are now beginning to cover an increasingly broader range of industries.

The second survey found that among the specific industries and businesses where ESs were in use, ten of the companies were in the software industry, eight companies in the data processing industry, and seven companies each in the finance and electrical machinery industries (see Figure 3). Furthermore, there were five companies each in the steel, transportation machinery, and electricity/gas industries, and, finally, four companies in the construction industry. Although in the first survey, a majority of businesses in the finance

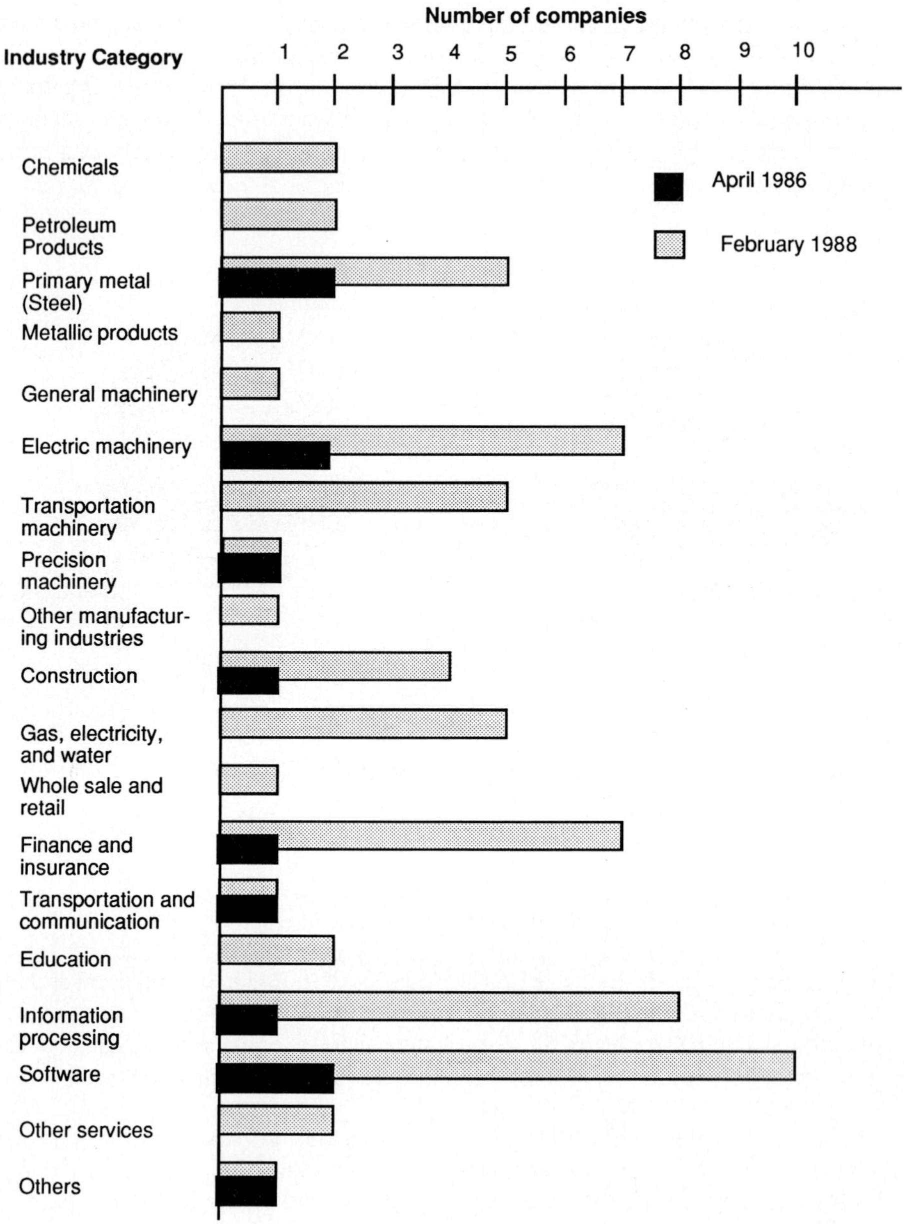

Figure 3 State of In-use Expert Systems by Industry (No. of Companies)

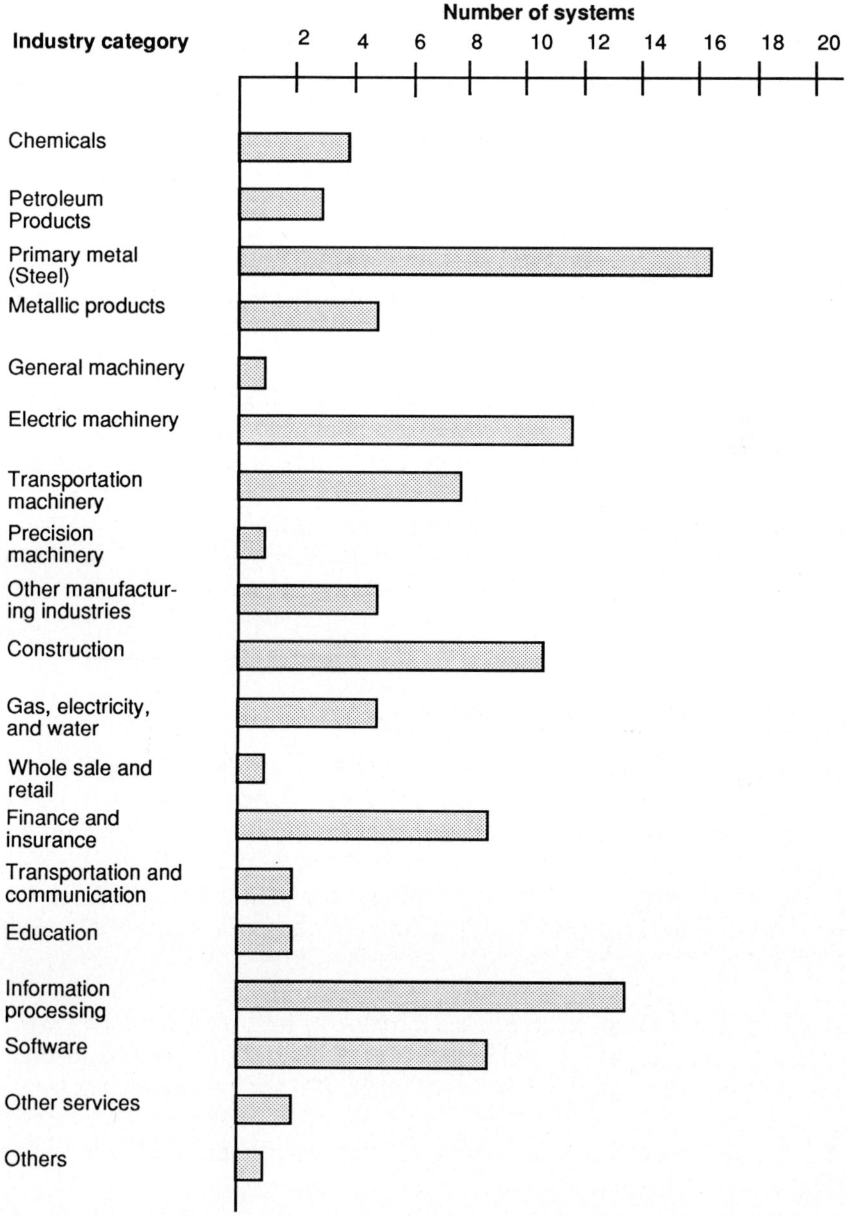

Figure 4 State of In-use Expert Systems by Industry (No. of Systems)

industry reported that they were not engaged in ESs development, in the second survey, businesses in this industry constituted the largest number which were developing ESs, in the computer user industry category. In terms of businesses using ES, in the banking and securities fields, they are used in connection with advice on assets management and investment consultation, while in the insurance industry they are used for checking the health condition of applicants.

In terms of the in-use ESs, the steel industry was far in the lead with seventeen systems among a total of five organizations. This was followed by fourteen systems in the information processing industry, twelve in the electrical machinery industry, and nine in the finance industry (see Figure 4).

The steel industry has been extremely progressive in the introduction of leading-edge technology, long ago having switched over to computerization. The main areas of ESs are the automated control of furnaces and the automation of the steel manufacturing process. In the case of the steel industry, they are not only eager to develop ES, but also aggressive to sell their original tools developed in-house (e.g. Sumitomo Metal Industries' SMI-MARKS-IT), and their original ES (e.g. Kobe Steel's welding specifications check system).

4. Target Areas and Size of Expert Systems

The second survey found that the three leading domains of ESs were diagnostics, planning, and design, in that order. Although design led planning in the first survey, figures for the two categories remain almost the same in the second survey. Of the total number of systems, more than one-third (40.0%, 126 systems) are diagnostic, 21.3% (67 systems) are for planning, and 19.7% (62 systems) for design. These three leading domains account for two-thirds of all ESs (see Table 1).

Using the number of rules in an ES as a measure of its size, the second survey found that the number of small-size ES, those with 100 rules or less, had increased since the first survey, from 17.4% to 36.1%. On the other hand, large-size ESs, those with over 1000 rules, had decreased, from 25.0% to 9.8%. These are significant changes (see Figure 5). They can be attributed to the many personal computers that have come into use as business tools, arising directly from the fact that the number of businesses that use personal computers has increased.

Category	April 1986 Respondents	February 1988 Respondents	No. of Systems
Interpretation	15 (15.3%)	20 (13.3%)	22 (7.0%)
Prodiction	25 (25.5%)	21 (14.0%)	25 (7.9%)
Diagnosis	64 (65.3%)	91 (60.7%)	126(40.0%)
Design	44 (44.9%)	45 (30.0%)	62 (19.7%)
Planning	35 (35.7%)	49 (32.7%)	67 (21.3%)
Monitoring	9 (9.2%)	9 (6.0%)	9 (2.9%)
Debugging	5 (5.1%)	8 (5.3%)	9 (2.9%)
Repair	10 (10.2%)	2 (1.3%)	2 (0.6%)
Instruction	18 (18.4%)	29 (19.3%)	34 (10.8%)
Control	19 (19.4%)	17 (11.3%)	21 (6.7%)
Others	8 (8.2%)	24 (16.0%)	30 (9.5%)
Total	98	150	315

Table 1 Application Fields of Expert Systems

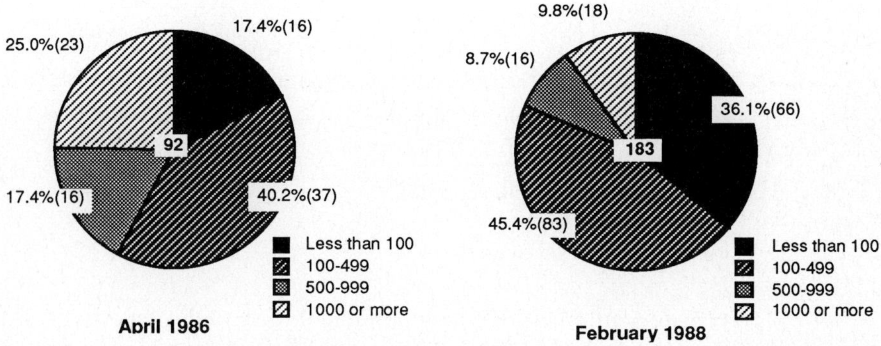

Figure 5 Size of Expert Systems

However, when figures are restricted to just ESs in use, ESs with 100 or less rules accounted for 17.6%, a decrease, while 17.6% of the ESs had more than 1000 rules. Large-size ESs thus increased their share of total ESs in practical use. A relatively large number of rules must be implemented for an ES to be able to cope with the rigors of practical use at the workplace.

5. Developmental Systems, Obstacles, and Future Trends

Results concerning the various development systems for ESs hardly differ from the results found in the first survey (see Table 2). In about two-thirds of the organizations, ES development was undertaken by their data processing (DP) departments. In one-third of the organizations, experts in the ES field carried out ES development, supported by their DP department.

System	April 1986	February 1988
DP department supported by domain experts	52 (53.1%)	87 (58.0%)
Domain experts outside DP department	24 (24.5%)	43 (28.7%)
Others	17 (17.3%)	18 (12.0%)
No response	7 (7.1%)	2 (1.3%)
Total	100	150

Table 2 Expert System Development System

Recently, a trend has emerged whereby personnel in the DP department who have gained expertise in AI technology provide AI training for domain experts, with the goal of creating a broader strata of capable personnel in the AI field as an AI technology transfer center. While there was also a gradual increase in organizations which rely mainly on domain experts to develop their systems for experts themselves, at the same time there was a tendency for these same organizations to switch over to the system in which the DP department supports the expert. In regard to the current state of the ES development field, the situation of ES is centered on domain experts as the expert support system; thus, ESs are being speedily developed by experts in those areas which had previously represented problems for experts. At the same time as ESs can reduce experts' work load, the departments achieve good quality of work on the part of regular personnel. Furthermore, regular personnel can do higher level work which experts do. This development system also ensures that, once development of an ES has been completed, the transition into the maintenance stage takes place smoothly, in view of the critical importance of maintenance.

In the first survey, the general opinion was that primitive problems regarding the implementation of ESs development (the effectiveness of ES, lack of knowledge in the area of AI technology, etc.) constituted obstacles to introduce ES (see Table 3). In the second survey, there were concrete problems concerning ESs development (e.g. the problem of knowledge acquisition). In particular, important matters such as system development methodology for the ESs and the need for adequate tools for knowledge acquisition were cited.

Obstacles Cited in 1986:

1. Inadequacy of the hardware/software environment.
2. Lack of understanding of the effectiveness of expert systems.
3. Lack of qualified engineers.
4. Lack of understanding regarding development and application of expert systems.
5. Inadequacy of existing technology.

Obstacles Cited in 1988:

1. Difficulty of knowledge acquisition.
2. Lack of qualified engineers.
3. Inadequacy of the hardware/software environment.
4. Inadequacy of existing technology.
5. Prohibitive cost to develop expert systems.

Table 3 Obstacles to the Growth of Expert System

During the two years between the first and second surveys, awareness of existing AI technology deepened, and the practical possibilities of ESs became more clear, as did the major obstacles to further expansion of ESs. Given the current state of technology, the areas opened to ES applications still remain quite limited, with many people expressing the opinion that the full implementation of ESs in the workplace still has many difficulties. (Ninety-eight organizations cited the insufficiency of existing AI technology.)

Regarding future developments in the ESs field, in the first survey, the largest number of responses cited as a goal of ESs development specialized applications for manufacturing, such as design, software development support, and diagnostics. In the second survey, the largest number of responses cited software development support (a "dream" system from the perspective of people working in the information processing field).

April 1986		February 1988	
1. Design	31	1. Software development support	30
2. Software development support	27	2. Decision support system	19
3. Diagnosis	26	3. Diagnosis	16
4. Prediction	21	3. Scheduling	16
5. Decision support system	18	3. Intelligent office automation	16

Table 4 Future Application Fields for Expert System - Top 5 -

There was also an increase in organizations looking forward to new ES applications for business offices, such as intelligent office information systems (see Table 4). Some organizations are also considering a broader and higher range of ES applications, such as decision support systems for their business strategies, as well as the transition from specialized ESs to larger-size ESs having a wide scope of capabilities.

6. Conclusion

The development of ESs in Japan is growing steadily increasing the number of practical applications. But there are very few cases where a "perfect" ES can be provided to a user for immediate actual use. It is no exaggeration to say that the real key to the success or failure of an ES lies in how well it can be maintained and enhanced under actual working conditions. In order to be improved on site, training in AI at the user site is necessary. But today, when adequate curriculum for such AI training has not yet been implemented, the unavoidable alternative is on-the-job training (OJT) of ES development. As ES applications grow, the focus of problems related to ES will tend to move from information processing departments to the actual workplace where the ES is being used. Clearly, as ESs progress, it will be necessary to have more advanced AI technology to broaden the scope of ES applications. The goal of making more effective ESs will entail solving a diverse set of problems, such as methods of connecting AI technology to existing systems, large-size ES development methodology, and knowledge acquisition.

References

1. Hirai, Y. (1987). Expert Systems Development in Japan, Japan Computer Quarterly, No. 69, pp. 3-22.

2. ICOT-JIPDEC AI Center (1988). Research Report on AI trends:AI Demand Trends, March 1988.

EXPERT SYSTEMS IN PRODUCTION AND SERVICES II
Th. Bernold and U. Hillenkamp (Editors)
Elsevier Science Publishers B.V., Amsterdam – Printed in The Netherlands
GDI, 1989

Expert Systems and Their Impact on Labor – Japanese Experience

Sei Dateki
Assisted by Junko Hirashi and Kinuko Fujihara
National Institute of Employment and Vocational Research
Tokyo, 177, Japan

Introduction

In this report, I will introduce the experiences of 22 companies which have already used Expert Systems or at least developed prototype systems. I found the name of companies using Expert Systems through newspapers or magazines and interviewed them in August 1988. Though only a limited number of companies have already introduced Expert Systems, I intended to select companies from various industries, in so far as they agreed to the interview.

The 22 companies include one computer manufacturer and one think-tank, which are system developers; nine manufacturers (four chemical companies, three engineering companies, one printing company and one metal working company); five financial and insurance companies; three construction companies; one electrical energy company, one retail trade company and one hospital, which are Expert System users. All of these are large companies with 600 to 60'000 employees.

I asked each company the following items:

1. Development of Expert Systems
1.1. Application of Expert Systems
1.2. Difference between previous computer systems and Expert Systems
1.3. Work distribution in developing Expert Systems
1.4. Persons engaged in developing Expert Systems
1.5. Acquiring and developing engineers for Expert Systems
1.6. Educating and training engineers for Expert Systems

1. Development of Expert Systems

1.1. Application of Expert Systems

The 20 companies using Expert Systems have 10 Diagnosis systems, six Planning and scheduling systems, six Consulting systems and six Design systems (Table 1).

The most advanced Japanese companies began the research and development of Artificial Intelligence (AI) including Expert Systems 5 to 6 years ago and began to build practical Expert Systems in 1985. From the beginning of development until 3 to 4 years ago, Diagnosis type Expert Systems were the most common because they are relatively easy to treat and their effects are clear to everybody. Recently, however, the application of Expert Systems is expanding to more active and strategic fields like planning and design in manufacturing. In addition, development of Expert Systems in financial and insurance industry has become active in the last 1 to 2 years (though the full-scale uses announced officially are only a few). The construction industry has been developing Expert Systems fairly actively, a little earlier than financial and insurance industry.

It seems that more Expert Systems than expected appeared, but the systems actually employed have been less than expected.

1. 2. Difference between Previous Computer Systems and Expert Systems

Previous computer systems were good at large volume, high speed calculations. Expert Systems have increased the potential for accomplishing all jobs

Field:	Name of system	Industry
Planing:	Production scheduling system	Chemical Petrochemical Metal working
	Work scheduling program	Super market Toiletry manufacturer
	Estimation of construction tender prices	Construction
Consulting:	Advice for the best investment	2 stockbrokers Bank
	Support for procedure of laws and regulations	2 construction
	Consulting for inheritance tax	Life insurance
Diagnosis:	Diagnosis of trouble	Petrochemical 2 chemicals Construction Automobile Precision machinery Metal working
	Evaluation for life insurance payment	Insurance
	Credit qualification check	Credit
	Consulting for medial examination	Hospital
Design:	Design of lens, semiconductors	2 precision machinery
	Piling methods, etc.	Construction
	Design of paper boxes for package	Printing
	Design of car interior layout	Automobile
	Design of power plant equipment layout	Electrical energy

Note: This table does not contain the Expert Systems developed by the system developers like computer manufacturer and think-tank because the number of these systems were too large to be shown in this table. Details are shown in the case study.

Table 1 Expert Systems in the Companies Interviewed

previously judged by man and have extended computer applications to such fields.

When Expert Systems are applied, they generally target the middle level jobs which are between the very high level jobs performed only by men and the simple, repetitious jobs.

Most companies consider Expert Systems only a new kind of software development method. None considers such systems to be very different from the previous computer systems. They can develop systems similar to Expert Systems using the old computer language. This method is not necessarily adequate for practical use, however, because it is very complex, time-consuming, expensive and difficult to maintain. On the other hand, in Expert Systems they need not to rewrite all the software, even if they add new conditions in the development and they can change them easily by adding rules. They can thus perform trial and error testing easily in the development, and it became possible to accumulate human experience more efficiently compared with the previous method. In addition, the appearance of high-speed computer system created the environment which made it easy to develop software to deal with human knowledge.

In Design Expert Systems for the precision engineering industry, the CAD system matured to the level of supporting and substituting man to a certain degree. Such a system is useful in situations when men tend to forget things or to use a certain standard method without considering the different designs. In the chemical industry, specialists prepared the production schedule depending on the data of sales and stock submitted by computers or, in diagnosis field, judged the cause of trouble from the data of stock input to computers. Now, however, such scheduling or diagnosis is performed by computers based on Production Planning Expert Systems and Diagnosis Expert Systems. In the consulting systems for life insurance companies, even before Expert Systems, typical patterns of evaluation for payment were systematized in computers which calculated the amount automatically. Patterns which differ from the typical ones should still be examined by specialists. Furthermore, in the consulting system, inheritance tax was previously determined entirely by specialists. To these fields, Expert Systems are being introduced and computer applications are being enlarged.

However, even now, computers can sense only 1's and 0's in spite of the brilliant discussion of AI On the other hand, man can proceed in ambiguous situations and can make conclusions and judgements considering a variety of factors. Expert systems cannot surpass man. Expert Systems only make it posto use a few more signs and deal with human knowledge a little better to support man.

1.3. Work Distribution in Developing Expert Systems

There are two kinds of user companies. One develops the Expert Systems entirely within the company without any outside support. The other develops Expert Systems cooperating with outside companies like computer manufacturers or think-tanks. In the latter case, there are again two types of companies. In the first type, computer manufacturers are in charge of all technological aspects of development including Artificial Intelligence; user companies supply only the knowledge of the specialist, the data and then needs for easy and effective handling of the system. In the other type, user companies have their own system engineers who can do the knowledge engineering. In this case, three kinds of people – the system engineers, the specialists in the user companies and the system engineers of computer manufacturers, etc, – work together in developing Expert Systems.

Some companies select various work distributions to suit the kind of systems. For example, they develop large systems using a host-computer together with the computer manufacturer and develop small systems using personal computer by themselves. Furthermore, some companies first develop the system with the cooperation of the computer manufacturer , but later acquire the ability to develop the system bythemselves. Most companies with their own AI engineers intend to accumulate the required skill for future self development. In this case, computer manufacturers or think-tanks etc. play the role of trainers for the user companies.

1.4. Persons Engaged in Developing Expert Systems

The primary persons engaged in developing Expert Systems are system engineers and the specialists in the work place of each company. An exception is the case in which all technological support is contracted to outside companies (i.e. computer manufacturers). Expert Systems are usually developed under a joint project with the cooperation of system engineers from the information processing department and specialists of various work places. Specialists provide the special know-how of their work, and system engineers with knowledge of Expert Systems listen to them and incorporate the specialist's knowledge into the computer systems.

In constructing Expert Systems, the capture of the specialist's knowledge is the most important problem. The methods to capture this knowledge vary by the company or by the kind of applications. For example, there are three general methods for acquiring the knowledge from the specialists:

(1) The specialists in the work place offer their knowledge and the system engineers with knowledge of Expert System listen and record it.

(2) The specialists in the work place learn computer skills and AI and record their knowledge by themselves cooperating with the system engineers of the information processing department, and

(3) System engineers with fairly deep knowledge of the equipment or work place ("a combined system engineer and specialist") listen to the specialists of the work place. The ability to understand the specialist's knowledge depends on the depth of knowledge about the special field itself.

In the third case, system engineers with deep knowledge of the equipment or work place are allocated to the project. Such system engineers have studied the field at a university or have work experience through job rotation. In addition, in some cases system engineers working in the factories play a major role in developing Expert Systems, cooperating with specialists and system engineers of the head office. They also learn AI There are not many instances of case (2). The ideal case is for the specialists to build Expert Systems by themselves using the easily handling software of the future. At present, however, companies are happy if they can employ the development style of case (3). Many companies employ style (1) and find some difficulties in capturing the knowledge of the specialists.

If user companies provide only the knowledge of the specialists and computer manufacturers support all the technical aspects related to AI, computer manufacturers supply the proper system engineers who can deal properly with the costumer's business or equipment. The user companies, therefore, do not generally require any new knowledge to build the Expert Systems. However, even in such a case, someone in the user company who has both job experience and computer intelligence knowledge must play the role of coordinator between user companies and computer manufacturers.

The need for "combined system engineers and specialists" is increasing even in the usual software development. Companies sometimes find it difficult to develop such system engineers. For example they are experiencing rapid technological change in software development every day. They must have specialists who can acquire this intelligence. On the other hand, jobs are becoming more complex and diversified. It thus becomes very difficult for the system engineer to understand the applied job sufficiently to develop the software if they stay only in the information processing section.

Many computer user companies develop some core workers who master the advanced computer software as system engineer specialists and let them stay in the information processing section. They also have some personnel who transfer between the information processing station and other work places. Some persons thus stay in the information processing section for a long time and some persons stay less. In some cases, relatively long experienced system engineers transfer to any other work place, stay there several years, then return to the information processing section again as system engineers. The situation differs from company to company and from person to person. This situation partly reflects the Japanese personnel management system.

In Japan, almost all large companies employ a personnel management system based on the generalist, not on the specialist. All persons transfer from one section to another, in some cases changing jobs through job rotation. Such rotation between the information processing section and other work places may become more important in the future from other viewpoints, because companies need system engineers with greater ability to understand the job itself in puddling complex systems like Expert Systems.The system engineers with work experience will become more and more important.

Needless to say, such opportunity to transfer the engineers differs by industry or job. It is relatively possible in office work but impossible, for example, in construction industry. The advanced software companies also attempt to develop system engineers with some strong specialities (for example financial problems, community business, sectors of manufacturing, communication) to be able to cope with customers' complex and sophisticated requirements. The primary method of training for this purpose is periodic job rotation or, in some cases, project rotation.

The persons who play the central role in technical aspects of Expert System development are system engineers (or research workers in the case of a large machinery industry developing the various equipment with AI and a think-tank). Few companies have an occupation called Knowledge Engineer. In most companies, system engineers cope with the problem mastering the AI language. The companies think that the method of Expert Systems is just a new skill for developing software. They, therefore, tbelieve that there is no need to distinguish between the system engineer and the knowledge engineer, now or even in the future. However, they usually consider the system engineer to have knowledge engineer's ability, very excellent system engineers with the careers as project leader and highly skilled in job analysis, system concept realization and consultation.

1.5. Acquiring and Developing Engineers for Expert Systems

All companies resolve the problem by using engineers within their own company. Some companies employ the new graduates who majored in AI or who are interested in AI Few companies, however, employ the mid-career entrants with AI knowledge from the outside labour market. Because there is almost no person who has mastered AI knowledge in the labor market. The only way to develop such engineers is to give the proper education and training to engineers within the company.

The human resources for system engineers and the method of their careers has already been introduced in one of my previous reports [1]. Though the science majors graduating from universities are more plentiful than others, a variety of people with relatively high educational backgrounds work as system engineers. In the machinery industry and the think-tank mentioned above, researchers who majored and got good marks in electronics, information engineering and mathematics in the former and in information engineering, communication, measurement, calculation, management in the latter, are developing Expert Systems. Most of them have graduated from post graduate courses.

1.6. Educating and Training Engineers for Expert Systems

It is difficult to acquire education or training for Expert Systems skills through school or public training now, because these skills are still at the developing research level and variable. The most effective way to master Expert Systems development skills within a company is now On the Job Training (OJT). The only effective way is to develop Expert Systems in order to accumulate expertise concerning tools, bargaining and understanding. In addition to OJT, engineers acquire knowledge from books or study meetings within the company (in some cases, each person studies and reports about a certain theme which is then discussed among all the participants. In other cases, a person who has attended an outside lecture on AIbecomes a lecturer and teaches skills to others. In still other cases, AI authorities from outside the company are invited as lecturers).

In Japan, all companies are devoted to developing system engineers within their own company. The situation is similar in the case of AI These companies always face rapid technological innovation in the software development, and learning new skills is a routine work. Most companies, therefore, consider AI or Expert Systems to be an extension of the usual software development skills, and as such, not to be special.

1.7. Who Has the Responsibility for and Takes the Initiative in Expert Systems Development?

In most cases, the information processing section and the user sector (e.g. the work place) commonly share the responsibility and initiatives for developing Expert Systems. The proportion of sharing is not necessarily fixed and varies on a case-by-case basis even within a company.

1.8. Resistance of Specialists to Expert Systems

Do specialists who provide the job knowledge resist Expert Systems because they may lose their jobs if the computer does work better?

Except for a few cases, there is little resistance from specialists. Most specialists welcome their Expert Systems because Expert Systems reduce their heavy work loads.

Several factors can explain the little specialist resistance that exists. One factor is that present Expert Systems are relatively small yet. The second and more important factor is that Expert Systems can only perform a part of the specialist's work, and that they support their work. Without specialists, Expert Systems cannot gain new knowledge to cope with the changing situation, and the final high-level judgement is committed to man. This situation will not change even in the future, so Expert Systems can never replace the specialist.

A third factor is the guarantee of employment. For example, in Japan, as a result of recent technological innovations, we have experienced significant labor reductions in the production process by using microelectronics equipment. However, very few companies dismissed employees. Instead, they relocate the employees to the busy areas within the factory and guarantee them the same wage even after the job change (table 2, table 3). Office automation technology is also used to deal with expanding business and to overcome labor shortages or to develop new services (e.g. new business opportunities) [2]. In Japan, the job security and wage guarantee are the basis of worker's cooperation in introducing new technology in spite of the large change in work. The situation is more or less similar in the case of Expert Systems development. Even when Expert Systems decrease manpower as a result of good efficiency, they are used to overcome labor shortages and to eliminate the need to increase employees to accommodate demand expansion.

(unit: %)

Size of establishment	Total	Relocated employees									Did not relocate employees
		Total	Relocated employees within the same establishment‡			Transferred employees to other establishments within the same enterprise‡			Transferred employees to affiliated company‡	Dismissed employees to encouraged retirement‡	
			Total	Section after Transfer		Total	Section after Transfer				
				Production section‡	Executive and Sales Section‡		Production section‡	Executive and Sales Section‡			
Total	100.0	29.5	28.0 (100.0)	(97.7)	(10.6)	3.3 (100.0)	(92.0)	(43.3)	1.2	0.4	70.4
1000 employees and more	100.0	44.8	43.0 (100.0)	(98.8)	(14.6)	6.1 (100.0)	(97.3)	(51.4)	3.1	-	55.0
300-999 employees	100.0	33.0	32.0 (100.0)	(97.5)	(12.8)	3.6 (100.0)	(93.3)	(52.0)	1.7	0.2	67.0
100-299 employees	100.0	25.8	24.2 (100.0)	(97.5)	(8.2)	2.8 (100.0)	(89.7)	(35.7)	0.7	0.6	74.1

Source: Ministry of Labor "Survey on Technological Innovation and Labor" (1982)

Note: ‡ The figures sum to over Total due to multiple answer.

Table 2 Employee's Relocation as a Result of Introducing Equipment with Integrated Circuits

(unit: %)

Size of establishment	Wage of workers who were transferred to other process or sector from where equipment with Integrated Circuit was introduced						Wage of workers who are still working where equipment with Integrated Circuit was introduced					
	Total	Previous wage was guaranteed	Wages were changed for new job				Total	Previous wage was guaranteed	Wages were changed for new job			
			Total	Wage of most workers increased	Wage of most workers decreased	Numbers of both workers were same			Total	Wage of most workers increased	Wage of most workers decreased	Numbers of both workers were same
Total	100.0	93.7	6.3 (100.0)	(40.5)	(15.9)	(41.3)	100.0	95.7	4.2 (100.0)	(88.9)	(1.0)	(7.2)
1000 employees and more	100.0	86.9	13.1 (100.0)	(14.7)	(5.9)	(79.4)	100.0	93.7	6.1 (100.0)	(59.5)	(-)	(35.1)
300-999 employees	100.0	94.2	5.8 (100.0)	(38.5)	(30.8)	(25.6)	100.0	96.2	3.8 (100.0)	(89.9)	(3.8)	(5.1)
less than 300 employees	100.0	95.1	4.9 (100.0)	(58.5)	(11.3)	(28.3)	100.0	95.7	4.2 (100.0)	(94.2)	(-)	(2.6)

Source: Ministry of Labor "Survey on Technological Innovation and Labor" (1982)

Table 3 Wage Change as a Result of Introducing Equipment with Integrated Circuits

In general, there are three types of specialists resistance.

(1) The first case depends on the types of workers. There are two kinds of people. One kind is contended with the present standardized work using old tools; the other does creative work but must spend a fairly long time doing routine or standardized work also. For the latter, Expert Systems are very effective, but there may be resistance from the former. In such cases, interviewed companies received cooperation from people who are open with their knowledge.

(2) The second case is the reluctance to develop Expert Systems because the specialists do not have enough reliance on Expert Systems (they doubt whether it is necessary or useful).

(3) The third case is that specialists do not intend to resist Expert Systems development, but they do not perceive their own knowledge based on concrete rules and find difficulty transferring their knowledge.

To reduce their resistance, specialists must be persuaded that Expert Systems do not replace specialists, but support them, and companies must convince the work place manager of the importance and effectiveness of preserving skills.

1.9. Total Manpower Needed for Developing Expert Systems

It is difficult to introduce the various cases of system development in one word. Total manpower for the development differs significantly from system to system, and companies do not necessarily use the same accounting methods for man-days (or -months, -years). Some include the days the specialists spend to provide their knowledge, and some exclude them. Some include the days when engineers were studying and discussing the selection of methods, and some exclude them. Furthermore, the scale of Expert Systems themselves differ, for example, depending on the hardware they use – mainframe, personal computer, minicomputer, LISP machines and work stations. Some small systems were developed in four man-months, and some large systems required more than 20 man-years.

2. Use of Expert Systems

2.1. Who Uses Expert Systems?

In general, there are two types of Expert System's use. In the first, the most skilled specialists who provided the knowledge themselves, use the system. In the other, less skilled workers use the system.

In the companies interviewed, the former type exceeded the latter. All systems in table 1 except the following are this type.

As examples of the latter, we found an advice system for best investment in one of the interviewed stockbrokers (young female workers with one or two years' experience of system use when explaining selections to customers at the counter), an evaluation system for life insurance payment (young workers with one or two years' experience get the results by using the system and the more experienced specialists check them before the final decision), a system for evaluation construction tender prices, a system for diagnosing electronic switchboard troubles in a communication-related construction company (both are used by junior or middle-class specialists, and they perform half the level of work of true specialists), a diagnosis system for concrete crack causes and repair, a piling method selection system in a construction company (slightly less skilled specialists or specialists in local branches use them), and a consulting system for selecting medical examination in a hospital (young doctors use it).

2.2. Changes in Work as the Result of Expert System Introduction

Are there any changes in the number of employees, kind and contents of job, work process, organization, responsibility, authority, the flow of work or information, role of manager and services?

The following merits of Expert Systems were suggested through interviews:

(1) Efficiency increased significantly, and it eased the shortage of specialists.

(2) It performed the routine work of specialists, decreased their burden and made it possible for them to devote more time to more difficult work.

(3) It became possible to provide higher quality goods or services to customers by using simulation etc.

(4) Accuracy of work increased.

(5) Wide common use of knowledge became possible.

(6) It became possible to maintain quality of service at a uniformly high level including the local branches.

(7) It became possible to maintain skills and knowledge of specialists even after they retired or when it was impossible to relocate them to a certain area.

(8) As a by-product of system development, companies received good suggestions for improving work because they must thoroughly ana-

lyze work load, job contents, human resources required and each person's ability before building the Expert System.

However, at present, effects of Expert Systems are not so large as to influence the number of employees or other problems suggested under the title.

Companies do not have very large systems yet, and specialists are as busy as ever in dealing with expanding demand, while shifting their work from easy tasks to more difficult ones. To worry about various problems at this stage is thus groundless apprehension.

Labor may be reduced when the large systems are developed in the future. Even then, however, they will only be able to restrain new recruitment. Company officers cannot imagine Expert Systems as having a larger effect than office automation or rationalization.

In an exceptional case, the company reduced the number of specialists in the design section of a printing company interviewed. Three designers of paper boxes for packages worked in the head office. By introducing an Expert System supporting design, the company was able to transfer one of the three designers to another section, using his experience and ability. There was no reduction in the local branch where they are still very busy. Another exception was a supermarket work scheduling program. The supermarket could save 200 working hours of part time help per month by effective labor allocation every ten minutes based on the sales prospects of the day. However, they used these saved hours to reduce overtime work and for better service and cleaning, so they did not dismiss anybody.

2.3. Required Ability for Expert System Users and their Training

Almost all companies devote themselves whole-heartedly to making Expert Systems easy for users to handle. Users can thus apply them after only a short explanation or a week's training at most, without any special ability required. All developers said that they should avoid developing complex systems which require users to have special ability. If they do not prepare easy handling systems, nobody will use them.

The only exception was the paper box design supporting system mentioned before. In this case, the company gave two month's education and training to designers because these designers maintain the system by themselves.

2.4. Maintaining Expert Systems

Almost all companies had headaches about this problem. Ideally, Expert Systems are maintained in user sectors by the users themselves. However, at present, systems are complex and it is difficult for the specialists to master AI skills. In most companies, therefore, the information processing section (computer manufacturers, software house or think-tank) maintains the Expert Systems.

Knowledge is changing every day, and new needs always occur. In order to construct a useful and practical system, it is thus necessary to input new knowledge continuously. However, there is no guarantee that the system will work well when they add new knowledge without adequate support by system engineers. This situation is not desirable for companies, as many busy system engineers (or researchers) spend endless time maintaining the system.

Companies are hoping for or developing software which will allow the Expert System users in the work place to develop the system themselves, without AI languages. The situation and selection may differ from company to company or from industry to industry, but in the future there may be work divisions of maintenance. For example, user sectors may do routine maintenance and the information processing section division do the major maintenance, for example, with the development of hardware. Alternatively the user sector may maintain Expert Systems using personal computers, and information system section may maintain the system using host-computers., like production scheduling. Some companies interviewed (construction, credit, printing, automobile and hospital) input new data automatically or with assistance from users.

3. Evaluation and Future Prospects of Expert Systems

Companies evaluate Expert Systems and their future possibilities relatively highly. They think thatExpert Systems do not replace specialists but support them very effectively. The applications are extending from diagnosis to active management fields like design, planning and forecasting. However, Expert Systems are not diffusing as rapidly as expected, and this trend is expected to continue even in future.

3.1. User Companies' Opinions on Expert Systems

Companies evaluate Expert Systems highly and they think there is yet a great potential to be developed in the future. As merits, they said Expert Systems perform the routine work and standardized work not necessarily routine; support men who sometimes tend to forget various factors; have the ability of diagnosis using voluminous complex data; and perform troublesome work like planning (scheduling), design etc. Such benefits are fairly large. Applications are extending from diagnosis to the active, strategic fields. It is certain that the whole integrated system will tend to contain little by little such a field as judgement. If there is clear know-how of the work but it is not on the computer or if the job contents, the work load and the share of each worker are clear, Expert Systems will be applied effectively.

However, as potential limits of Expert Systems, the companies suggested that their ability is yet very low compared with men who possess a very high intuitive judgement ability even in the situations, creativity and inductive reasoning. If they can put the implicit human knowledge in an explicit form on the computer system , then the system can replace man more and more. This is difficult, so Expert Systems do not replace the specialists but support them effectively. In some cases, high cost of development may be another limit of Expert Systems.

As to the dangers of Expert Systems, they suggested the problem that men depend only on the judgement of computers. For example, doctors sometimes intuitively sense the nature of an illness when they meet the patient, and they are usually right. Expert Systems have no such ability. Situations should be judged with sufficient breadth of experience and consideration.

Companies are not so anxious about the danger of using a black box, because the specialists stay at the work place after the introduction of Expert Systems, and the danger will be avoided when the companies prepare a clear maintenance system and standardize knowledge construction.

Diffusion will not be as fast as originally expected because there are yet many problems in (1) hardware, (2) software and (3) the ability to capture the specialist's knowledge. There are numerous problems in software efficiency in particular, and capturing the specialist's knowledge becomes a bottleneck as it takes more and more time as the systems become more complex and sophisticated.

As to software, it is difficult to modify and maintain systems, the processing speed is slow and there is little interoperability.

In capturing the specialist's knowledge, only system engineers with AI skills can do this at present, and it seems difficult to do this automatically, using equipment.

To train system engineers with AI skills, it is necessary to prepare a development manual in order to standardize their work instead of the present training system based on OJT. Now, however, they cannot understand the situation well enough to do so.

Hardware changes may significantly affect the speed of Expert System diffusion. If they have higher processing speed and larger memories, the Expert Systems are expected to make greater progress. Interoperability of hardware is also important for the future expansion of Expert Systems.

3.2. System Developers' Opinion on Expert Systems

The manager of a think-tank described Expert Systems as follows: They found fields to which Expert Systems can be applied very effectively. The problem is that is difficult to accurately forecast the effect, profit and cost. In addition, they found it difficult to measure the effect quantitatively, because most cases aim at the qualitative work improvement.

Several thousand Expert Systems may be being developed. Through this, AI thinking methods and development skills are being diffused. However, the practical use of the systems in the working environment is just beginning.

The speed of diffusion is slower than expected. The developers think it is because:

(1) Most companies introduce the systems without sufficient analysis of needs in work places because they are afraid to be behind other competitors.

(2) The boundary of AI is not clear, so there are both over-promotion and over-expectation on the one hand and underestimation of Expert Systems on the other hand, because they looked at poor systems.

(3) The lack of interoperability impedes the rapid diffusion of Expert Systems. Because many user companies want to link the Expert Systems to the systems they already have, using the mainframe, personal computers or work station in order to use the system for actual work.

To train system engineers with AI skills, they are now preparing quite different curriculum. They intend to train the engineers from the wide viewpoint that they should master various system construction methods like OR, statistics This will enable the engineers to select the best methods for each problem and to think that AI is only one of development tools which is used if it is appropriate for that problem.

Computer manufacturers have high expectations about Expert Systems. However, they also feel the speed of diffusion is a little slow and the managers suggest that these systems may be a little too complicated to be sold rapidly.

References

[1] DATEKI, S. YAHATA, S. and MATUMOTO, S., Ability Development of Information Processing Engineers and their Career Formation: Focusing on Software Engineers, in NIEVR Report No. 2, Changes in Work Patterns and their Educational Implication, March 1987, published by National Institute of Employment and Vocational Research, Japan

[2] DATEKI, S., Employment and Human Resource Development in the Service Sector - Technological, Structural Change and Labor -, NIEVR Report No. 3, Feb. 1988, published by National Institute of Employment and Vocational Research, Japan

EXPERT SYSTEMS IN PRODUCTION AND SERVICES II
Th. Bernold and U. Hillenkamp (Editors)
Elsevier Science Publishers B.V., Amsterdam – Printed in The Netherlands

The Social Impact Study of the Fifth Generation Computer and A I

Hajime Karatsu
R&D Institute
Tokai University
Tokyo Japan

Creative prospective power is required to forecast the social impacts brought about by newly developed and innovative technology. We have a tendency to extend our experience of the past to forecast the future and make errors all the time. According to such mistakes, much comedy and tragedy occurred. The steam locomotive invented by Trevithic was forced to be guided by a red flag waver just in front of the train under the regulation of safety.

In concern with the 5th Generation Computer (5th G.), unexpected errors or poor conclusion would be brought from the method of extending the past to the future.

The basic difference between the traditional computer and the 5th G. is that the former is for information processing and the latter is to realize knowledge processing. The 5th G. is expected to realize man-machine conversation easily, so called "user friendly" and "easy programming". In one word, the target of the 5th G. is the popularization of the computer.

According to the computer white paper of Japan, only 2 % of the population of Japan handles a computer today. However, the number of computer users may jump up to the level of two digits rapidly. At the beginning of the history of the automobile, only a man specially trained as a driver could handle it. But today, the car is an intrinsic part of our civilization as a tool easy to be used by anyone. Without the car, almost social activities would hardly work well. It just fits the name "motorized society".

According to the analogy mentioned above, we may naturally get the conclusion that technological condition to construct the computerized society will be realized by the 5th Generation Computer.

The computerized society brought about by the 5th G. is not the same as discussed in the past in e.g. the world of "1984" by George Orwell, but will be newly created in the next era in which computer power is not concentrated in one hand but distributed and handled throughout society.

I am presently chairman of the social impact study committee of the 5th Generation Computer Project of Japan. The first issue of our committee was to study the possibilities brought about by the 5th G. applied to the field of low productivity in Japan. As you already know, the Japanese industries attained fame not only for its high productivity but also for its high quality. On the other hand, statistics show that in fact the productivity of Japan as a whole is rather low compared with other industrialized nations. This means that some sectors of the Japanese economy pull the average down by poor productivity. These sectors comprise for example agriculture, retailing, education or administration.

At the conference of FGC5'81 held in Tokyo, I pointed out 5 issues which could be improved in Japan by introducing 5th G. computers:

1. Application to low productivity fields;
2. Internationalization of Japanese society;
3. How to cope with a highly educated and aged society;
4. Limited natural resources and energy;
5. Individuals.

Issues of no. 1, 3 and 4 deal with improving the productivity in our industrial and social activities by using the intellectual processing ability of the 5th G. machines. Item 2 is concerned with machine translation and mutual understanding between different cultures stimulated by bilateral dialogue.

In our committee for the study of the social environment and the impact of advanced information technology, we selected the following 11 topics:

1. Survey of the knowledge industry;
2. Enquiries about the nature of "user friendly" man-machine system;
3. Metamorphosis of matured industries;
4. New businesses initiated by the 5th G.;
5. Impact on Administration;
6. Innovation in enterprise (organization, productivity, decision making);
7. Innovative organisational structures enabled by the 5th G.;
8. Education and training;

9. Risk management of and with the 5th G.;
10. Employment and occupation;
11. Life style and way of thinking of individuals.

I would like to discuss these issues briefly.

First of all, the 5th G. will be applied in the industrial sector. It aims at improving efficiency and productivity. In this sector, only competitiveness through high productivity can assure the future of an enterprise. Medical applications will be the second important field. The reason is quite simple and clear. It concerns life and death of human beings. Thirdly national security will be by its very nature an important application field.

Following these three areas, educational applications will be widely spread in order to increase the productivity of teaching and training students of all levels from primary school to the graduate courses. To pursue and to match the change caused by the progress of our society and social conditions, we are forced to learn an enormous amount of new things. We have presently no experience in dealing with such a great challenge. It forces us to rationalize the ways of education in every educational field. By comparison it will be rather easy to introduce the 5th G. to the consumers and private life.

In concern with the improvement of productivity, you might raise the question about unemployment. The machine should be installed on the job site for the purpose of eliminating workers or clerks. You would think, then, that unemployment is caused by the machine.

I am a member of the rationalization committee of Tokyo metropolitan Government and in charge as chairman to head the subcommittee for Office Automation (OA). At the end of last year, a plan for OA was sent to the municipal council as subject for discussion. A member of the session asked me, "What do you think about firing clerks when OA works well ?"

I answered, "Of course, OA eliminates quite a number of different jobs in the offices. However, there is no need to discharge any personnel." Today, Tokyo city holds many different institutions for the purpose increasing welfare. Libraries, athletic sport houses, museums, homes for aged people, etc. All institutions close at 5 o'clock every evening and stay also closed on Sundays and holidays. A closed door library is no library any longer but just a vacant building. According to the answer of the city authorities, we cannot open the house because of the shortage of personnel.

Then, welfare cannot be increased without Office Automation, shifting the personnel from clerical work to libraries, museums, sport centers and so on. This way of thinking will be quite important as a model for predicting and shaping the computerized society.

To shift the personnel from one job to another, flexibility of job assignments must be established before such kind of innovation can take hold. Someone may hesitate to explain it, however, you must recognize that our social environment is under the rule of free competition. When the robot was introduced to the production shop floor, almost all scholars and politicians were afraid of a harmful jobless rate.

On the contrary, in Japan, we made efforts to use robots to overcome the shortage of workers brought by the the rapid economic growth rate until the oil crisis of 1974. And again, robotization was accelerated to increase the productivity as the survival strategy against the pressure of rising costs brought by wage rises and high oil price.

We can come to the conclusion that Japan sustained the jobless rate at the lowest level by attaining high productivity realized by robots. This conclusion will be better understood if you try to imagine what would have happened if Japan had not introduced robots, Japan would have lost competitive edge of its industry and an enormous amount of workers would have lost their jobs.

Today, almost all nations are making efforts to introduce automation to the shop floor and office, in order to enhance their competitive entrepreneurial power. To respond to the job rotation boom expected in the near future, efficiency of education and training shall be improved by utilizing the 5th G. To my judgement this can be realized by the developing a flexible job assignment structure for our society.

I would like now to explain a new idea brought about by the 5th G. As you know, modern aircraft maintains stability by means of computer control. But they still have the traditional shape of an aircraft with main wings in the front and a large tail at the rear, all of which contribute to a stable flight.

An aircraft could also fly safely only with the help of a computer and a gyro. Then, such a big size tail as that of current aircraft becomes unnecessary. Consequently, an aircraft could be equipped with a smaller tail, reducing its weight and air drag. The main wing needs not be shaped like an arrow with its pointed edge facing forward. Wings attached in reverse would be more efficient. A computer would guarantee the stability of flight. An aircraft based upon such new concepts is called a control configured vehicle.

This new aircraft is inherently unstable. It cannot keep flying once its computer fails. However being unstable, it is capable of flying askew. Of course, current aircraft cannot do this.

It occurred to me that the human body is also essentially unstable. Humans can stand straight up thanks to their brains, that is, the computer of the body. When their computers stop functioning, humans just fall down. However, because of this instability, humans are capable of movements which four-legged animals can never imitate. For example, horses can never perform ballet-like movements.

Further speculation makes us realize that the organization of enterprises and government offices is pyramid shaped. The purpose of building a pyramid-shaped organization is to have the center of gravity placed lower, so that the organization remains stable when there are some defects in its information system network.

No pyramid organizations are necessary, when computer control is so sophisticated that it can reach the level of perfection. There is an example of a company with no pyramid structure, that is, a company managed by a super person. Such an organization should be able to act more quickly with greater mobility.

What is the point of giving all these examples? In short, I want to note that the shape of an aircraft changes with the introduction of new techniques. That is, the aircraft is designed around the control concept of the computer. Similarly, when computers are incorporated into society, it may be desirable that society takes an alternative form to permit the realization of higher efficiency and mobility. I feel that the social impact of the 5th G. must be considered with all these prospects in mind.

Someone may have a suspicion that nothing will be left to be done by human beings when the 5th G. is introduced everywhere in our social activity. Even diagnoses by medical doctors are said to be performed by utilizing the computers, with lower misjudgment rates.

A good answer to the question was brought by our study of an airline company. An authority of the company said that most of the aircraft accidents are caused by pilot mistakes. For example, when a plane approaches the airport and a thunderstorm threatens to break over the runway the pilot has to consider either to abort landing or to continue the approach. Only a few seconds' judgement divides the fate of the plane. In such a critical state, the computer may play a dependable role as a decision consultation machine, acting as a substitute for a hot-headed pilot. A computer never loses its head.

Basically, I think that the computer cannot excess the ability of human beings. However, sometimes a human being loses his mind while the computer always works well without getting excited.

The popularization of the computer will be quite effective for enlarging the intellectual activity of handicapped people, which can be comparable to the merit brought by the wheel chair. It opened their world. Today it even enables athletic games, namely the Para Olympics.

So far, I have explained about the target of the 5th G. project and the possibilities of its application. These expectations can be realized only when we prepare a framework for the society using 5th G. systems such as new laws, regulations, culture and educational level, etc. We say "New wine needs a new bottle". Without these preparations, we do not know what kind of backlash will happen in the future.

In the medical field, a diabetic patient must go quite often to the hospital to have the level of his urine sugar checked by a medical doctor in order to adjust his diet. Today, it is technologically quite easy to measure the urine sugar at home and send the data by telephone line to get the consultation. However, in Japan, this kind of remote medical treatment is not generally utilized because of the regulation of the health insurance law. This is quite ridiculous! When I asked the authority of law, the answer was as follows: The health insurance organization will pay only when the patient calls in at the hospital, otherwise it will not pay. Why so? The hospital might call the patients every day for which the organization should pay as a medical examination, if the restriction is cleared. It is concerned with the moral of the medical doctor! In general, Japanese patients cannot enjoy such kind of convenience by high technology.

Another strange story goes as follows: In Japan, on-line banking systems play a role for payment by credit card without checking by the holder of the card. This service includes charge for electric power, telephone charge and so on. In the case of private entrepreneurs, the settlement between companies by utilizing the on-line system is restricted by the policy of the Government, in fear of not being able to detect the stamp-duty tax evasion when money flows through the computer and telecommunication network.

For almost all nations, such kind of trouble and friction may occur between the 5th G. and traditional law, culture, habit, social structure. Therefore, we must study and prepare the way to cope with the new technology.

Science and technology are always double-edged swords. We must handle them cautiously. Almost all that I have mentioned above is the bright side of the 5th G., however, the biggest and most grave problem is the issue concerned with the degradation of the human activity, in other words, "intellectual laziness" which speeds down the energy of our society.

In the past, civilization was developed by people who could spend enough time for it, not bothered by heavy and dirty work which was turned to the shoulders of slaves. However, they lost social activity gradually and finally went to ruin. I am afraid now that the 5th Generation Computer may have a potential of bringing laziness to our society.

It is quite hard work to forecast the style of the future based on the 5th G., and unexpected phenomena might occur. To overcome such a hazardous incidents, we must prepare a feedback system which always observes the development of our society not unlike a weather station. It should issue necessary information to adjust the direction of our project for a soft landing.

Evaluation and Operational Systems' Progress Reports

EXPERT SYSTEMS IN PRODUCTION AND SERVICES II
Th. Bernold and U. Hillenkamp (Editors)
Elsevier Science Publishers B.V., Amsterdam – Printed in The Netherlands

Evaluation Criteria for Expert Systems

Brian Oakley
LOGICA
London W1A 4SE, UK

1. Summary - Evaluation Criteria for Expert Systems

In considering the evaluation of Expert Systems, one has to give special attention to the aspects in which they differ from conventional systems, and to the weaknesses in early Expert Systems that delayed their widespread use. There are, essentially, three factors that explain the many years in which Expert Systems have been worked on but hardly used:

1. The cost effectiveness of the Run-Time System. This factor is just like that for any conventional system, but is sometimes difficult to measure since the efficiency of the system may depend upon the particular problem the system is tackling within the range that the system is designed to tackle.
2. Knowledge representation efficiency. It is becoming increasingly clear that the way in which the knowledge is represented and stored has a considerable influence on the problem solving speed, on the ease of extending the knowledge base and on its verification.
3. The quality of the Human Interface. Unlike a conventional computer system, an Expert System must have a good human interface, for the user must be able not only to obtain an answer, obtain advice from the system; the user must also be able to question why that particular advice is given.

These are key factors to take account of in the evaluation of any Expert System. But for any "serious" system on which lives, health, money, even happiness, are to depend it must be possible to verify and validate the answers that the system will give in any particular set of circumstances. Because of the inevitable lack of completeness and rigor in the knowledge base and rules, this presents a particular problem for the evaluation of Expert Systems.

The paper will examine these issues, and consider how far the available toolkits and shells help the constructor of Expert Systems to deal with them.

2. Evaluation Criteria for Expert Systems

2.1. Comparison with Conventional Computing

a) When one sets out to evaluate a conventional computer system one does not usually question whether it gives the right answer, one con reasonably assume that a computer system, based on the verities of mathematics and boolean logic, will give the right answer if it gets the right data and is properly programmed. But the Expert System, based on inference computing, has no such certainties. It will almost inevitably have an incomplete rule base, some of the rules may be incorrect in certain circumstances, some of the rules may be contradictory. So though there is a probability of the answer being correct, there is no certainty. This means that much more attention has to be paid to the quality of the advice that an Expert System produces, rather than to the matter of speed, storage, etc., that tend to be the way of characterizing a conventional system.

2.2. Classifying Expert Systems

b) The heart of an Expert System is the Knowledge, so one element in the evaluation of such a system must be the quality of the Knowledge and of the process of linking that knowledge to infer some advice. So one way of classifying Expert Systems would be to consider the nature of the knowledge, what domain it comes from. One of the problems with current Expert Systems technology is that no satisfactory and widely accepted way of classifying Expert Systems exists. One has only to consider the success of Linneus at classifying nature to recognise how classifying helps scholarship and understanding of a subject. He may not have achieved Darwin's insight into what caused the diversity of nature but he achieved a classification that has largely stood the test of time, now that DNA studies enable us to provide a scientific test for family relationships.

c) Attempts have been made to classify Expert Systems by the nature of the equivalent mental process: Do they provide help with Diagnosis, Monitoring, Planning, Scheduling, etc. Table I attempts to classify systems that Logica have built in this way. It turns out that it is not very informative. To classify an electromyographers assistant together with a train brake fault warning system as both being diagnosis systems serves to cloud the picture rather than clarify. On the other hand the fact that one comes from a medical domain, the other from a mechanical engineering does seem of benefit to the librarian and the domain specialist.

d) Yet a classification based purely on domain is clearly inadequate. How about a matrix classification of which one dimension is "domain", the other "technical property"? This helps both the domain expert and the knowledge based system expert.

- Large Administrative Systems
  1) Social Security System
  2) Accountancy package help system
- Product Formulation
  Systems for Foodstuffs, Oils, Glues, Drinks, etc. etc.
- Medical and Engineering Diagnosis
  Electromyographers Assistant
  Brake fault monitoring
- Building Management Regulation Interpretation
- Aircraft Mission Planning
- CAD/CAM system and Job Shop Scheduling
- Air Traffic Control
- Business Start–Up Advisor
- Audit Trail Analysis
- Real Time KBS Validation
- Stock Market Investment Assistant

Table I: Logica's Expert Systems

2.3. Technical Properties of an Expert System

e) For a conventional computer system it would be typical to consider the type of machine on which the system runs, the speed of performing a test problem, and the memory required. One might also require some information on the mean time to system failure, and the security of the system. An experienced customer would also enquire into the Quality Assurance methods used, how the system has been verified and validated. All these have some relevance for an Expert System, but they are not enough. For a conventional system one might ask what tools had been used to create the system. This gives a clue to how to gain an insight on Expert System has been constructed.

f) In Table II are listed the properties that one might look for in a conventional computer system, but also the properties that relate to the technical features an expert system might employ. An inspection of the list shows that these are the headings one would use if one was classifying the properties that can be created

I. Common to all Computer Systems

1. Machines on which the system will run
2. Speed for some test program
3. Memory Required
4. Robustness, or Mean-time-to-failure
5. Security
6. Validation and Verification

II. Special to all Expert Systems

1. Base Language

2. Interfaces: 1) Packages
   2) External Languages

3. Knowledge Representation:
   1) Rules
   2) Rule-sets
   3) Frames
   4) Inheritance
   5) Uncertainty

4. Inference Technique:
   1) Backward chaining
   2) Forward chaining
   3) Mixed chaining
   4) Use of demons

5. Explanation features:
   1) Why?
   2) How?
   3) What if?

6. Cost to buy

7. Maintenance available?

Table II: Technical Properties of Expert Systems

from a shell or toolkit, like Xi Plus or Bold Work. Of these features the "Base Language" used needs little explanation, and is not of any great consequence except to the designer. Was LISP or Prolog used? Or if the system stems from Japan was a Guarded Horn Clause language used? The "Inference Technique" can be readily deduced, and is hardly worthy of classification any longer, though some of the more advanced features may be worthy of comment. The external interface capability is important if the Expert System is to be embedded in some external software system, rather than being a stand-along system. But the two features that really do matter are the "Knowledge Representation" form and the "Explanation Features". They deserve some explanation.

2.4. Failures of Early Expert Systems

g) There seems to have been three reasons why it has taken some forty years for Expert Systems to come into wide use. One reason is obviously the cost of the run-time system. Because Inference computing tends to be very demanding on computer time it has taken a long time for delivery machines to be available at a widely affordable cost. It is all very well to use a special LISP processing machine, five years ago typically of the Symbolics type, but at least in Europe one cannot afford to distribute such machines, say, to every bank manager. The Personal Computer has altered all that, even though it requires pretty powerful machines to run anything other than trivial systems. Much more efficient compilers for LISP and Prolog have helped to reduce the cost of computers used for design. The other reasons for the failure of early systems in use relate to the inability of the systems to be readily understood by the domain expert and the user, problems of knowledge representation and human interface.

2.5. Knowledge Representation

h) Practice has convinced those with experience of constructing Expert Systems that it is essential to represent and store knowledge in a manner that enables the stored information to be conveyed to the domain expert in a way that he will readily understand and appreciate. If there is a "language" for a domain, then it is desirable that that should be used; for example the language in which chess moves are represented is essentially universal. Perhaps the best reason for this is that in order to validate the system the domain expert will have to examine the stored knowledge to confirm that it is correct and complete. But another very practical reason is that it seems almost inevitable that a knowledge base, once constructed, will require extension sooner or later. The original expert will probably have moved on by then, so even if it was determined that only one expert be employed, in the event this is rarely practical for long. There are, of course, a variety of ways of representing knowledge, rules, rule-sets, frames, etc. Some care is needed to find the right way to represent a particular type of knowledge, in order to obtain operating efficiency, and to return clarity for the domain expert.

2.6. User Interface

i) At the other end of the Expert System creation lies the user. As was pointed out at the start of this paper, unlike conventional computer systems, Expert Systems lack the ability to produce the single correct solution to the problem, except in very exceptional circumstances. It seems that a simple user interface that relies on giving a single answer to the user's query is doomed to be unsatisfactory. The user will need more information about the quality of the answer and how it was obtained. What are the key rules that lead to a particular answer? How likely is the answer to be correct? What if one of the parameters of the system is altered? So "Why?" "How?" and above all "What if?" facilities turn out to be very important, even essential if the system is to be useful. This often leads to the user interface becoming a major part of the system. So in classifying an Expert System it is useful to know just how flexible is the user interface.

2.7. Validation and Verification

j) In the list of possible attributes, validation and verification are treated as if they are simple. This tends to be far from the truth even for conventional computer systems. For Expert Systems there seems to be a fundamental problem. Verification can be considered as the process of establishing that the developed system confirms with its specification - "We have built the system right". Validation is the process of establishing that the specification for the system is correct - "We have built the right system". It is becoming possible to apply logical tests to establish that the system does conform with its specification. Formal specifications are not easy to write or to verify, but the process for an Expert System may be easier than for a conventional system, especially if the system has been written in some logical language.

k) But how does one Validate an Expert System? How does one establish that all the rules needed for handling the particular field that is supposed to be covered by the system are there, that the rules are correct, and not contradictory across the problem domain? Of course for small problems this may be practical by inspection. A system usually does not even know what the limits of its knowledge are. (A human expert often doesn't too, though he thinks he does - but that is another story!). So it does help to provide the system with clear boundaries; within the boundaries all necessary knowledge needs to be represented; outside there can be no Validation.

2.8. Parallel with Text Books

l) The fact has to be faced that there is no real way to satisfy oneself that the specification of an Expert System is complete. It is useful to compare an Expert System, not with a conventional computer system containing some algorithm that is demonstratably correct according to the laws of nature, but with a text book. The critic is the nearest one can come to providing a validation. The well informed critic may notice errors, and omissions. By chance he may be able to satisfy the potential reader that the book is sufficiently error free and complete description of its domain that it is worth purchasing. But he is most unlikely to be able to confirm that there are no errors, no important omissions. (It is a well known fact that the standard text books for fields like chemistry and medicine contain errors that go uncorrected through successive editions. One author re-quotes the errors from his predecessors).

m) So the conclusion must be that though one can create a table of technical properties that will help to describe an Expert System in a way that gives a good feel for its technical properties, there is no real way of providing an absolute Validation that the system will produce the right answer in all circumstances. After all, as the man said "What is truth?". What one has to look for is the good critic of an Expert System. It is interesting to note that it will be useful if he is conversant with the technical terms used to classify the system. But it will be essential that he knows the domain covered, so that he can make informed comments on the correctness and completeness of the stored knowledge.

EXPERT SYSTEMS IN PRODUCTION AND SERVICES II
Th. Bernold and U. Hillenkamp (Editors)
Elsevier Science Publishers B.V., Amsterdam – Printed in The Netherlands

Evaluation of Expert System – Applications in Industrial and Services Environments

Manfred Moldaschl
Institut für Sozialwissenschaftliche Forschung
München, FRG

Abstract

When dealing with expert systems researchers, engineers and manufacturers tend to stress the advantages of the new technologies whereas social scientists often concentrate on the risks involved. My contribution will also be concentrating on these risks as I am of the opinion, that the potential benefits of these new technologies will only be able to be exploited to their fullest extent when we are aware of the risks involved and develop ways and means of avoiding them. According to my central thesis these risks are not so much the result of AI-technologies themselves, but are far more the outcome of the overestimation of their performance capacity which subsequently leads to inadequate forms of application which neither make the best use of the technological potential nor of the personnel involved. This tendency toward overestimation is particularly distinct in the prevailing "machine centered approach", the risks of which have found little attention so far. This lack of attention causes unintentional effects for the companies which in some cases have a diametrically opposite effect to the actual objectives such as increasing productivity improved reliability or relieving experts.

This article advocates a "contrasting" viewpoint in software engineering, whereby the specific potential inherent to man and machine is analyses and selectively developed instead of trying to make machines function like human beings and vice versa.

---

1. Introduction

"Every social scientist is faced with the task of acquiring knowledge in order to master the present and of creating ignorance in order to design the future."

J. Kucynski

"Knowledge which has not been acquired by the senses can create no other truth than one which will be harmful."

Galileo

These two statements were not made with "artificial intelligence" in mind and yet they touch on two aspects of a central problem: the significance of practical and sensory experience and the role of human ignorance in the further development (generation) of human knowledge. In other words – the central problem in the use of expert systems is the production and reproduction of human knowledge and human experience.

In the following my basic premise will be that the above mentioned problem can pose itself in very different ways, depending on company objectives and expectations in the use of XPS and the possible forms of utilization which are opted for. It would seem important to me to clarify this viewpoint, because in the current discussion on XPS the potential effects are often directly regarded as stemming from technology "per se"; this holds true for such negative effects as the loss of empirical knowledge, as well as for positive effects up to those of a "more humane society" (Schank, 1984, for example).

Yet also in those cases where it is accepted that the effects can only be interpreted in the context of the conditions and objectives of technology utilization, the discussion usually tends to focus on the direct effects and consequences of an intended form of utilization. It is a common experience, however, also within companies, that things often run a very different course to the intentions of a given company or to what technology assessment has anticipated. In my opinion, this has to do with the fact that the unintentional and the systemic effects are often underestimated and in fact are so manifold, that it is impossible to anticipate them all.

In my following considerations I would first like to specify some of the framework conditions of XPS and subsequently outline some of the unintentional effects and feedback mechanisms. With regards to the various sectors affected by the use of XPS, such as society, company and employees, I will be concentrating on the last mentioned area, with special priority given to the risks involved.

2. Context and Objectives of Company Utilization

The risks of jeopardizing the generation and the preservation of human expert competence, are likely to vary according to the type of company problems which are to be dealt with by the use of XPS. For example:

- Problems of company performance capacity; coping with increasing flexibility requirements and complexity (for example the rising number of product variants, greater integration, JIT).
- Increased cost pressure in certain areas, for example when a disproportionately large number of employees are to be found in planning and service departments (while personnel in the manufacturing departments is decreasing).
- Problems of having experts available for important tasks (shortage of experts).

It is understandable that in the first case XPS would be utilized more for solving technical-organizational problems, whereby it remains open, as to whether this would be brought about by supporting the experts or by establishing the highest degree of automation possible. In the second and third case problems of personnel management take the foreground, whereby in the third case it is uncertain as to whether the solution lies in supporting or replacing the experts. The latter is likely to be the usual objective in the second case.[1]

The manner in which the rationalization potential of AI-applications is utilized also depends on the general organization patterns and the utilization of human labor. In the last years the concepts of "paradigms" or "philosophies" of work design were often referred to. We would like to group the range of existing rationalization strategies around two poles: namely the approach determined by Taylorism and the Human Centered Approach.

1 In the third case the utilization depends on the source of the shortage, that is the company interpretation of the source, whether this is personnel policy, labor market or any other factor.

3. "Computer Aided Taylorism" and "Computer Aided Craftsman"

What is referred to as "Taylorism" in Europe has been the dominant pattern of work design in the past decades. This "traditional" pattern of rationalization is characterized by three prominent features. The first is the principle of simplifying tasks by establishing a maximum degree of division of labour. Taylorism is usually only identified with this feature. The second, more important feature, is the transformation of the work planning into scientific terms: this means extracting the empirical knowledge held by the workers, eliminating subjective components and interests and feeding it back to the workers in the form of standardized work instructions (compare Volpert, 1985). The priority of technology has emerged as the third feature, a standpoint and an understanding which regards man as a basically unreliable, subjective source of mistakes to be replaced as far as possible by the use of exact algorithms and technology. One should be aware of the fact that these basic features of Tayloristic approaches may very well continue to exist even when Taylorism is declared to have been "overcome" in the course of a partial reduction of the division of labor.

As we know, the Tayloristic rationalization approach is particularly predominant in those areas where mass production and a low level of employee skills prevail (see Lutz, 1976). The company size also plays a certain role.

In those areas where high quality products are manufactured in small and medium size series and a sufficient number of skilled employees are available Tayloristic principles were not able to establish themselves to a very large extent. The German machine building industry is a good example for this. Here the supply of skilled workers has been guaranteed by the "dual system" of vocational training.[2] This can be regarded as a result of, yet also as a precondition for the success of this and other branches of the West German industry.[3] Features of this type of work organization are a low degree of division of labor in terms of skills and hierarchical structures and a high degree of employee participation on the one hand, and on the management side a pronounced awareness of the central significance of skilled personnel. This type of work organization has been termed "professional organization" (Kerr, 1954). This design pattern focuses its considerations strongly on human labor and its tasks,

---

2 Government defined vocational training of skilled workers according to specified occupations, usually 3 1/2 years of apprenticeship, with alternate training in companies and education in public vocational schools.

3 International comparative investigations have shown that countries with lesser developed systems of vocational training, such as Great Britain and the United States show a higher degree of in-plant division of labor under similar conditions (e.g. Lutz, 1976, Sorge at al., 1982).

and selects technology according to its capacity for supporting human skills in the best possible way (as evidenced by the concept of the "Computer Aided Craftsman", Jones, 1984). This approach, however, continues to be an exception. At present the so-called Human Centered Approach is more a target concept, a basic "design philosophy" (see Corbett, 1986 and Rosenbrock, 1987).

As far as we can see at present the Tayloristic approach continues to prevail, also in the ideas, expectations, objectives and concepts expressed by manufacturers and potential users in the context of XPS application. This is clearly evidenced by the following objectives commonly brought forth:

- The reduction of the dependency on experts by "conserving" their knowledge
- The immanent potential for accessing and distributing expert knowledge
- The relief of experts by automatizing the processes of judgement and decision making.
- The elimination of "inconsistencies" between expert opinions
- The reduction of training expenditures through the technology of XPS themselves (the so-called explanatory component) and by reducing the number of experts required

It is likely that this approach will continue to prevail due to the fact that it is just as deep-seated in engineering circles as the "Man-is-a-Machine-View" is among AI experts. According to one of the fundamental concepts entertained here, human thought and action are held to be basically identical with computer procedures and can therefore be automatized. "Skills" are regarded as a huge accumulation of facts and rules, and "learning" as progressive amassing of facts and rule bits.

4. The Actual Risk: The Overestimation of AI

In our opinion the main danger in the application of XPS lies in overestimating their performance capacity, also due the before mentioned mechanistic misunderstanding. Expert systems extend the limits of what is technically feasible and yet are confronted by the general limits of formalizing human competence on the one hand and the fundamental limits of the feasibility of planning company processes and sequences (Moldaschl, 1988 a).

The first limit which is systematically underestimated is the extent to which human competence can be formalized. "Professional Qualification" is not the same thing as knowledge, and "knowledge" is by no means identical with the knowledge of elementary facts and rules. Otherwise it would suffice to read a book or undergo theoretical instruction in order to be able to ski, drive a car or learn how to operate a printing machine. The capacity for thought does not remain restricted to the application of knowledge formulated as rules and you will find that AI-experts rarely have much to say about the individual's scope for taking action. It is not my intention here to attempt to place criticism of AI on a psychological basis. I would like to remark however, that the "mastery" achieved by experts is based on practical experience, on the daily sensorial experience of dealing with materials, machines and human beings. It is only through taking practical action, through sensorial experience that knowledge becomes that, which the German word "Können" denotes, a term which is somewhat inadequately translated as skills and which refers to a certain degree of mastery having been achieved. The "feeling for material" or "intuitive feeling" for taking the right course of action which are based on a certain degree of mastery can, for the time being, not be reproduced by technological means. Hubert and Steward Dreyfus (1986) have pointed this out from a philosophical standpoint in a most impressive manner.

With the above mentioned thoughts in mind try and think of something which you are particularly capable of doing, such as giving a critical assessment of a scientific paper or driving a cross-country motorcycle over a difficult course. Can you imagine that just by talking to somebody you could explain these things in such a way that the other person would be equally capable of doing them? Or what about writing down some of the relevant rules on a sheet of paper? Now how would the inexperienced person understand this knowledge which has been extracted from its empirical background, and how will he or she be able to act in an effective manner? This is indeed the situation of the XPS user who does not happen to be an expert in the particular area.

A second, fundamental restriction which the methods of artificial intelligence are confronted by, is the limit to which company operational sequences can be planned. Open systems and complex processes, as are typical for modern companies, possess such a multitude of potential sources of disturbance which are impossible to fully anticipate and thus they also hold a high degree of incalculability.[4]

---

4 In several enterprises I made a curious experience in dealing with managers and system engineers, where I found that the very same people who vehemently opposed socialist economy planning pushed total planning systems in their own enterprises. As one foreman at an FMS told me: "Hardly have we managed to overcome the system's growing pains the symptomns of old age beginn to set in!"

There is no planning perfect or system complex enough to fully anticipate all these factors. Also, the more complex systems become the less scope they offer for flexible control and the more prone to failure they become through technical defects, coding mistakes - two "Mariner" probes, for example, were lost due to a point instead of a comma in the program (Valk, 1987) - or also by human errors (remember the Exocet incidence in the Falkland War.)

Yet it is in the very nature of human intelligence to be capable of dealing with unclear and contradictory information, to cope with open, uncertain and new situations. The capacity of human intelligence for handling ambiguous contents and knowledge gaps is based on our innate potential for learning. This means transforming knowledge deficits into knowledge by taking action, by experimenting, and thus using a given lack of knowledge as a source of acquiring new knowledge.

Human competence remains indispensable for complex technical systems. But the question remains open as to how will it be integrated? Instead of developing software, however, which would be able to give human beings the best support possible for doing that which they can do better than computers, the current developments are directed towards achieving a technical simulation of such competence, in order to replace [5] those persons holding such expert knowledge. And this is happening at a time when the individual within the company is playing an increasing central role: fewer and fewer workers are confronted with an increasingly complex machinery. Therefore overestimating the self-regulation capacity of technology poses a serious danger to productivity, process security and mental health. And it is the technology-oriented, "Tayloristic" viewpoint which tends to succumb particularly strongly to such overestimation.

5. Intentions and Unintentional Effects

Resuming the last arguments, there are two sources of risks, two general types of effects to be considered. On the one hand there are the effects resulting from the effective performance and rationalization potential of XPS; and on the other hand there are effects which have primarily to do with the overestimation of technological potential. In the following I would like to briefly outline some of the possible unintentional effects resulting from the wrong assessment of human competence and the overestimation of technical performance capacity. In doing so I would like to restrict myself to describing direct and counter-productive effects on the company level.

---

5 This replacement may occur in a number of different ways: replacing parts and aspects of expert work in order to accelerate work speed; dividing expert work into development and a larger number of application functions; and in some rare cases, replacing experts altogether.

- The companies want to become independent of experts yet make themselves dependent on a form of technology which is only capable of handling routine operations. At the same time however, in the course of increasing automation special situations and disturbances are becoming more and more common occurrences.
- Companies want to overcome the shortage of experts yet are producing such a shortage at the same time by dispensing with the training or recruitment of human experts.
- Companies seek to reduce their training expenditures yet are generating a lack of skills, due to the fact that the "explanatory component" of XPS is neither capable of replacing practical experience or vocational training; and also because this component is not capable of providing explanations in the true sense of the word , due to the fact that the computer has no genuine "understanding" of the field it is being used in.
- Companies would like to bypass the inconsistencies between different expert opinions, yet invariably generate inconsistencies between model and reality – inconsistencies which users are subsequently confronted with and cannot handle adequately.
- Companies are trying to avoid mistakes and disturbances by objectivizing human knowledge, while inviting what they would like to avoid, due to the fact the system is only capable of partially representing the complex interrelationships.

Of course there are other, less technology centered approaches which are in danger of losing the potential benefits of XPS through an inadequate use of technology and personnel, for example when they

- try to take an excessive work load off the shoulders of experts and at the same time expect that they now make more decisions in less time and additionally monitor the conclusions the system has arrived at,
- try and take the "burden" of routine work off their hands and at the same time cut off their source of potential practical experience – such as the case of a supervisor in a power plant who is only supposed to intervene in the case of an emergency, yet who does not know how the system reacts to intervention.

These are only a few of the problematic effects which may directly result from the utilization of XPS without being intended. The question should also be posed as to what other possible positive effects, intentional and unintentional will arise, as well as indirect effects (for example on departments and employees not at all involved with the use of XPS). And finally it would be very interesting to investigate how the companies are reacting to these effects. Positive feedback loops are conceivable, such as an increased use of technology to cope with problems which only became pressing after the introduction of XPS (skill problems, migration of experts, etc.).

Before we go on to the question as to how companies might react to the problems looming up on the horizon, I would like to mention a few more company risks, which may result from the employee point of view. With regards to qualification the following risks should be mentioned.

- The present job held by an expert will be subdivided into that of a knowledge engineer and one or several data suppliers for the system or system user, associated with a loss of status and dequalification of experts-or an overburdening of poorly qualified users.
- The expropriation of expert knowledge. Individual knowledge does not actually disappear altogether, however it is no longer held by the individual and that means the danger of loss of status and control, or of job loss.
- The loss of expert knowledge through lack of use in the case of extensive automation (use it or lose it).
- The stagnation of expert knowledge due to the loss of possibilities for gathering experience and learning (also due to the necessity of having to adhere to system guidelines under time pressure).
- Qualification is reduced to man-machine "interaction", associated with a loss of communication and social support in learning situations and the danger of deficient and solely machine based qualification.

These risks relating to employee skills are associated with severe stress factors for personnel:

- Loss of status and control, or the risk of such loss both cause emotional stress, as does overstrain
- So-called users are left alone with the system during the learning period, resulting in overstrain and a feeling of insecurity
- Although skills waste away, stagnate and are no longer specifically developed, they are still called for in emergency situations in order to avert serious consequences of disturbances (stress is caused by contradictory work requirements-emergency dilemma, or Harrisburg-syndrome; see Hirschhorn, 1984)

– Although neither experts or lesser qualified personnel are able to verify data provided by the system under time pressure, they are nevertheless responsible for the results if bad comes to worse (anxiety and stress caused by the dilemma of responsibility).

Load Dilemma
 Thoroughly checking system decisions – and making more decisions in shorter time

Harrisburg Syndrome
 Intervening rapidly and effectively – and having no practice

Dilemma of Responsibility
 Having to follow the system – and being responsible in case of damage

---

Table 1: Some Contradictory Job Requirements

While these effects are hypothetical in the context of XPS utilization, they are by no means new. They are typical for highly automated systems, yet not XPS specific. By increasing the degree of automation and technical mediation they serve to intensify the problems. In our investigations of FMS (Flexible Manufacturing Systems) or of PPS (Production Planning Systems) we frequently encountered such discrepancies between the anticipated effects and reality as well as between the demands made on employees and their scope for taking effective action. Thus these discrepancies are by no means the never-ceasing pessimistic apprehensions of social scientists, but are widespread facts which affect productivity and cause "inexplicable" failures, or failures which are explained away as being "human failure".

6. Correcting the Miscalculation - or "Correcting" Reality?

We have been mainly concerned with the risks which arise through an overestimation of AI technologies, on the grounds that the effects have less to do with the technology itself than with the way in which it is used and the objectives pursued. If it is true that overestimation of this kind causes such grave problems one might expect that the expectations would soon be corrected by practi-

Picture 1: Dilemma of Responsibility

cal experience. In agreement with Mertens et. al. (1988) one should assume that the expectations held by the companies and society concerning this new technology may follow a quasi natural curve: overestimation – frustration – realism.

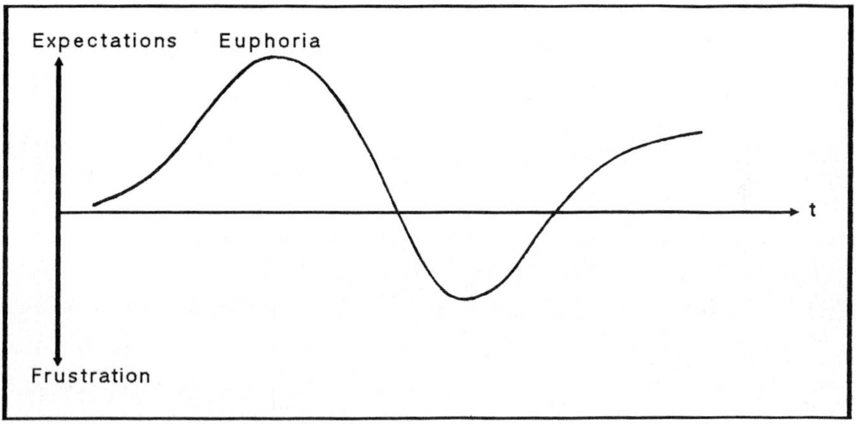

Picture 2 The Expectations Curve (Mertens et al.)

Investigations concerned with other applications of information technology in the manufacturing and office sector (Moldaschl, 1988 b, Weltz, 1988) have shown that this expectation curve needs not be an inevitable consequence, however. An attitude of overestimation may remain despite frustration and may lead to the attempt to solve the problems arising by an increased employment of technology. The reasons for such frustration are either looked for in the wrong area or are not recognized at all.

Some of the reasons for this blindness to the above mentioned problems and risks could be:

- The compensatory efforts of employees by which the discrepancies between formal requirements and actual conditions are covered up as far as possible at the price of considerable additional effort, personal risk and strain. Such efforts help to further sustain the illusion of complete control.

- The reversal of the cause and effect principle, for example when the lack of employee motivation or competence is held responsible for the discrepancies between planning and reality.
- When the Tayloristic approach has become so firmly entrenched in engineering structures that it is no longer perceived as a paradigm, and is no longer viewed from a relative standpoint as being one of a number of possible approaches.

A curious but typical example of the last mechanism is exemplified by the following incident. A software engineer built up a highly centralized and automated control system for an FMS. The system never worked because of the new problems – whether organizational, technical or social – which kept continuously arising. So the engineer revised the system again and again, until it was a completely new and in fact worker-oriented system. But he did not seem to be particularly aware of the fact for he told me: "The system was perfect, but the circumstances have been lousy". Which means to say the model was alright, only reality happened to be "wrong".

This implies that all the pleas in favor of the expert and assertions of not wanting to replace him, are not worth very much in practical terms, because we are lacking the ways and means of pursuing a better course of action. This also means that a supervisor, for example, can derive no feeling of safety from

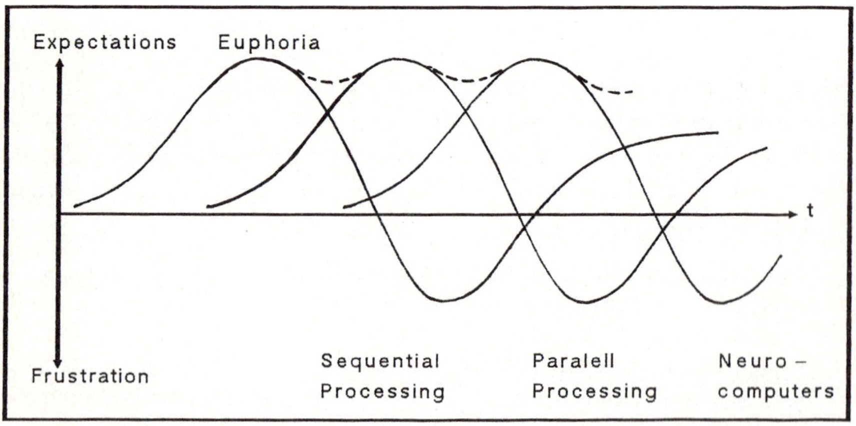

Picture 3 New Stimulation for Overestimation

"knowing" that he is basically not replaceable, as Margaret Boden implied at the last conference. Nor should we rely on the Mertens-curve. The image of an oscillation continuously being continuously re-excited might be more apt. The current discussion on Parallel Processing and Neuronal Networks is adding fuel to the flames of the concepts of omnipotence entertained in AI-circles.

Which ever way the level of expectations may turn: the present discussion gives us more reason to fear that the company reality will have to adapt to the restrictions set by expert systems, than providing us with the hope that XPS-technology and its forms of introduction and utilization will be adapted to the reality of work; to human potential and thus to a humane, low-risk and future oriented organization of work. An indication in this direction are the highly optimistic forecasts voiced by promoters, manufacturers and potential users of AI-products which make little mention of risks or brush them aside as a minor issue, as Peter Schefe for example, stated in the summary of the last GDI-ILO-conference (1987). This has systematic causes which go far beyond mere marketing considerations.

Deeply concerned and worried, yet not without hope, two influential AI-critics concluded a paper with the warning:

"Should calculative rationality triumph, no one will notice that something is missing."

Dreyfus/Dreyfus (1986, p 206)

7. Political Options

With regards to political control measures and research policies there are two central demands resulting: Firstly the need for policies which will promote technical and organizational alternatives to the predominant Tayloristic course of development.

There have been a number of practical efforts in this direction in several companies. Similar efforts in other areas in which information technology is applied have been receiving government support in the Federal Republic.

The explosive government support of technology development in the AI sector must be augmented by a massive promotion of theoretical and methodological alternatives such as the "Human Centered Approach" (for example Corbett, 1986) and the "Contrastive Work Analysis" (Volpert, 1987). "Contrastive Analysis" means: See what people need to do their work and what man can do better than the computer. Ask in what way these functions and human competence could be granted optimal support by system design. These concepts also form the foundation of a "forward assessment" with regards to desirable and undesirable future developments.

Secondly there is the necessity to control and substantiate the effects of promotion measures by evaluating AI-systems where such measures were employed as well as those which did not receive such support ("backward assessment"). The discussion has reached a point where further policies can not be developed without the results of empirical assessments.

8. Summary

It is impossible to speak of "the" effects of the use of expert systems. It is only possible to investigate their effects together with the company framework conditions and the rationalization strategies directed towards these specific conditions. Therefore scenarios concerning the effects of expert systems must include the above cited factors as central components (1st thesis).

Rationalization courses and scenarios display a range of variance between the two poles of "Computer Aided Taylorism" (Volpert, 1985) on the one hand and the "Human Centered Approach" on the other. So far there has been a predominance of Tayloristic solutions (2nd thesis).

The Tayloristic paradigm (production knowledge is expropriated, formulated in scientific terms, and "returned" to the manufacturing area as highly standardized instructions, human labor is regarded as a disturbance factor to be excluded, and top priority is given to technology) is likely to prevail in the companies also when AI-systems are employed, as it conforms with the mentality usually found in AI circles. Hence XPS act as "trend amplifiers" (3rd thesis).

Expert systems increase the gap between the reality of planning and the "actual reality". The discrepancy between the formal planning models and the restricted calculability of complex manufacturing processes - as evidenced by the use of information technology to date - is certain to increase with the spreading of formal models. Therefore XPS act as "failure-amplifiers" (4th thesis).

The greatest danger in the use of expert systems is the fact that their performance capacity is overestimated and the discrepancies are not recognized. It is very likely that expert systems will not primarily be adapted to complex reality, but that reality will have to adapt to fit the expert systems. Reality will be reduced to that which can be formalized and fits in to the expert system (5th thesis).

The consequences - the limitation of the generation and reproduction of knowledge and skills - must not only be determined for the individual employee, but also for the company and society. This is particularly necessary due to the fact that the significance of the individual employee grows along with the rising degree of automation and decreasing number of persons involved in the ongoing manufacturing process (6th thesis).

9. Conclusion

With regards to political control measures and research policies there are two central demands resulting: Firstly the need for policies which will promote technical and organizational alternatives to the predominant Tayloristic course of development. Secondly there is the necessity to substantiate the effects of promotion measures by evaluating AI-systems where such measures were employed as well as those which did not receive such support. Thirdly, guidelines and methods such as the "Contrastive Work Analysis" should be developed to support the assessment process and the human-centered design process.

Literature

BERNOLD, T. / HILLENKAMP, U. (Eds.) (1988): Expert Systems in Production and Working Life. Amsterdam: North-Holland.

BODEN, M., Should Supervisors be Afraid of "AI"? In: BERNOLD / HILLENKAMP (Eds.) (1986).

CORBETT, J.M., Human Work Design Criteria and the Design Process: The Devil in the Detail. In: Brödner (Ed.): Skill Based Automated Manufacturing, IFAC.

DREYFUS, H.L. / DREYFUS, St.E., (1986) Mind over Machine. The Power of Human Expertise in the Area of the Computer. Oxford

HIRSCHHORN, LARRY, (1984) Beyond mechanization - Work and technology in a postindustrial age. Cambridge, Mass.: MIT Press.

BILL JONES, (1984) Division of Labor and Distribution of Tacit Knowledge in the Automation of Metal Machining. In: T. Martin (Ed.): Design of Work in Automated Manufacturing Systems. Oxford: Pergamon.

KERR, CLARK, (1954) The Balkanization of Labor Markets, in: (E. Wright Bakke, et. al. (Ed.)) Labor Mobility and Economic Opportunity. Cambridge, Mass.: MIT Press.

LUTZ, BURKHART: (1976) Bildungssyteme und Beschäftigungsstrukturen in Deutschland und Frankreich - Zum Einfluß des Bildungssystems auf die Gestaltung betrieblicher Arbeitskräftestrukturen. In: ISF München: BETRIEB - ARBEITSMARKT - QUALIFIKATION. Frankfurt: Campus.

MERTENS, P., BORKOWSKI, V., GEIS, W., (1988) Betriebliche Expertensystemanwendungen. Eine Materialsammlung. Berlin: Springer.

MOLDASCHL, M., (1988 a) Grenzen der Mechanisierung geistiger Arbeit. Expertensysteme in der Produktion. In: Die Mitbestimmung, 34 / 1988 / 9.

MOLDASCHL, M., (1988 b) Widersprüchliche Arbeitsanforderungen. Mentale und emotionale Belastungen in der Produktion. ISF München.

ROSENBROCK, H.H., (1983) Social and engineering design of an FMS. In: WARMAN, E.A. (Ed.). Cape '83. Amsterdam: North Holland.

SCHANK, R.C., (1984) The Cognitive Computer. Reading, Mass.: Addison Wesly.

SORGE, A., HARTMANN, G., WARNER, M., NICHOLAS, I., (1983) Microelectronics and Manpower in Manufacturing - Applications of Computer Numerical Control in Great Britain and West Germany. Aldershot.

VOLPERT, W., (1983) Zauberlehrlinge. Die gefährliche Liebe zum Computer. Weinheim: Belz.

VALK, R., (1987) Der Computer als Herausforderung an die menschliche Rationalität. Informatik-Spektrum 1987 / 10, Springer Verlag.

VOLPERT, W., (198?) Contrastive Analysis of the Relationship of Man and Computer as a Basis of System Design. In: (P. Docherty et. al. (Editors)) System Design for Human Development and Productivity: Participation and Beyond: Amsterdam: North Holland.

WELTZ, F., (1988) Die doppelte Wirklichkeit der Unternehmen und ihre Konsequenzen für die Industriesoziologie. In: Soziale Welt 39 / 1988 / 1.

EXPERT SYSTEMS IN PRODUCTION AND SERVICES II
Th. Bernold and U. Hillenkamp (Editors)
Elsevier Science Publishers B.V., Amsterdam – Printed in The Netherlands

Lay-out Design Work in the Automotive Industry

Norimasa Kishi
Nissan Motor Co. Ltd
Central Engineering Laboratories
Yokosuka, Japan

1. Introduction

Based on a practical example of Lay-out Design Work, our activities and methods at Nissan are described. In addition associated problems of developing and introducing expert systems are covered. The system in question is aimed at assisting designers mainly in routine design modifications. It offers the following advantages:

- proper guidance of the design procedure
- Ease of concentration on design constraints
- Expansion of knowledge and know-how within the system.

Expert systems incorporating the know-how of automotive designers are expected to be increasingly introduced in routine design work.The perspective is that they could produce better design efficiency and reliability. A specific mode of assessing its impact is proposed by the comparison with the previous introduction of robot technology.

2. Preliminary Work

In the initial stage of our AI research we considered the fields in which we could apply AI. This was in 1982, just before the AI boom in Japan. As the definition of an expert system, using specific expert know-how and empirical rules stored in a computer, we can obtain the same solutions as an expert. From the beginning we conceived this technology as being a form of computer technology, which can assist in easing our intellectual work load. Therefore, a first preliminary study was conducted to clarify its application fields and to analyze its target work.

2.1. Application Fields.

AI can be used for a wide variety of applications in an automobile company. Examples of typical work to which AI can be applied to is shown in Fig. 1. AI systems can be divided into three or more broad categories.

- Systems applied to the automobile itself are mainly provide vehicle functions which are close to human action. E.g AI control, in this case fuzzy control, can be used to produce automatic speed control systems. In a related application AI can also be applied to brake control systems.
- The main objectives to apply AI systems to vehicle development and manufacturingin are the potential reduction of the overall development time and to achieve higher design efficiency. In the area of design and test work, expert systems are being used to make CAD systems more intelligent. In the factory they are used in production-planning and scheduling-management.
- The applications of AI to vehicle maintenance aims to improve customer service. E.g. the application of expert systems to failure diagnosis or trouble shouting, contributes to better automobile servicing.

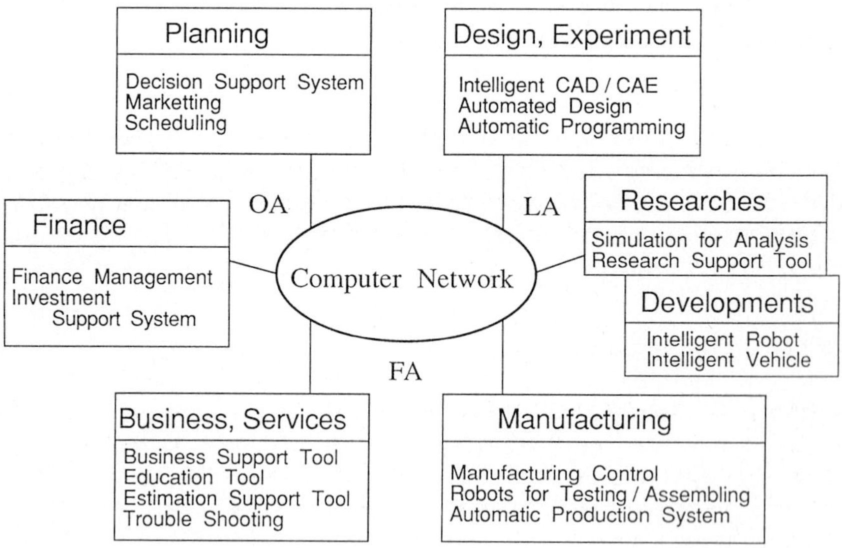

Figure 1 AI Application Areas

2.2. Automotive Design Work Analysis

The area of design to explain our development of expert systems is described here. First the work that went into developing our expert systems was analyzed. The overall process involved in producing automobiles is shown in Fig. 2. In the planning process, market trends are applied in determining the concept and major performance targets of the new car. Next in the general design the concept is translated into specifications of units and performance values such as fuel consumption, acceleration and driveability. After the general design process is completed, work proceeds to the detail- design stage. Generally speaking three kinds of closely related design work are carried out, performance design, parts design and layout design. After all of the parts are designed in this phase, manufacturing begins. The finished car then goes to the market.

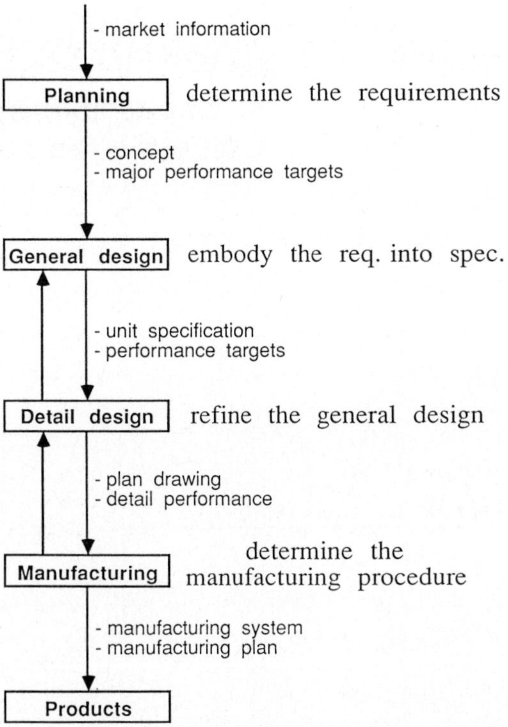

Figure 2 Outline of the Total Production Process

The contents of design work car be broken down into three levels. As roughly sketched in Fig. 3, work in the automobile design process consists of routine work, intelligent work, and original work. The volume of original work decreases gradually downstream from process to process. Conversely, routine and intelligent work increase as they proceed from to process. Original work is defined as a work that involves entirely new design. It requires creativity and problem consciousness.

As for intelligent work, it might be defined as work which depends on the engineers experience and knowledge. More precisely, remodeling and redesign are carried out on standard parts. Routine work involves retrieving existing design data, ordering standard parts, writing up documents, and so on.

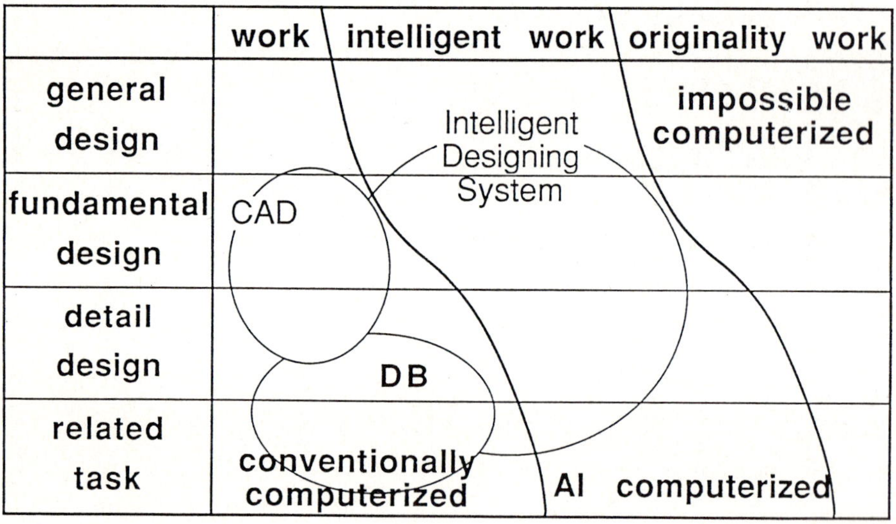

Figure 3 Design Process

Focusing on this specific area, a closer study of the engineers' work was made. The process of design is illustrated in Fig. 4. System specifications are provided in the upper levels of the design process. In realizing the car concept, designers perform intelligent work to determine the design procedure. In this process much interactive refinement along with trade-offs and compromises between competing alternatives are made as to reflect the engineer's intent – based on the car concept – as closely as possible within scope of the design specification. When the engineers encounter design conflicts, that means trade-offs and compromises, they base the design on their own knowledge of effective solutions. These design conflicts occur frequently. For example, a designer wants to make a car more sporty, he will increase acceleration performance, but this may result in lower fuel consumption and safety. In reality, conflicts are seldom solved theoretically based on mathematical methods, but must usually be treated using trial and error procedures based on know-how and design knowledge.

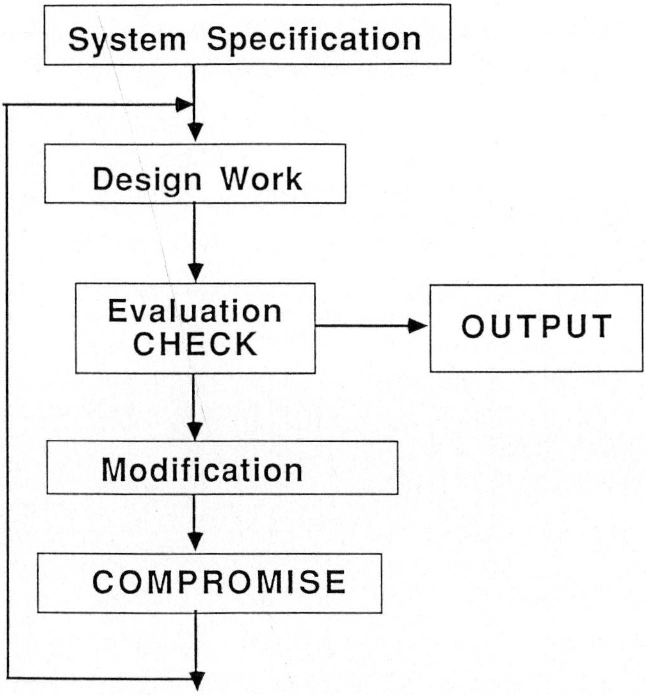

Figure 4 Design Process

2.3. An Image of an AI Support System.

In the computer support phase, there are three levels on which solutions are obtained in our study. On the first level, the designer uses his own judgement, and satisfies the requirements by modifying the parameters through trial and error. In this case, the designer selects parameters to be modified, and the computer makes a recalculation and outputs drawing and data for remodeling.

On the second level, the computer itself modifies the parameters to satisfy the design requirements based on stored know-how and design rules. It computes the remodeling and outputs the results. The designer merely indicates whether he is satisfied with the results or not. This judgement is made, based the design concept.

On the third level, fully automatic remodeling design is carried out by the system, which even judges whether the results are satisfactory.

How AI techniques applied to design work is depicted in Fig. 5. The designer makes use of engineering information as a form of knowledge. This informat-

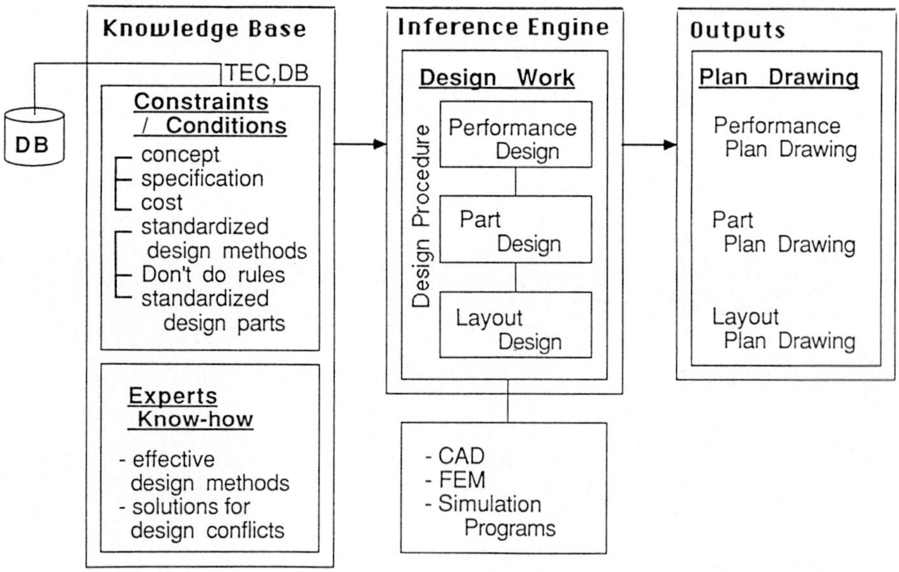

Figure 5 Block Schema of the Application of AI to Design

ion is normally retrieved from a database, and it consists of concept specifications and so on. In making the design, the computer uses expert know-how on design methods to infer the suitable procedure for the design, and it puts out production drawings. To adapt the specification to the concept when design conflicts arise, the computer uses conflict-solving know-how to find an effective solution.

2.4. Expectation for AI Advantages.

The advantages expected to derive from AI in the context of assisting designers in working more effectively are as follows:

- Good utilization of engineering information.
- Effective design procedure guidance.
- Effective solutions to design conflicts.

The first point concerns the engineering database, which is complicated by nature, must be set up in a way that provides designers with an effective access. The knowledge-base should be written in their terminology, this is designer language, so that it will be easy to understand. This information in the knowledge base can be easily added and deleted is one advantage of AI.

The second issue concerns the the car concept which matches model design with user life style. This requires that design work be carried out using flexible, and not rigid or routine procedures. By inferring design knowledge through AI, the expert system can provide a procedure well matched to the design objective.

Turning to the third point, we have to realize various kinds of closely related design conditions and restrictions exist in design work. These require from the designer often to make compromises in their efforts to satisfy design requirements.

3. Application Example

3.1. User and Target Design Work.

The practical expert system we developed is briefly described here. The user is a designer having sufficient knowledge and know-how and is capable of judging the effectiveness of the design procedure based on its concept.

The system assists the engineer in laying out the pedals, shift lever, parking brake, knobs, steering wheel, and so on. These are the fundamental parts related to driving operations. It's aim is to produce high design efficiency and reliability by providing an appropriate design procedure and carrying out design calculations. The system consists of three computers as shown in Fig. 6. The first machine on the left provides the design procedure through inferencing. The middle carries drawings and calculations And the one on the right is a convention CAD terminal used for checking interference between parts.

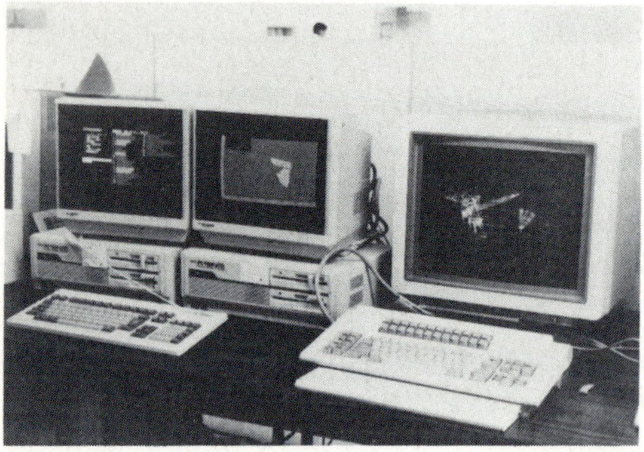

Figure 6 Designer's Workplace

3.2. Design Knowledge

Layout design rules are based on knowledge of how parts can be located within a given area. The knowledge of experts in layout design is collected, classified in a hierarchical order and represented in the form on production rules. This knowledge is broken down into six categories according to its relations and consists of three types of constraints.

First are the space constraints. These limit the area in which parts can be located. For example, all parts must be located above the floor panel and within the dash board. Second there are the human factors. Driveability and operability should be as much as possible based on these factors. For example, parts like the shift lever and pedals should be located where driver can access them easily.

Finally there are dimensional constraints. The shape, physical size, and function of each part must be taken into consideration.

3.3. System Functions.

The system has two main functions. One is to assist in the layout process itself, and the other is to support efficient problem solving. The first function consists of an inputting function, a procedure advice function, a calculation function and a confirmative function. In actual design, the order in which the compartment is laid out will vary according the model type or the concept of the vehicle to be designed. The priority assigned to parts and vehicle parameters is also varied to give each vehicle an image which directly reflects its design concepts. Therefore the function provides the means to the extent that the designer can execute his job easier. This function consists of a design modification function, relationship display function, and design history function.

3.4. System Evaluation.

Even though problem solving with this system is carried out on the first support level, evaluation results reveal that it is able to decrease the design work load and increase product quality. These results are attributed to the higher speed at which each design evaluation can be performed and the wider variety of design approaches which theses time savings permit. Since automatic parameter confirmation virtually eliminates design validity checks, the engineer is free to give his undivided attention to the design work at hand.

4. Considerations of the Impact

4.1. Interest and Reactions.

The interest and reactions we received regarding the AI systems is summarized in Fig. 7. The affirmative group consisted mainly of those who thought that the systems will be applied to their own work. The negative group were those who thought that it would be applied to somebody else's job. Before the trial, the affirmative group was optimistic, but the other was skeptical. However, both thought of AI as being almighty. After deciding on concept and requirements of our system we demonstrated and explained all of these points to the design engineers. Through these activities, some designers stated that they wanted us to develop expert systems of various kinds to assist them in their work. Compared to members of other departments, designers are more familiar with computers because they use them in their daily work.

After the first trial explained above, the affirmative group changed their view somewhat, and thought of the system as a useful support tool. The negative group, on the other hand, would not budge from their position, and asked questions like is this really artificial intelligence?

The affirmative group felt that the AI systems were compatible with their job and work place, while in the negative group only a few members agreed. Differing from the affirmative group, who felt that knowledge is important, they kept asking work can't be performed without using computer systems?

	affirmative or positive	negative
Application	for themselves	for someone else
Supportive-ness	1. little 2. much	1. none 2. little
Expectation	1. almighty 2. supprot tool	1. skeptical 2. Is it AI?
Evaluatiom	compatible with their job	resist reorganization
Afterthought	Importance of the Knowledge Base	Couldn't be done with a conventional computer system?

Figure 7 Summary of the Reactions Regarding the Application of Expert Systems.

Our engineers response to the system is briefly commented. We held the trials in two stages. Only a few managers agreed to participate in the first round. Even though they would bear very little of the expense and work load. This was because of the lack of clearly defined time limits. Therefore, we pretty much had to carry out the first trial which was the feasibility study by ourselves.

We built a simplified model of the expert system to see if it would be adaptable to these management areas. It incorporated fundamental knowledge, and it was put together mainly by our AI research members. Then, after the managers saw the system demonstrated they became willing to spend time to provide us with their knowledge. They now felt that the system was worth while and could help in carrying out their work.

After gaining this acceptance, we embarked on building a prototype of the system. This was the second trial. The negative group, on the other hand, would not budge from their position, and asked questions like is this really artificial intelligence? The affirmative group felt the AI systems were compatible with their job and work place, while the negative group feared that introduction of those systems would require reorganization their work.

4.2. Comparison between Introduction of Expert System and Robots.

A good comparison can be made between the introductions of expert systems and that of robots. The impact of expert systems on human workers is summarized in Fig. 8. In the early development phase, we chose to think of robots as mere machines. Machines do not always work perfectly. They sometimes break down which is their weak point. As with a child, man can bring up the robots to the point where they perform well. AI is an area of a computer technology. As such, the weak point of expert systems is their lack of knowledge. Corresponding to the example of the robots, man can foster the growth of expert systems, in this case, by expanding their knowledge.

As for application areas, robots are applied to heavy and tiresome work, whereas expert systems are applied to complicated repetitive routine work and thus tiresome work. This means that both systems are to assist human beings. One in physical, the other in intellectual work.

In addition, when robots were introduced, since their operation was based on computer languages, production engineers, however had trouble using those. Therefore they devised what they call 'ladder ' language which was closely related to their field of work and needs. The same can be said for design expert systems. These systems can be used much more effectively if design language is the language of the designer is used to express expert knowledge.

During the development phase, when we introduced robots at Nissan, we set up two lines in the initial trial. A conventional line manned by human workers was set up in parallel to the robot line. The robot line worked well at times, but experienced trouble at others, falling below the human line in efficiency. When trouble occurred, humans took over and modified the robots so as to improve the robot line operation. In this way, a single line was eventually achieved. Even in Nissan's fully automated lines, many workers are still assigned to maintain and teach the robots.

Our expert system was to be introduced in almost the same way. Designer worked in parallel, one using conventional methods and the other using the expert system. When the expert system could not provide the proper advice, designers made improvements to its knowledge base. In the near future, many workers will be assigned to maintain the knowledge stores in expert systems.

	Robot	Expert System
Way of Thinking	Machine	Computer
Target of Work	heavy boresome	complicated boresome
Use	Assistant Human in Charge	Assistant Human in Charge
Weaknes	Machine Trouble	Knowledge Growth
Planning of Trial	individuak work gradually	individual work gradually
	Physical Power	Judgement
Education	necessary Robot-language Robot Controler to teach	necessary Design-language CAD-Terminal to operate
Impact	Maintenance People	Knowledge Engineer
New Job	Robot Researchers	Domain Expert

Original Work

Figure 8 Comparison between the Introduction of Robots with Expert Systems

This means that expert systems will not become a rival to humans, even though they may reduce the amount of intelligent work performed. In the case of robots, robot-maintenance-work and new robot-research-work appeared. In expert system as well, knowledge-engineering-work will appear. Of course, expert system will require domain experts to up-grade their knowledge and skill.

5. Some Comments

The value of knowledge is considered. A framework to facilitate the acquisition of accurate knowledge is constructed. Many methods have been proposed for doing this. However, it is very difficult to express knowledge based on experience in words, even if the knowledge engineer is present and observes the expert reasoning process. This is a key factor which must be reckoned with in establishing effective means for acquiring knowledge.

Let us assume that an expert system is developed which is effective in reducing cost and that it is put into practical use. Under the present situation the person who first developed the system, that is the person who provided the know-how, will get the credit. However, what is actually important is how the know-how in the system will be maintained in the future. The person who maintains the know-how will probably received no credit. Under present patent laws, the inventor is compensated for the use of an original invention, however, in the case of an expert system he can incorporate high levels of know-how which makes work much more efficient. It is, however, difficult to identify which part of the know-how is actually effective. Of course with why- and how-reasoning, we can find out how many rules to employ in a particular know-how inputs. But once the system is placed into operation, we tend to look at the rules and more at the results output by the system. Consequently the people supplying know-how can't tell clearly whether their contribution is being used effectively or not.

In Japan, engineers usually provide ideas through a suggestion system. This could be a useful tool to acquire additional knowledge and improve the system. It has not been made clear , however, what the proprietary rights are for the intangible intellectual ideas which make the software of expert systems. If some kind of index could be devised for assessing the significant of intellectual contributions, experts would probably take a more active part in providing know-how. This increases input would make it possible to develop system software with a totally different potential for growth than that we have now.

EXPERT SYSTEMS IN PRODUCTION AND SERVICES II
Th. Bernold and U. Hillenkamp (Editors)
Elsevier Science Publishers B.V., Amsterdam – Printed in The Netherlands
GDI, 1989

Fault & Condition Monitoring on Trains

Barry Skingle and David Mulvey
Logica UK Limited
London W1A 4SE, UK

Introduction by Brian Oakley

In 1987 Logica developed an Expert System for London Underground that monitored the braking and traction system of an underground train. The primary purpose was to help the driver restart fast after the brakes had been applied automatically. There are eight different causes for automatic application of the brakes so the task of the driver in establishing what the cause was and deciding that it is safe to re-start is not trivial. On the other hand the task is well bounded and not really difficult for an inference system. The system was extended to include the monitoring of the many traction motors on the vehicle.

From receipt of the "Introduction to Proceed" until the system had been tested on a train, including developing a special purpose computer to run the system, because of the noise and dust environment in which it has to run took just six months. The system must be one of the first mobile Expert Systems, if not the first, and can be loosely described as a Real Time system though it is not actually operating against a fixed time schedule.

Perhaps the real interest in the system is that it has "safety critical" features, in the sense that a mistake could lead to serious driver errors. So it was essential that the system should be vigorously verified and validated. London Transport had to carry out a careful set of validating tests before the system could be used.

Because the system was to provide information both to the train drivers and to the maintenance engineers it was necessary to communicate the knowledge in the system in two forms, in the different ways appropriate to the classes of users. By representing the knowledge to the drivers in a form they could readily understand it proved possible to test the rules on them, obtain corrections and additions, and amend the system at a turn round time of about 40 minutes. The drivers proved very co-operative, and showed considerable interest in the system, presumably because it makes their task easier without disturbing the way they are used to working. The lesson of matching the knowledge representation to the domain expert was, once again, underlined.

Abstract

This paper describes a knowledge-based system for fault diagnosis and condition monitoring on underground trains. The system provides timely and appropriate advice on fault recovery and performance degradation to both train drivers and maintenance staff.

The system operates in the difficult environment on board an underground train. Factors such as magnetizable tunnel dust, wide temperature and humidity ranges, and vibration preclude the use of standard disc-based computer hardware. The Logica solution involved building a microprocessor-based system, encapsulating problem-solving knowledge on board the train. The hardware is rack-based and uses a Motorola 68000 processor.

Care was taken in choosing appropriate facilities for representing and structuring the problem-solving knowledge. A task hierarchy is used to structure the problem-solving knowledge. Within tasks, rules are represented in a specially-developed language. A limited set of monitoring points on the train provides the necessary information to the system.

The system was developed directly in C on a personal computer. The code was tested using hardware and software simulators of the train. The system was then cross-compiled and down-loaded to the microprocessor system and installed on a test train.

The system passed the specified series of acceptance tests on the test train, and was then accepted.

The work reported here brings together ideas on: diagnosis and condition monitoring, structuring problem-solving knowledge, selection of development and delivery systems, integration of knowledge-based elements, deployment of knowledge-based systems in demanding environments, and acceptance testing of knowledge-based systems.

This work has clearly demonstrated the practicality and potential value of knowledge-based techniques in embedded systems operating in hostile environments, exemplified by underground trains.

---

1. Introduction and Background

In 1990, London Underground Limited (LUL) plans to begin a programme for the replacement of its rolling stock. In a radical review of the operation and design of the underground trains, LUL commissioned Logica to conduct a practical development study to investigate advanced techniques for fault diagnosis and performance analysis on the trains.

With future train control systems LUL intends to provide facilities for drivers to be advised on what to do if the train develops a fault in service. It also intends to provide systems status information and assistance in the location of faulty components for maintenance.

Fault diagnosis and condition monitoring has become an important area of study within the expert-system field (Harmon, 1986; Moore, 1986). Many systems have been built which can carry out fault diagnosis in consultation with a user (White & Fredericksen, 1985). Knowledge-based toolkits have become available for building fault and condition monitoring systems on small and cheaply available personal computers. Systems have been written which run on PCs and are interfaced with the machine being monitored (Milne, 1987).

2. Fault and Condition Monitoring on Trains

LUL are interested in monitoring faults in and the condition of a wide variety of systems in underground trains. For the work reported here two representative train systems were selected:

- fault monitoring of the safety-brake system;
- condition monitoring of the traction system.

The safety-brake system protects the train against many abnormal events which could endanger the train if the brakes were not applied. For example, the safety-brake system will apply the brakes in the following circumstances:

- passing a red signal;
- exceeding safe speed settings;
- driver's safety device released;

- pressure loss from brake air system;
- parting of couplings between vehicles.

In addition to these reasons, the safety brakes may also be applied if a component fails in the safety-brake circuit. The possible faults include:

- failure in relay coil;
- fuses blown;
- micro-switch open circuit.

The driver has to ascertain whether a component has failed, or whether the application of the safety brakes is legitimate. He has a variety of switches and control handles in his cab which allow him to configure the safety-brake system in response to various triggering states. It is important to get the train safely underway as soon as possible; time spent stuck in a train underground is both unpleasant and causes disruption to the service.

The traction system of an underground train covers the control of electric motors, each with its own axle, mounted on a bogie. The motors can operate in either series or parallel. Top speed can be achieved only if the motors operate in parallel. Selection of the configuration is made by the driver using a control handle in his cab.

A train has perhaps 16 separate electric motors. Motors may operate outside of their expected performance profile or they may entirely burn out. Motor controllers may malfunction, resulting in the delivery of too little or too much power. The train's wheels may spin, reducing applied power and possibly damaging equipment. Drivers do not notice when minor degradations in the performance of a single motor occur. Each minor degradation contributes to further deterioration in performance until a serious fault occurs. If minor faults are recognized in the early stages costly repairs and potential delays to the underground service can be avoided.

3. Requirements

LUL require a system offering accurate and timely advice to both drivers and maintenance staff.

The current approach to monitoring the safety brakes is based on a programmable-logic system. It consists of a number of monitoring relays in the safety-brake circuit. When the safety brakes are applied an array of lights in the driver's cab is illuminated. LUL require a train-based system that will determine the reason for the application of the safety brakes, provide the driver with clear but succinct advice on how to make the train operational, and aid maintenance staff in locating a failed component. As few monitoring points as possible should be used, to reduce the chance of component failure within the monitoring system itself.

A method of monitoring the condition of the traction system must be provided that is as independent as possible from the type of control system used. This means focussing on the fundamental parameters of the traction system: axle speed, line voltage, motor current and driver's demand. The detection of various conditions outside the expected performance envelope will help in carrying out early maintenance to prevent potentially more serious faults from developing. No train-based system exists at present to help with this task.

One of the major issues involved is the environment within which the system must operate, which includes a number of harsh features:

- restricted space for hardware;
- magnetizable tunnel dust;
- severe vibration;
- wide temperature and humidity range;
- conducted and radiated electromagnetic interference.

These environmental factors rule out the use of standard disc-based hardware.

4. Knowledge Representation

A number of Logica projects have demonstrated the validation and maintenance benefits of representing knowledge in application-specific terms (Bustany & Skingle, 1988). This experience led us to pay close attention to the choice of facilities for knowledge representation. We were particularly interested in facilities for representing and structuring the necessary problem-solving knowledge. Other workers (for instance, Reichgelt & van Harmlen, 1986) also recognize the importance of matching knowledge representation and inference regimes to the requirements of the application, and the importance of identifying problem-solving knowledge.

Through interviews with engineers from LUL we developed an understanding of the safety brake and traction systems. For the safety-brake circuit we also used circuit diagrams supplied by LUL to investigate possible faults and appropriate remedies. For the traction system a performance envelope defining the operation of a healthy train was agreed using traditional current-speed characteristics. Reasons for performance outside the agreed envelope were then identified.

We developed a paper-based intermediate representation for the knowledge to be incorporated. An initial paper model of the knowledge base using this derived representation was submitted for consideration and approval. The engineers at LUL found it straightforward to interpret and refine the knowledge. After a few iterations the knowledge base was accepted.

The problem-solving knowledge is broken down into a number of tasks and subtasks. Each task contains a number of rules. The rules encapsulate inference steps. The action of rules can result in either the generation of advice, or in the selection of a new subtask. In this way the system's attention is quickly focussed as irrelevant areas of the search space are eliminated.

Two types of advice are generated by the system. The first type is to help the driver get the train moving and is expressed in terms familiar to him. The second type of advice is for LUL maintenance staff, to help in localizing component faults. In this case the standard LUL terminology is used for describing components and circuits.

The rules used within the tasks refer to monitoring points. These may be:

- physical monitoring points, for instance detecting low voltage at points in the safety-brake or round-train circuit;
- virtual monitoring points representing, for instance, periods of acceleration that are not directly measured by transducers.

For the safety brake system the tasks were structured to:

- check if the brakes have been applied;
- if they have, determine whether this was due to a legitimate operation or component failure;
- determine which component, or group of components is responsible;
- deliver appropriate advice.

Sections of the safety-brake circuit are successively eliminated by checking the associated monitoring points until the fault location is localized.

For the traction system, the tasks are used to search for particular conditions. If the stored history of traction performance does not indicate a condition the next, less serious condition is checked for. For instance, conditions such as motor failure are checked for before persistent wheel spin.

5. Architecture

The system operates in two modes: condition monitoring of the traction system or fault diagnosis of the safety brake system. The system is internally divided into six subsystems:

- System Manager;
- Traction Data Preprocessor;
- Device Drivers;
- Inference Engine;
- Knowledge Base.

The Traction Data Preprocessor filters data from the traction monitoring points to remove interference. The information necessary to identify a faulty train is recorded in the traction history. To reduce the amount of information, readings are stored only when the train crosses specified speed boundaries, or when the state of the train changes significantly. A significant change occurs when the current in the motors falls outside a specified range, or when a change occurs in the demanded or actual configuration of the motors. A journey is defined as a run between two stations. A history of readings from previous journeys is stored during system operation.

The Inference Engine subsystem operates on the tasks and rules in the knowledge base, taking input from the monitoring points (via Perform Next Activity), and the Traction Data Preprocessor. The Knowledge Base contains the safety-brake and traction knowledge represented by tasks and rules.

6. Development

The environmental characteristics of the tube train described above precluded the use of the usual software tools, including even PC-based software packages. Train-based systems have to be compact, board based and resistant to electromagnetic interference.

Because of these constraints we decided to develop the system in C using an IBM PC XT 286. A MICE 2+ in-circuit emulator was utilized during development to aid testing of the code.

The tasks and rules stored in the Knowledge Base are represented as C structures. The knowledge base contains 11 tasks and 40 rules and occupies about 13 kilobytes of memory.

Logica built a hardware simulator of the safety-brake circuit using miniature relays. For our software simulation of the traction system we used a finite-state machine controlling routines calculating motor current. This approach allowed us to test the system from the relative sophistication of the development PC.

7. Delivery

For the train-based system a rack-mounted microprocessor system was constructed. The CPU card contains 512 kilobytes of RAM, 80 kilobytes of EPROM, a real-time clock and three serial interfaces in addition to a Motorola 680000 10MHz CPU. The completed code amounted to approximately 50 kilobytes.

An important requirement was to minimize the number of monitoring points on the safety-brake circuit. In contrast to the 17 monitoring relays used by the existing, conventional monitoring system, this system operates with eight digital monitoring relays.

It was essential to store the knowledge base in EPROM, as normal secondary-storage devices could not be used on-board the train.

One important aspect of proving the practicality of knowledge-based technology on underground trains was to achieve acceptable performance times. In practice the system operated with no perceptible delay.

8. Testing

An important element of this work was the formal accaptance by LUL against a specified series of tests. After testing with our purpose-built hardware and software simulators the system was installed on LUL's test train and trial runs were carried out on the test track at South Ealing. Logica conducted a number of tests to check the correspondence of the actual train with the agreed definition of train behaviour. A number of changes to the knowledge base were made. Turnaround times of 40 minutes were achieved in:

- detecting a required change;
- modifying the C-based knowledge representation on the PC;
- cross-compiling the code for the 68000 processor;
- burning the revised code into EPROM;
- installing the new knowledge base on the train.

When the system operated to Logica's satisfaction LUL configured and exercised the train to produce the necessary acceptance-test conditions. The system passed its tests and was signed off by LUL.

9. Conclusions

The work reported here brings together ideas on:

- diagnosis and condition monitoring;
- structuring problem-solving knowledge;
- selection of development and delivery systems;
- integration of knowledge-based elements;
- deployment of knowledge-based systems in demanding;
- environments;
- acceptance testing of knowledge-based systems.

This project has demonstrated the feasibility of embedding knowledge-based elements to perform real-time diagnostic tasks in an operational environment. By adopting an application-specific means of representing the knowledge we were able to retain benefits of the knowledge-based approach even though it was impractical to deploy conventional expert-system tools.

Acknowledgements

This paper is the result of work carried out by Logica for London Underground Limited (LUL). The authors would like to thank the staff of LUL, particularly Mike Abbott, Charles Horsey and Ranjit Croos-Fernando, for their help and assistance. We also acknowledge the contribution of the other members of the Logica team: Graeme Smith, Bharat Patel and Barry Thurlow. Special thanks are due to Graeme Smith for his help in preparing material for this paper.

References

Harmon, P. (1986). Expert Systems Strategies, 2, no 8, Cutter Information Corp.

Moore, R. (1986). Expert Systems in Process Control: Applications Experience. In Proceedings of the 1st International Conference on Applications of Artificial Intelligence to Engineering Problems, Southamptom, England

White, B. & Fredericksen, J.R. (1985). QUEST: Qualitative Understanding of Electrical Systems Troubleshooting. In Sigart Newsletter, no 93

Milne, R. (1987). On-Line Artificial Intelligence. In Proceedings of the 7th International Workshop on Expert Systems and Their Applications, 437-451, Avignon

Bustany, A.G. & Skingle, B. (1988). Knowledge-Based Development via Application Languages. In Proceedings of The 4th Australian Conference on Applications of Expert Systems, Sydney

Reichgelt, H. & van Harmlen, F. (1986). Criteria for Choosing Representation Languages and Control Regimes for Expert Systems. DAI Research Paper no 287. Department of Artificial Intelligence. University of Edinburgh

EXPERT SYSTEMS IN PRODUCTION AND SERVICES II
Th. Bernold and U. Hillenkamp (Editors)
Elsevier Science Publishers B.V., Amsterdam – Printed in The Netherlands

ExperTAX SM – Impacts on Work, Qualifications and Training

Karl M. Wiig
was consulting partner with Coopers & Lybrand, Dallas
now principal with The Wiig Group
Arlington, Texas, USA

1. Introduction

In the early 1980s, the senior management of the accounting firm Coopers & Lybrand (C&L) observed that accounting firms were becoming increasingly "knowledge oriented". The value of their services to clients were becoming more knowledge based. Advise and judgmental assessments of client situations increased while manual and clerical work of audit sampling, manipulating numbers, and finding and handling documents decreased. As client operations became more computerized, and as auditing and other accounting services became more automated, it was evident to C&L's management that within the not too distant future, "C&L's computers would audit the clients' computers" making the human contributions almost exclusively knowledge based. With these premises, C&L's management started an expert systems group and in 1985 commissioned ExperTAX^{SM} , a comprehensive artificial intelligence (AI) based system designed to spread its best tax advise expertise throughout the firm.

C&L developed ExperTAX^{SM} to support its internal audit and tax planning service. The system is designed to make available the firm's most insightful and up-to-date expertise available to the managers and accountants in the field. ExperTAX^{SM} was first released for firm-wide use in November, 1986, and is now in its fifth release. It incorporates expertise from over 40 corporate tax experts and is now updated several times each year. It provides expert advice on tax accrual and planning for client firms and includes interpretation of the latest tax law changes. It is used in all of C&L's 95 US offices and is deployed on IBM PC/AT compatible computers. In mid 1988, it had been used in over 1,000 client engagements and is now in mandatory use for all client engagements for the industries that its expertise covers. At the present, ExperTAX^{SM} is being expanded to include additional specialty expertise for other industries.

ExperTAX^{SM} operates both as a "peer reviewer" and as an "expert consultant" to assist the auditor and tax specialist. It is designed to be used by the field staff who are able to interpret its output, perform the field work independently, and then present the results to their managers for review and approval. Previously, it was required that managers participate actively in the planning stages to lead the conceptualization of the engagement, even though they at times had limited expertise. With ExperTAX^{SM} the expertise that is made available to the field staff consists of the best knowledge and judgements of the 40 experts and that expertise typically is better than the tax managers' expertise, thus providing a superior quality service to clients.

ExperTAX^{SM} is the first of several systems designed to change the way C&L will do business. It is a building block in a deliberate management strategy to exploit AI to improve the firm's viability and competitive position. An important aspect of ExperTAX^{SM} is that it is maintained by the firm's tax department as a major professional function within that operation, rather than by the firm's AI or traditional information systems organization.

2. Perspectives of Strategic Advantages

C&L along with other institutions has started to derive strategic advantages from the application of AI. The advantages take many forms depending on the particular approaches that are adopted for different applications and the manner in which the AI systems are created. A few significant applications are well publicized whereas others are kept quiet and may be totally unknown. It is becoming clear, however, that the potential economic leverage that is experienced with the application of knowledge technology (KT) may be of considerable strategic importance. Figure 1 indicates the potential economic leverage from automating human skill functions for various categories of work. The dominant target areas for conventional automation and automation with knowledge technology have been indicated. Practical applications indicate that the economic leverages from knowledge-based systems in particular are becoming strategically important. As the industry has increased the capability to use expert systems to support knowledge workers' intellectual functions it is observed that the leverages can be substantial[1].

---

[1] E. Feigenbaum et al.: The Rise of the Expert Company Times Books, New York, NY 1988.

Up to now, many advanced firms have developed significant systems in support of their strategies and have formulated deliberate plans to change the way that they are doing business. As a result of the nature of the strategic advantages that are sought, the benefit streams that are realized through deployment of AI systems are typically quite complex. The direct benefits are not always economic in nature – they may lead to longer-term improvements in products and services provided, thus resulting in advantages of competitive strengths, greater market penetration, and better customer satisfaction that places the firm in a better competitive situation at a later date. In such situations, the new capabilities often result in better services that lead to increased customer loyalty and ultimately create benefits in support of the institution's mission.

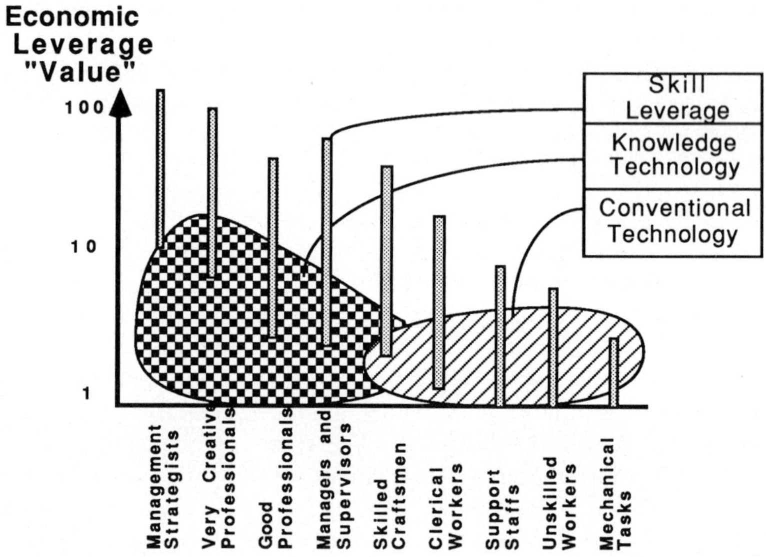

Fig. 1 Example of Potential Economic Leverage from Automating Human Skill Functions.

In order to conceptualize, build, and implement AI-based systems, it must be recognized that several activities need to be performed. The creation of ExperTAX^{SM} was no exception. Business uses for contemplated AI-based systems need to be considered in the context of how knowledge within the organization must be built, deployed, and controlled; i.e. managed. Knowledge must be elicited, analyzed, and modeled using methods and approaches that fall within the realm of KT. Computer-based approaches and systems need to be created to automate the relevant portions of knowledge and reasoning using AI technology. Expert systems must be integrated with a number of other environments: the business environment, the workplace environment, the knowledge workers' (i.e., the users') perspectives and cognitive world, and the information system or technical environment. Figure 2 shows a conceptual representation of relations between KT, AI, Knowledge Management, conventional computer sciences, applied philosophy, psychology, and social sciences. As can beseen from this figure, the issues associated with managing knowledge, (i.e., considerations for how to leverage and exploit knowledge for business

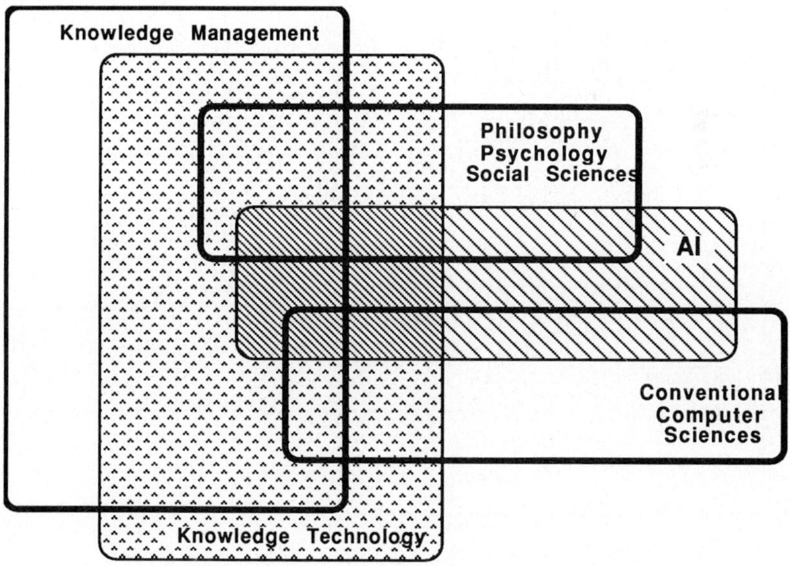

Fig. 2 Relations Between Knowledge Technology, Artificial Intelligence, and Other Areas.

purposes) and KT (which consists of methodologies for how to identify, assess, build, and deploy knowledge), often are associated with functions outside computer sciences, AI, and other support disciplines such as philosophy, psychology, social sciences, and semantics and linguistics.

The particular activities that were undertaken to conceptualize, develop, and maintain ExperTAX^{SM} involve all of the areas indicated in Figure 3. They included general business considerations such as strategy setting and conceptualization of the knowledge-based system (KBS). Specific KT activities involved specification of the role ExperTAX^{SM} should play in delivery of tax advisor services, elicitation of knowledge from experts, modelling of knowledge, etc. In order to build ExperTAX^{SM} , it was also required to engage in AI and computer sciences activities for selection of reasoning methods and knowledge representations, rapid prototyping, and final system design.

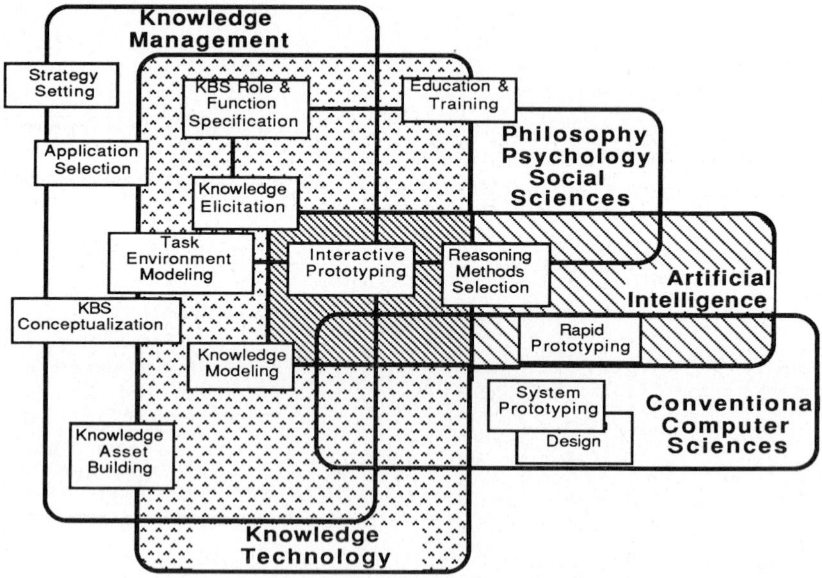

Fig. 3 Relations between Knowledge Technology Activities and the Major Technical and Management Areas.

As we consider the impacts of the creation of ExperTAXSM within C&L, it is of importance to recognize the nature of the activities that were undertaken. These activities span considerably different disciplines and perspectives as

indicated above, and require broad qualifications on the part of the imple-mentors. On the other hand, due to this extensive investment in the capabilities of the system, the qualifications and training required to use the system are considerably reduced as discussed below.

ExperTAXSM is implemented to operate on PC/AT compatible computers with 640k memory. It uses a proprietary environment implemented in LISP. The implementation required an investment "well over one million dollars[1]" and required almost two years. ExperTAXSM was designed and implemented by members of C&L's Decision Support Group's expert system development team. It is a "stand-alone" system that supports a major business function and is used sporadically by its users who have numerous other functions beyond use of the system. It includes over 6,000 "clauses" (rules, facts, and other declarations), and the system is therefore a "medium-sized" system. (Figure 4)

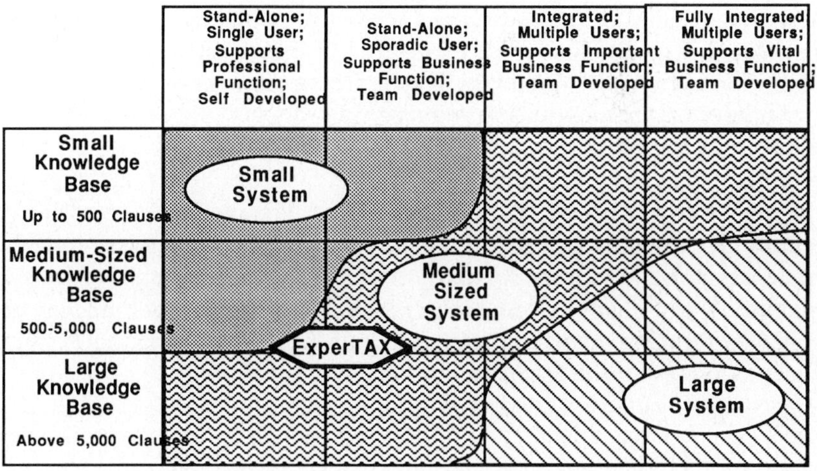

Fig. 4 Size of ExperTAXSM in Relation to Other Classes of Expert Systems.

[1] D. Shpilberg et al.: ExperTAXSM: an expert system for corporate tax planning. Expert Systems, Vol 3, No 3

3. Use of ExperTAX^{SM}

The "old way" of preparing for tax accrual and planning involved time consuming methods using a thick paper questionnaire and an unmanageable user manual that was difficult to grasp and memorize. The costs of performing the function as prescribed were high compared with the benefits from following the methodology in detail. As a result, the methodology was frequently only partially followed. The procedures were updated infrequently and updates were very costly, both to perform, and to distribute to the user community.

The "new way" of preparing for tax accrual and planning using ExperTAX^{SM} is still performed within the same time and resource budgets as before. Benefits of the new way of doing business are significant, however. The major benefits are timeliness and quality of services to clients by always considering the best expertise that is available to the firm. Updates are much less expensive and are frequent. And the methodology is easy to use for the field staff and their managers.

The clients are appreciative of the extra value of the advice they now receive, particularly since the quality of the advice has increased significantly without any increase in cost to clients. Since the reports and information requirements follow well designed formats that are directly relevant to the clients' situations, the clients find great value in the relatively low effort required to produce the needed information. The users find that the system is easy to use because of the uniform information requirement and reporting formats. As a result, interpretation and implementation efforts are reduced, as are errors associated with omission, commission, and interpretation. ExperTAX^{SM} has been found to require very little user training since the system supports directly the concepts and perspectives that accountants are well trained in. Users have developed significant confidence in the system, particularly because its frequent updates makes it contain the latest changes with well considered reasoning and judgement as supplied by the more than 40 experts. Each release is also verified and validated using strict procedures to ascertain good quality control.

ExperTAX^{SM} is maintained by C&L's tax department by five tax professionals who are supported by a large group of experts. The professionals who are in charge of maintaining the system all have accounting backgrounds. They also, however, have additional training in knowledge elicitation and modelling and in AI technology and knowledge encoding. The ExperTAX^{SM} knowledge maintenance environment has been specially developed to be used by non-AI professionals and is equipped with editors and truth maintenance facilities.

The initial version of ExperTAX^{SM} produced excessive output reports. Users were subjected to information overload and had difficulties setting priorities for the issues that were identified by the system for inclusion in the tax accrual and planning. As the tax specialists who now are maintaining the system became proficient in knowledge-base maintenance, they were able to streamline the reporting functions to become less redundant and to only include relevant considerations. The initial systems implementors, who were AI professionals, were not able to provide the required level of discrimination to achieve this level of efficiency.

4. Work Impacts

Major impacts of ExperTAX^{SM} include the fact that work now can be carried out further in the field with fewer visits and fewer consultations with managers. Auditors and tax specialists are freed from drudge reasoning and are devoting more energy and time on creative and interesting aspects. There are less concerns with with errors of omission and interpretation of particular situations. The physical workplace has not changed with the introduction of the expert system. Personal computers were previously part of the workplace equipment and users were already computer literate.

5. Qualification Impacts

There were no changes in the qualifications required of users, i.e. of auditors and tax specialists. No additional skills were required of them to operate or utilize the system. The maintenance staff, however, required considerable additional training as discussed below. They were not required to have different academic qualifications. It was noted, though, that the accountants who became members of the knowledge maintenance team had considerable additional interests in areas ranging from psychology to linguistics to computer sciences, and it possible that this constitutes a "hidden" requirement to perform knowledge maintenance.

The implementation team consisted of professional expert system implementors with backgrounds in AI, conventional computer sciences, knowledge engineering, systems science, and psychology and philosophy (epistemology). It was clear in this case, as in most of our other expert system projects, that these qualifications are universally required to create systems that are powerful and well matched to the applications environment.[1]

6. Training Impacts

As indicated above, the users did not require formal training in the use of ExperTAX^{SM}. The required training consists of a 45 minute example session to gain familiarity with the operation of the system. The system is equipped with liberal "Help Functions" and it has not been needed to create a users manual.

The tax specialists who join the maintenance staff, however, need to go through a training period of about one month to acquire the required understanding to maintain the system. They are trained in several areas:

- Relevant areas of computer science;
- Aspects of cognitive psychology;
- Epistemology, Linguistics, and Semantics;
- Knowledge Elicitation and Modeling;
- Workflow and Task Environment Analysis;
- Knowledge Codification and Shell Operation; and
- Training in the ExperTAX^{SM} knowledge maintenance system.

The expert system maintenance professionals are selected from the most qualified tax professionals as they will be responsible for codification and continued development of the strategic knowledge assets that also are competitively crucial to the firm.

7. Conclusion

There are a number of considerations that result from the experiences with ExperTAX^{SM}. C&L's management have decided to implement additional systems for other areas of their accounting practice. It is expected that these systems also will require little user training. It further expected that the new systems will be maintained by the most capable representatives from the user community, and representatives from those communities have therefor been included on the development teams. ExperTAX^{SM} is expected to continue to evolve into other

[1] For a further discussion of these factors, see Wiig, K. M.: Knowledge-based Systems and Issues of Integration: A Commercial Perspective. AI & SOCIETY Vol 2, Springer-Verlag 1988 pp 209-233.

areas to free its users from additional drudgery and to improve the service to clients. It is not expected that the "people content" will be reduced in the next few years, although it is expected to happen in the next decade or two.

The appreciation for several new skill areas need to be developed in expert systems implementors and in the managers who are responsible for installing this technology in their operations. Some of the areas that need to be under-stood are:

- Understanding business and knowledge worker operating environments;
- Understanding knowledge tasks and functional relations and characterization of such tasks;
- Cognitive science, including different types of knowledge holders and their behaviors;
- Task environment analysis;
- Knowledge codification, i.e.: elicitation, analysis, rational reconstruction, and modeling;
- Knowledge encoding and automation of human reasoning;
- AI architectures and programming;
- Man/machine interfaces, including natural language understanding and generation; and
- Conventional computer science and technical integration with information systems.

The requirement to develop such a broad perspective in the business leaders is motivated by the need to provide them with the understanding to envision opportunities and to include new capabilities in the strategies that the firm will follow.

After having operated ExperTAX^{SM} for over two years, it is clear that the nature of work supported by the system has changed to the better for the tax and audit specialists. Their work has become more interesting and they have received continued assistance from the system. The system is also providing them with unique opportunities for training in the reasons behind the expert advice provided by ExperTAX^{SM}. The system has, in fact, become a vital link in the training of junior personnel. The qualifications for tax and audit personnel have not changed. In summary, the benefits outweigh the costs of the system by a very large margin.

EXPERT SYSTEMS IN PRODUCTION AND SERVICES II
Th. Bernold and U. Hillenkamp (Editors)
Elsevier Science Publishers B.V., Amsterdam – Printed in The Netherlands

Summing up: The Perspective of Emerging Training Needs

Peter Schefe
Fachbereich Informatik, Universität Hamburg
Hamburg, FRG

1. Scope

Both case studies (viz. Senker et al., 1988) and general reviews (viz. Jahoda et al., 1988, Koenemann, 1987) seemingly support the opinion that the (if any) unique effects of expert systems on conditions of work and resulting training needs are superposed and concealed by the effects

(1) of information technology in general;

(2) of the organization of work.

Roughly, I would agree, however, the new quality of expert system technology, especially the declarative, logically tractable knowledge representation schemes will account for specific impacts – admittedly – fine grained and dependent on application contexts (viz. Schefe, 1988). As to the second issue, we have to set up a framework of conditions for our judgement. According to the ongoing discussion on automation, there are at least two: a Tayloristic, technology-centered and a human-centered approach. We will follow this alternative in outlining the new needs for 'knowledge acquisition' of the worker (blue or white collar) as users and operators of expert systems, leaving out considerations on education needs for computer scientists, managers, instructors a. o. For the new emerging qualifications we give

(1) an overall characteristic;

(2) contents derived from the 'new' mode of interaction with expert systems;

(3) contents derived from expert systems installation, use and maintenance.

2. Emerging New Qualifications

We observe a common need for a more generalistic qualification, however, with different interpretations: first as an ability to adapt to changing specializations, with purely technical contents, sustaining the effectiveness of the production process; second as an ability to explore and create new specializations, with complex socio-technical contents, sustaining effectiveness of the production and the autonomy of the individual.

This corresponds to the dichotomy of training for functionality and performance on the one hand and education for autonomy, responsibility and competence on the other hand. "Training what is needed", i. e., conceiving of courses mostly conducted by industrial actors (viz. Paonessa, 1987) aiming at introducing new technology effectively, i. e., securing acceptance, would smoothly fit into the former framework. Training methods will be chosen according to the limited tasks at hand; training on the job or training for the job will be tuned to short-term economic considerations.

In the long run, learning to learn will be a base qualification, as the value of specific abilities and attainments will be temporally constrained. A meta-competence necessary to maintain autonomy of action is the ability to judge the feasibility, usefulness and social accountability of socio-technical innovations. Clearly, this cannot be acquired in a course, but only in a life-long social process with open access to, if not participation in, innovative developments. Admittedly, this is rather wishful thinking than a realizable idea, nevertheless, it is a requirement of humanization.

3. Formal Operating Skills

The distinction to be made pertains to both the technical and the educational aspect. Within a technology-centered approach, the aim is to design adaptive, user-modelling, i.e., non-transparent, simplistic interactive components; within the opposite approach, user interfaces are intended to be adaptable, transparent but complex. Accordingly, the requirements are short-range specialized skills without understanding of the interaction model on the one hand, and long-range, generalizable explorative, only partially specialized skills including (at least some) background understanding of deep issues.

User-friendliness, in first context, is understood as simplicity or readiness to adapt to the naive user. There is overwhelming evidence from interviews (Schefe, 1987) and case studies (Senker et al., 1988) that expert systems operation will be much more simplified than conventional software products are today. "Two to three days training for a clerk will suffice" was a typical answer. These assumptions are mostly based both on conventional interaction interface design and special 'explaining' capabilities. Only on the far horizon (as opposed to university researcher's opinions in particular) appear natural language conversationalists - computers as 'partners' etc. - to be ideals of a system, as additional training would be reduced to almost zero. From this point of view, expert systems will weaken the position of those demanding higher qualifications of the workforce.

Although ease of learning to operate a system is a desirable achievement, simplistic non-transparent interfaces will be boring in the long run. Thus, expert systems should not be 'communicative' and adaptive but inspectable and adaptable, they should not model the user, but the user should be able to build a model of the system. From this, it can be inferred that training scope and extent will not be reduced but enhanced, and furthermore, that training cannot be on the job exclusively, but knowledge will be acquired within a broader context of enhancing the competence of action. This includes general knowledge of system's interface adaptation techniques determining its behavior, of available presentation techniques and ergonomic layout of machinery. For the skilled worker, a shift will occur from knowledge of concrete processes and machinery to knowledge of algorithms and abstract structures. The worker should be prepared to understand and appropriately apply the system. Not at all should his training be restricted to operate the system available. This is even denied in applier's interviews, being in favor of generalistic learning. However, it has to be secured that contents do not become arbitrary, or subjects to quick change without enhancing the cognizance of workers in the long run. Thus, the competence of acquiring new knowledge from available resources independently, will be crucial.

A well-supported participation in the design-process would be the last opportunity to enhance the cognizance of the work force.This is true for skilled clerks, too. Employees working in offices will bother with the new technology more than those working in technical domains, because they are lacking the technical background and have to fear imminent replacement. On the other hand, clerks and other people not acquainted with computing machinery, may readily accept the new technology, if their status is upgraded, e. g., if they can do things they could not have done before, as Senker et al. (op. cit.) are reporting. Thus, this group deserves special educational care.

4. Content-oriented and Communication Skills

Within the – prevailing – Tayloristic framework, expert systems will be a means of further formalization, atomisation and enhancement of control of mental work. Downgrading of both content-oriented and social-communicative skills will be the probable result. User-operators will be constrained to data gathering, monitoring and solution filtering, i. e., executing formal control without competence of decision. Accordingly, training needs for the workforce will be restricted to generalized, mostly depleeted of content formal skills, and short-range superficial domain knowledge, to "what is needed".

Furthermore, systems will serve as a training tool saving costs for highly qualified pedagogical personnel. As explaining capabilities of expert systems are quite limited (Schefe, 1988), this will result in a further deskilling effect concerning contents and communications. The strength of this effect will vary with the degree of qualification. It will be high for process operators and people doing routine processing within both white and blue collar jobs. It will be low for expert people who are more able to adapt to new situations.

Whilst, in the technology-centered approach, contents- and communications-oriented qualification will loose importance, within a human-centered approach, expert systems may serve as a medium of knowledge concerning production processes and service procedures, ensuring autonomy of knowledge application and decision making. This approach requires a considerable increase in education and training needs, i. e., life-long generalized, but content-directed learning, non-formal, socio-communicative competence, ability not only to use but also to judge the function of an expert system as a medium and a methodology of analysis of knowledge-intensive processes in social-technical settings, at least to be aware of their socio-technical scope and limitations, in order to participate in their installation and maintenance.

As an innovative technology, expert systems may offer the opportunity to introduce innovative educational programs that narrow this gap providing with a deeper understanding both of work contents and organization. As to the technical content, such a program may be differentiated according to different degrees of system complexity and to qualification levels. There will be, particularly in the production area, a lot of rather simple 'handheld' devices that would allow even for a trained non-specialist to change the knowledge base by adding and subtracting rules (viz. Gupta/Arshak, 1987) in a simple format, performing a function similar to a note-book.

For a complex system comprising hundreds or thousands of rules, only a highly skilled technician or engineer will be able to fully understand and modify its 'knowledge base' with its rather complex problems of knowledge representation and processing, especially those of interfacing declarative and procedural knowledge. Qualifications that help climb the career ladder will increasingly overlap with computing and formal abstraction skills. The maintenance of such systems would be reserved to specially trained engineers, if not computer scientists. Although an awareness of the increasing importance of inhouse training can be observed, the base qualifications required for engineers – ability of abstraction and structuring a knowledge domain – will be left to non-industrial educational institutions. This seems to be appropriate for the remote future – depending on changes in the general educational system. For the time being, qualification deficits are considerable.

There are some efforts by industrial companies, especially producers, to address this problem, however, aiming at short-term acceptance, not critical assessment of the new technology. E.g. the knowledge base maintenance personnel should not only know about basic techniques of knowledge acquisition, analysis and representation as well as inference, not exclusively those occurring in the system at hand, but also about weak points of the current techniques. Furthermore, awareness of social problems induced by their work is a crucial requirement, the more so as the maintenance personnel may otherwise gain the role of a new elite in the process of knowledge industrialization.

As a consequence, learning must take place within a human oriented framework, reinforcing socio-communicative competence, making people aware of their own role within a working process, calling for common, not (only) competitive efforts.

References

T. Bernold, U. Hillenkamp (eds.) (1988): Expert Systems in Production and Services, Impact on Qualifications and Working Life.(North Holland) Amsterdam etc.

Jahoda et al. (1988): Expert systems. Present state and future trends: Impact on employment and skill requirements (A review of AI literature). International Labour Office, Geneva.

J. Koenemann (1986): Auswirkungen von Expertensystemen. Ansätze einer Technologiefolgenabschätzung auf dem Gebiet der Künstlichen Intelligenz. Fachbereich Informatik, Bericht Nr. 123.

C.J.Paonessa (1987): Artificial Intelligence Technology: Human Factors in Planning and Implementation of Expert Systems. In: (Bernold/Hillenkamp, 1988).

P. Schefe (1988): Expert systems. Present state and future trends: Impact on employment and skill requirements (An assessment). International Labour Office, Geneva.

Senker et al. (1988): Expert systems. Present state and future trends: Impact on employment and skill requirements (Case studies). International Labour Office, Geneva.

Training and Retraining

EXPERT SYSTEMS IN PRODUCTION AND SERVICES II
Th. Bernold and U. Hillenkamp (Editors)
Elsevier Science Publishers B.V., Amsterdam – Printed in The Netherlands

Public Vocational Training Sector and Dual Systems

Andreas Drinkuth
Industriegewerkschaft Metall
Frankfurt, FRG

1. Introduction

If you talk about training and retraining for Expert Systems (ES) you can't understand it apart from existing and future applications and the philosophy behind their development.

One also has to see how limited the diffusion of ES has been so far. So it may be too early to talk about an institutionalized training system. One can't base a training system entirely on the currently dominant direction of the development of ES. On the contrary: we have to discuss the different developments phases very critically. What is at issue is the quantity and quality of work in the future.

2. Applications

ES today are used primarily in the sciences or in technical institutes. For example:

- data management;
- to answer specific questions about technical processes;
- to give you suggestions for experiments;
- literature searches;
- to observe and monitor experiments.

The developers of the ES are often the users as well. Chemists and physicists use ES to store and to retrieve data during their experiments. In industry ES are used for diagnosis and planning in narrow technical fields. But the goal is to use ES more widely and to allow complex machines, different computer systems or computer aided equipment to communicate among themselves with the help of ES. The goal is for production to be guided by programmes rather than people. The ES orders, repairs or steers the flow of production. Other applications for ES are in the robotics or pattern recognition which is a very important interface. ES are also a central building block for CIM. Some other fields of applications are in education or logical programming.

So if we look where ES are being developed and who is working with them, then you see that the target group for training today is primarily in the scientific field. That means that universities, colleges and companies should be training these scientists and students.

3. The Dominant Development Philosophy

Current ES operate according to "if-then-rules". The assumption is that thought-processes can be reduced to a series of "if-then-statements" and thus means that human experts think and behave in the same way. The knowledge of human experts is understood as a collection of facts and rules. All one would have to do is mine the experienced-based knowledge of the human experts as raw material for filling in the shell of the ES. So the theorists of Artificial Intelligence don't see any fundamental differences between the cognitive abilities of humans and machines. In principle it should be possible, they think, to recognize the methods which guide human perception and evaluation. According to this view the computer "understands" reality by constructing an internal model. With the help of its knowledge base and the rules of the computer generates "logical" responses to the particular problem.

According to this logic you don't need people to teach and pass knowledge along because this knowledge so defined can be stored. The problem so far is that we don't have enough of the specific knowledge and the "if-then-rules" in particular fields. They do concede that one of the main problems to run an ES is the area of common-sense-reasoning. But this is often fundamental to comprehend reality. Siekmann, one of the German theorists for AI says: "ES can simulate the intelligence of a specialist but not of a three year old child".

4. Critique

Behind this philosophy lies a mechanistic view of how intelligence processes work. They neglect the fact that learning can only take place in and through reality, through lived experiences. One can't reduce human behavior and activities to a series of "if-then-rules". A human expert evaluates a situation in its entirety and in part intuitively, without checking a long list of facts and rules. She (or he) has a feel for material and a sense for machines. Her (or his) mastery is based on practical experience with material and machines. Associated thinking, analogies, intuition and a feeling for things are impossible or nearly impossible to program. Computer procedures are not identical with human thought and behavior. Human behavior and learning grows out of experience in specific social, political and cultural context and one has to be aware of this context, when acting in a particular area.

One can't reduce intelligence to the manipulation of symbols. If one ignores these fundamental differences between human experts and ES and brings these assumptions into the training for ES, then there is a danger of losing touch with reality. Then one would see the computer world as the real reality and not of a necessarily reduced model of it. If one follows this logic, then the real world becomes in a sense second hand. One doesn't have to experience it directly. Training doesn't need to deal with real problems. It can be limited to the computerized reproduction of these problems. In other words: to the manipulation of symbols. The result will be that the contact with reality is sharply limited. The other danger is that of a "double reality". And even that the computer model be taken as more real and that reality has to conform to this model. If that were to happen it would change our everyday behavior and that of companies.

5. Demands for an Alternative Conception of ES and Vocational Training and Retraining

Broedner says: "People can think thanks to their hands, they can work thanks to their heads". That is, a person learns through his hands on the basis of real experience and that in turn enables him to work. This demand must be considered in the philosophy behind ES and in the contents and methods of training for them. This alternative philosophy accepts the contradiction and complexity of reality and the necessity of sensory experience. It considers how ES can be used to support and augment human intelligence, for example to order facts, to monitor appointments, to check procedures or to take over monotonous work.

We need development- and application-ideas that begin with human experts and support them, that gives them experimental training and qualifies them to work with the appropriate ES. The problem solver is not the ES but the person. That brings us back to the opening question: How should work and technology be designed and organized so that they support human beings and not the other way round.

Finally I would make some recommendations for vocational training and re-training:

- Training programs should be based on real and not on simulated experiences. And it is on this basis that training on the specific ES should be built.
- We need concepts for development and application of ES that put the human in the center.
- The point of the training should be to train people to solve problems with the support of ES. That's all the more important that people have this general understanding because specific jobs which are done by people today may be done by machines tomorrow. The understanding of the problem and knowledge and use of the ES as a whole to solve this problem are two sides of the same coin. Both have to play a role in training for ES.
- The dual system of vocational training that we have in Germany appears to allow for this connection between theory and practice. However, in the apprenticeship-training the ES must be seen as an aid in solving problems and not as a problem-solver itself.
- Today the additional training system in Germany is too theoretical. It needs to emphasize practical training which is connected to the specific work of the trainees. In addition, training on ES is currently only for scientific experts because in most cases they are the developers and users, what I mentioned above. With the extent of spreading of ES into other fields of application it should also include other skilled workers.
- At a high-school level polytechnical training should also be developed that would make it possible for a student to work both toward the possibility of going to university but also learn a skill at the same time.

References

Siegfried Bleicher, "Kontra-Standpunkte zur Künstlichen Intelligenz", in: Logistik im Unternehmen, Juli/August 1988

Peter Häusler u.a., "Künstliche Intelligenz und Bildung in der Bundesrepublik: Eine Bestandsaufnahme", herausgegeben vom Institut für die Pädagogik der Naturwissenschaften an der Universität Kiel, 01.12.1986

Industriegewerkschaft Metall für die Bundesrepublik Deutschland, Siegfried Bleicher, Hrsg., "Künstliche Intelligenz - Kontroversen um eine neue Technologie", Dokumentation einer Fachtagung der IG Metall am 16. und 17. Oktober 1987 in Berlin, Frankfurt 1988

Industriegewerkschaft Metall für die Bundesrepublik Deutschland, Siegfried Bleicher, Hrsg., "Künstliche Intelligenz oder die Rationalisierung geistiger Arbeit, Werkstattbericht, Oktober 1987, Frankfurt am Main

Industriegewerkschaft Metall für die Bundesrepublik Deutschland, Siegfried Bleicher, Hrsg., "CIM - oder die Zukunft der Arbeit in rechnerintegrierten Fabrikstrukturen", Ergebnisse einer Fachtagung der IG Metall, Frankfurt am Main 1987

Manfred Moldaschl, "Grenzen der Mechanisierung geistiger Arbeit - Expertensysteme in der Produktion", erscheint in: Die Mitbestimmung, Oktober 1988

Peter Schnupp, Ute Leibrandt, "Expertensysteme - Nicht nur für Informatiker", Berlin/Heidelberg 1986

Stiftung für Kommunikationsforschung, "Wird das Denken überflüssig?", Stenografisches Protokoll einer Arbeitstagung vom 18.10.1985 im Wissenschaftszentrum Bonn-Bad-Godesberg

Walter Volpert, "High-Tech ohne Mensch?", in: UNIVERSITAS Berlin, 3/88

Wechselwirkung Schwerpunktheft "Künstliche Intelligenz" Nr. 27, November 1985, Berlin

EXPERT SYSTEMS IN PRODUCTION AND SERVICES II
Th. Bernold and U. Hillenkamp (Editors)
Elsevier Science Publishers B.V., Amsterdam – Printed in The Netherlands

The Changing Role of the Instructor in a World of Technology and Expert Systems

Dr. Orley R. Herron
President
National College of Education
Evanston, Ill, USA

The expert systems and other new technologies that we are discussing today present both a challenge and an opportunity for educators, whether they work with students on the college campus or in the corporate or business world.

I would like to speak with you this morning from my own perspective as an educator and as a college president – about how these new technologies are changing the way we deliver instruction and about the impact they may have on the instructor's role.

I represent the National College of Education, a 102-year-old college that will soon become a university. For more than a century, the National College has been involved in teacher education, and beginning about ten years ago the College expanded into other academic areas. Our graduates are employed in the corporate and business community, in hospitals and other health-care facilities, in government or human service agencies, and in schools.

As I have talked with our recent graduates and with the community leaders who serve on program advisory councils, on the President's Council and the Board of Trustees, they have reinforced our belief that in today's workplace it is vital to include computers and related technologies in each student's academic program. They have also emphasized the need for high-quality continuing education and professional development, whether it is delivered through college programs or on-the-job training.

Two major forces impact on our graduates' careers. The knowledge base is expanding rapidly but the half-life of knowledge in many professions has decreased now to only two to four years. At the same time, the workplace is becoming technologically more sophisticated. Persons at all levels of employment – entry-level or middle management, or even senior management – will require some kind of continuing education or on-the-job training to stay current or to upgrade existing skills.

The Carnegie Foundation for the Advancement of Teaching estimated in 1985 that more than 21 million adults, some 13 percent of the labor force, were enrolled in some type of organized course outside of traditional higher education during that year. (Eurich, 1985, p. 20.)

Serving numbers of that magnitude represents a major problem for our society, and technology is one of the best advantages we have at our disposal. At the National College of Education we have seen first-hand the quality of achievement that is possible when faculty and students have access to the appropriate technology and are willing to use it. For example:

In the language laboratory on National College's Chicago campus, students are learning English as a second language. They are able to work at their own speed through five levels of a computer-assisted tutorial program until they are ready to go into regular college classrooms.

In the Demonstration School at the Evanston Campus, we are teaching young children to use microcomputers for problem-solving and decision-making. They are likely to be part of the next generation's high-tech users.

In other settings, a science instructor may use computers to demonstrate experiments that are too difficult or dangerous to perform in the laboratory, or a medical student may use expert systems to learn diagnostic skills.

Colleges and universities across America are investing in unprecedented amounts of hardware and software, while the faculty and students are developing new ways to use it. As we integrate expert systems and other kinds of technology into the university curriculum, we will fulfill two important goals: first, to provide students with more in-depth experiences with computers during their formal college instruction, and second, to provide better continuing education experiences. We believe that, as consumers, our students will eventually need to be familiar with the same kinds of technologies that are being used in their chosen area while still in college, rather than waiting to learn on-the-job.

Despite all the advantages, some educators are concerned that the new technologies will change the dynamics of the teaching/learning process (Bok, 1985, p. 2), or even be a threat to the instructor's traditional academic role. Based upon what we know about education, changes will occur in how we teach, in what we teach, and even when and where we teach, but overall, the quality of instruction will probably improve. I believe the question is not whether we should use the newer technologies in higher education or in continuing education, but how best to do so.

Carnegie Mellon University recently advertised for students to participate in an experimental course. The course description (Corbett, 1988) read like this:

- "Essentially no lectures."
- "Class attendance required only every two weeks."
- "Learn on your own time."
- "Schedule quizzes when you feel ready."

Corbett (1988) projected a success rate of 84 percent – approximately five of every six students – and promised that one of the instructors, a computer functioning as an "intelligent tutor", could give students immediate help whenever problems occurred. The other instructor, a faculty member, would meet the class at two-week intervals and be available to students upon request.

This delivery system contrasts strongly with more traditional college and university teaching. Today, in many institutions the lecture-hall is still the most prevalent teaching site. Class sizes may range from a small class of 25 or 30 students to 400 or 500 in a larger one. Classes meet in an assigned room, at prescribed times, and for a prescribed number of weeks.

We know that in teaching/learning process, students usually learn more when they are actively involved. According to a recent study by the Carnegie Foundation, college students in a traditional delivery system reported that they participated actively in the classroom only 5 percent to 20 percent of the time. Classroom observation and follow-up interviews confirmed that the findings were closer to 5 percent. (Newman, 1985, p. 61.)

Thus, a key feature of the newer technologies is that they enable us to provide individualized, self-paced instruction for students. Instead of sitting passively in a lecture hall, the students can participate actively in the process.

As changes occur in the delivery system, we would expect to see an impact on the instructor's traditional role. Formerly the instructor was viewed as being the "expert" and was often an authority figure. The instructor's job was to transmit the knowledge he or she had gained from years of study to the students who enrolled in the class.

According to Ehrmann (1984), the focus has shifted from the instructor to the content that is to be learned. The instructor's role has changed from an "expert" and authority figure – to a facilitator and manager of the learning environment. The new "expert" – a computer – may even be considered a "third partner" in the learning process.

In theory, faculty members will be freed up from having to teach large lecture-hall sessions, and in practice, most will spend more time in informal teaching activities. Faculty will also have to spend more time on assessing learner needs, and locating or developing the appropriate technology-based resources. (Ehrmann, 1984, pp. 7-12.)

A parallel example at National College is the experience we have had in establishing our adult programs in which the instructors are learning facilitators, as opposed to a more traditional classroom role. The dynamics have shifted, yet faculty and students feel that much has been gained.

The use of technology in the curriculum will force educators to consider how learning occurs. Many professionals agree that when cognitive psychologists and computer scientists work together to build expert systems, there will be more emphasis on how human beings think, reason, learn, and remember, and how they use experience to make decisions and solve problems. (Lyman, 1988, p. 18.)

Young children often learn in proportion to the time spent on task and the interaction with concerned adults. With adult learning, however, the process is more sophisticated. In traditional higher education the burden of learning a subject falls squarely on the student, regardless of whether the instructor's teaching style matches the way the student learns. Now there is a chance that an expert system will diagnose the student's individual learning style and respond appropriately.

Smith and Dunn (1985) believe that as colleges and universities join the information society, both instructors and students will benefit from the ability to share resources and communicate via computer networks. These abilities will further change the instructor's role.

Based on current practices in higher education, it is likely that college faculty will incorporate computers and other types of technology in the classroom, in the occasional lecture or small group experience, to demonstrate and teach concepts that were previously considered too difficult.

For example, Simonche, a faculty member at the University of North Carolina, has set up a computer simulation that enables students to participate in "the critical events that affect U. S. history." By means of the computer, students are called on to make decisions at key points in history, evaluate the results, and defend their positions. (Simonche, 1987, p. 20.)

In another institution, Kemeny, a professor-emeritus at Dartmouth College, affirms that having access to a computer has radically changed the way he has taught mathematics in his 43-year career. Earlier he would have liked to teach several topics that were considered "too hard" for students at a particular level. Now these topics and others can be included in the curriculum. (Kemeny, 1987, p. 44.)

In the "electronic university" faculty members will have a wealth of academic resources at their fingertips – or at their terminals – and we are discovering new applications every day. Instructors can access the college library, tutor a student, or give out the next day's assignment without leaving their desks, and with the appropriate technology, they can bring resources into the college classroom from all over the world. (Moeller & Hania, 1987; Young, et al., 1988.)

With the rapid expansion of the knowledge base and with equally rapid technological growth, it is no longer possible to expose students to all of the information they will need throughout their lives. In the university of the future the instructor will be expected to teach each student how to access information from a world-wide array of computerized data bases; how to analyze and synthesize the information, and how to apply it.

Instructors in higher education, industry and the corporate world must themselves be skilled users of technology for their students to realize its full potential. However, with rapid changes in technology, many instructors may require continuing training and support.

At present, college and university faculty are usually hired because of the expertise they bring to an institution in teaching, scholarship and research. In the future, some search committees may expect instructors to be competent in the newer instructional technologies in addition to their academic discipline. Faculty members are likely to work in instructional teams, rather than alone in their offices, and at least one person on the team will probably have these special abilities. (Smith & Dunn, 1985; Hocking, 1985.) Before we can reap the full rewards of the new technology, higher education institutions and other employers must be willing to provide the appropriate hardware, software and training. The irony is that higher education institutions right now are probably the least physically equipped to be competitive, and the least able to purchase the necessary equipment.

The problem goes even further. A recent report to the U. S. Congress from the Office of Technology Assessment, a nonpartisan congressional agency, stated that, at the elementary and secondary school levels

"Today's classrooms typically resemble their ancestors of 50 years ago more closely than operating rooms of business offices resemble their 1938 versions." (Chicago Tribune, 1988.) This report estimated that school districts in America need to spend at least $4 billion dollars to provide an adequate supply of microcomputers – one for about every three students – despite the fact that the schools have spent more than $2 billion dollars for computers in the past ten years, We do not have a comparable figure from the higher education community, but the principle is the same.

As we move ahead, there will have to be more involvement from government and the corporate world to help underwrite the cost of computer hardware and software on all levels of education – in the elementary and secondary schools, where children are now expected to become computer literate, through public and private higher education.

I believe we should encourage the development of partnerships between higher education institutions, federal or state government, and the corporate community as a way to meet this important challenge. IBM is the premiere example of this notion. They are making a difference relative to this issue by being the largest corporate donor in the United States. That leadership is vital for this problem – for this opportunity – to be effectively addressed.

You and your organizations are all in critical roles in this sense. You all see the opportunity. Too many of us – as education specialists – only see the problem. You need to be the catalyst, because without that ingredient, change can be a very slow and deliberate process. I salute you for what you have done to this point. But I challenge you to "close the sale" and bring this enormously important situation to a successful conclusion.

References

Bok, D. (1985, Fall). Looking into education's high-tech future. EDUCOM Bulletin, 2-10, 17.

Corbett, A. (1988, August). An intelligent tutoring system. T.H.E. Journal, 12.

Ehrmann, S. (1984, September). Technology could change the goals of a college education. Educational Technology, 7-12.

Eurich, N. (1985). Corporate classrooms: The learning business. (p. 20). Princeton, N. J.: Carnegie Foundation for the Advancement of Teaching.

Hocking, J. (1985, August). The computer in higher education: not just another mechanical devise. Educational Technology, 19-23.

Kemeny, J. (1988, May/June). Mathematics: How computers have changed the way I teach. Academic Computing, 44.

Lyman, P. (1988, March/April). The computer revolution in the classroom: A progress report. Academic Computing, 18.

Moeller, J., Jr. & Hania, A. (1987, October). Creating the computer-integrated campus: A vision of the future. Academic Computing, 6-9, 61.

Newman, F. (1985). Higher education and the American resurgence. (p. 61.) Princeton, N. J.: Carnegie Foundation for the Advancement of Teaching.

Report of the Office of Technology Assessment. (1988, September). Chicago Tribune.

Simonche, J. (1987, September). Computer simulations: The teaching of history and the goals of a liberal education. Academic Computing, 20.

Smith, P. & Dunn, S. (1985, July). Tomorrow's university: Serving the information society. Educational Technology, 7.

Young, L., Thearling, K., Skiena, S., Robison, A., Omohundro, S., Mel, B., & Wolfram, S. (1988, May/June). Academic computing in the year 2000. Academic Computing, 8-12, 62-64.

EXPERT SYSTEMS IN PRODUCTION AND SERVICES II
Th. Bernold and U. Hillenkamp (Editors)
Elsevier Science Publishers B.V., Amsterdam – Printed in The Netherlands

The Training Costs Associated with Artificial Intelligence Applications in Manufacturing

Courtland M. Hilton and Karl G. Kempf
Intel Corporation
Components Technology and Manufacturing Group
Knowledge Applications Laboratory
Chandler, Arizona, U.S.A.

Abstract

It is obvious that the introduction of AI-based applications into a manufacturing community which has only a cursory exposure to AI concepts will entail a substantial user training overhead. Indeed, this has been our experience after the installation of a number of expert systems built in PC-based shells and the initial delivery of two custom systems built in Common LISP. In addition, there have been a number of surprises concerning training needs. Some of these training needs have centered on the user and were not anticipated at the time of application conceptualization. More interestingly, some surprises which have been encountered involved personnel other than the user. We describe these surprises, and propose a training model which we hope to employ in the future to eliminate them.

---

1. Small User-built Intelligent Job Aids

One of Intel's major proprietary advantages lies in its extensive knowledge "base", contained largely in the minds of its thousands of excellent process, product, and manufacturing personnel. These human experts are generally consumers of software technology, but are not software developers. Intel's strategy to exploit AI technology dictates tapping this large resource base by synergistically combining a few large central AI development programs with a broad base of small user developed intelligent job aids (IJA's) or expert systems. The IJA's are typically being written and deployed by the manufacturing site's local experts thus enabling the preservation of critical knowledge as well as promoting and accelerating the multitasking capability of our workforce. The IJA's typically address issues of diagnosis, prescription, interpretation, or classification. The following four systems are briefly described to provide a representative flavor of our efforts.

1.1. Applications Overview

Swept CV Plot Interpretation: A swept capacitance and voltage plot is used to detect the presence of certain microcontaminates in the semiconductor fabrication process. The interpretation of non-standard plots is widely regarded within Intel as a difficult and expert task. This IJA development was motivated by the sole corporate expert's desire to train local site technicians and engineers in the principles of proper interpretation and to thereby free his time for other tasks. The IJA was developed on a PC using an inductive shell called FUSION [1]. The system has about 150 multiple antecedent rule equivalents (MARE's, see footnote [2] for more detail) in its knowledge base, uses graphic images to help guide the user, and supplies global and context-sensitive help through a hypertext utility. The system has been deployed to all of Intel's semiconductor plants, with plans in place for its incorporation directly into the measurement instrument, thus providing for future automated interpretation of the plots as the CV test is performed.

E-test Advisor: Device electrical test (E-test) is performed at the end of the semiconductor manufacturing process to assure top component performance and to identify any potential device problems that may be pending. Product engineers and technicians are routinely called on to identify faulty manufacturing steps based on the test vector information. This IJA was developed when a large series of personnel changes threatened the integrity of the collective site knowledge. A device engineering group leader, who had significant software development skills, developed this system on the local VAX using the rule based expert system shell EXSYS [3]. The rule based system has about 300 rules. Process data required during the consultation is automatically supplied through an ancillary program that queries the main engineering database. The tool found its most popular use in the training of new device technicians, although it is also used when particularly difficult problems arise. The system is not integrated with the test equipment, covers only one major process and was

---

[1] 1stClass and 1stClass Fusion are IBM P.C. based expert system shells, products of 1stClass Expert Systems, Inc. of Wayland, MA. They are inductive systems, representing knowledge in the form of examples and decision trees rather than in productions.

[2] Multiple Antecedent Rule Equivalent (MARE) is a in-house metric used to compare the size of expert systems developed using Fusion with those developed in other PC rule based systems. It inherits all the frailties of "rule counting" metrics. A single MARE is a knowledge tree branch that extends from the root to a single tree leaf. Its knowledge could be represented in a multiple antecedent production.

[3] EXSYS, a product of EXSYS, Inc. of Albuquerque, NM, is a rule based expert system shell which runs under VMS, UNIX, and MS-DOS.

found to be difficult to write and maintain. The difficulty in adding new knowledge to the system has contributed to its lack of growth.

Tester Interface Repair: Our device testers are integrated with our VAX based engineering database via a special interface and gateway. When an interface failure occurs, the performance of the test floor is hampered. At one particular site interface failures were occurring about twice per week and required about an hour of the sole local expert's time to diagnosis and repair. This IJA was written by the local expert using the expert system shell 1stCLASS [1] (a limited version of FUSION mentioned above) to facilitate the performance and training of the technician staff. This no-frills system has about 40 MARE's. The expert invested a total of about twenty hours total in training to use the IJA software, writing, and deploying the IJA. The expert estimated the IJA allowed technicians to handle about 80% of the trouble calls. Through use of the IJA the technicians are now competent in the interface repair; the IJA is no longer in use.

Polysilicon Doping Diagnosis System: Thin electrical conductors made of phosphorous contaminated (doped) polysilicon are used as "wires" in many semiconductor devices. A particular process of phosphorous doping has, for various reasons, proven to be less repeatable than other manufacturing steps. To compensate for these difficulties, this IJA was developed by an area technician and engineer in about eight hours. Its use has saved them about ten times this amount of time over the half year by allowing the manufacturing operators to correct the equipment/process problem or to do initial system diagnosis prior to calling for technical assistance. The IJA was developed using FUSION and has about 90 MARE's. The IJA is integrated with the station computerized logs and statistical process control system to allow automatic invocation of the IJA during times of need. The expert's sense is that the system may soon not be needed as acceptable diagnostic skill acquisition has resulted from the operators use of the system.

1.2. Training the Users

Training the expert in the creation of IJA's: Our training model was tailored to capitalize on the existing strengths of Intel's engineering staff. We took as a given that the staff possessed basic PC skills and set such skills as a prerequisite to further training. If a PC skills deficiency exists, supplemental training is readily available through local corporate training programs. Our observations led us to conclude that the engineering staff was accustomed to articulating or expressing their diagnostic knowledge in either the form of process and equipment troubleshooting (decision) trees or in the form of verbal advise. Consequently, we provided no knowledge acquisition or knowledge representation training. Instead, we chose FUSION, an expert system shell in which knowledge is represented through trees or examples, for our entry level tool. The shell required basic computer literacy and allowed many experts to intuitively represent their knowledge in a familiar fashion. Experts were taught the use of FUSION in an intensive hands-on two day (16 hour) course.

Based on surveys we found our original training model and curricula met the perceived needs of about 90% of our students. The remaining 10% were deficient in PC skills and thus were not able to properly assimilate all the course material. However, as measured by the number of IJA's produced and deployed, we felt our training model and curricula only accomplished about 30% of our instructional goals. Our perception is that the experts have demonstrated the need for further skills training in problem and resource definition, understanding and abstracting their problem structure, and ancillary software use.

Surprise 1. Problem and resource definition: Some experts did not view the creation of an IJA as requiring a formal problem solving methodology. Intrigued by the IJA technology and fooled by the magnitude of their task, they would plunge straight into system programming rather than lay the foundations of project success through problem definition, scoping, and resource planning. Although some experts would select problems of insignificance to solve, more often than not the scope of their project was initially forecasted to be smaller than required. One result of this incorrect scoping was that the expert developing the IJA would tire and quit or deploy an incomplete system. Systems without enough depth to achieve a "critical mass" are not only ineffective and quickly ignored by the target users but also create an expectation among the user community that IJA's will be useless.

The best approach we have found to date to alleviate this problem is having the experts manually prepare the decision trees for representative portions of their project. However, due to the press of other activities, this prerequisite condition is often ignored or only superficially completed. Even with this preparation the experts often find the tree they have manually prepared is of too course a granularity to be used as a complete guide when programming the IJA. We are considering the distribution of a suite of completed IJA's together with their resource requirements to perspective developers as a means of further helping them properly scope and resource their projects.

Surprise 2. Problem decomposition and abstraction: We found, counter to our expectations, that some experts not only had difficulty in expressing their detailed troubleshooting knowledge in the form of decision trees, but also were unable to decompose their solution methodology into a hierarchy of logical modules or contexts (tops-down decomposition). This lack of abstraction skill often led to false starts, ineffective structures, and frustration. The frustration was generally exacerbated by the expert's strong perception that the IJA technology would be valuable to them if they could only get it going. Our providing one-to-one assistance to the expert or having the expert develop multiple prototypes has been found to help attenuate the problem. This trial and error approach places even stronger requirements for user friendly development tools. Which experts will or will not suffer from this difficulty has not seemed to correlate to the expert's value to their organization. Our sense is that experts can be screened for this difficulty rather quickly through a brief observation of their problem decomposition efforts.

Surprise 3. Ancillary software: To obtain the flexibility required by our applications the integration of an IJA with ancillary software is often required. It was our naive expectation that the user would develop whatever ancillary software was required. We have found that the creation of such software is almost always beyond either the inclination or the capability of the expert to develop. Likewise, we have observed that training in the use of the ancillary software needs to be in as great a depth as the training in the use of the expert system shell itself.

Surprise 4. Computer literacy: In spite of the required course prerequisite of basic PC skills we found that about 10% of the experts did not possess sufficient familiarity with PC environment to allow them to be effective in developing their IJA. We have plans to make the prerequisite requirements more explicit and facilitate the experts registration in corporate PC skills classes.

Training of IJA Users and Trainers: The use of the completed IJA's was so simple that Intel's standard training procedure was not followed. A simple one-to-one session between the expert, technicians, trainers and operators was all that was required. We are not aware of any significant problems with this approach. However, there were implementation problems. Some technicians felt their jobs trivialized while others exhibited the standard reticence to change. In some locations inadvertent barriers to the availability of or distance to the deployment computer prevented facile access to the IJA's. Although managerial mandates that the IJA's be used are possible, the most effective implementations appear, not surprisingly, to be those where the IJA is integrated into an existing CIM environment. Many of the barriers to IJA use could be removed by proactive supervision and management.

1.3. Training the Non-users

One of the primary roles of our managers and supervisors is to create an infrastructure and environment for success. Our training of these groups, while brief, sought to emphasize the necessity of their proactive involvement in the infrastructure development.

To inform, educate, and garner program support from managers, we presented a special two hour overview of AI applications and user developed IJA's to senior and middle managers throughout our domestic manufacturing sites. The presentation focused on how the use of AI applications can improve productivity, promote greater flexibility, and generate higher revenues. Infrastructure and resource issues were highlighted several times throughout the presentation. Emphasis was placed on the role a proper environment would play in the system viability and use. An example IJA solving a real problem was also demonstrated, followed by a sample IJA development prototyping session. The response to these meetings was universally positive. The most senior management funded the program's expansion. However, most other managers, in the daily press of previous commitments and activities, did little proactively to create the needed infrastructure and resource the development efforts, although they did permit IJA development training classes to be held at their sites. In retrospect, it is clear we did not train the managers in their new role, we only told them what it was. Additionally, we did not reach down to the first line engineering and manufacturing supervisors; as they wield much of the day to day resource power, omitting them had significant ramifications.

2. Custom-built AI Systems

The Knowledge Application Laboratory also addresses larger scale problems which are not amenable to solution using PC-based expert system shells. An example can be found in our work on manufacturing scheduling, specifically the scheduling of semiconductor wafer fabrication facilities (fabs).

2.1. Application Overview

Fab scheduling is a difficult problem for two reasons. First, there is the magnitude of the combinatorics. The typical fab employs a number of processes (~5), each with a number of products (~10), each with a number of lots in production at any given time (~15). Furthermore, each process consists of a number of steps (~150), each with a number of possible target machines (~4), each with a number of qualified operators (~4), not to mention tools such as diffusion boats or lithography reticles. Scheduling consists of making assignments of specific lots and particular operators to individual machines at designated times, and for any given assignment decision there are a large number of possibilities each of which interacts with a large number of other assignments. The second difficulty inherent in fab scheduling is the dynamic nature of the problem. Progress in technology assures that the processes, products, and machines change on a yearly or quarterly basis. Economics force changes in product quantities and product mix at a quarterly or monthly rate. Training and turnover modify the operator skill set on a monthly or weekly basis. And, of course, the delicate nature of the process and the equipment give more than adequate opportunity for daily or hourly surprises.

Given the combinatorics and the dynamics, three distinct scheduling problems can be identified. One is Fab-Strategic scheduling where the time-frame is months and quarters. Here manufacturing management makes decisions about the scheduling ramifications of ramping up new processes, adding more equipment, altering operator training, and so on. The next problem is Fab-Tactical scheduling where shifts and days are the relevant time-scale. At this level, shift managers and area supervisors are concerned with scheduling around broken equipment, handling rush jobs, coping with absent operators, and related difficulties. The third problem is Fab-Real-Time scheduling which is concerned with the minute by minute execution of the schedule. Fab floor personnel are interested in being warned about impending scheduling difficulties, alerted to schedule breakage and its implications, and advised about schedule repair.

At this point in time, we have prototype implementations of a Fab-Strategic scheduler and a Fab-Tactical scheduler in the hands of our users for preliminary evaluation. The Fab- Strategic system schedules by reacting to a simulator. With access to a frame-based model of the fab, the simulator "runs" production until some machine finishes processing a lot. At this point, the simulator turns control over to the dispatcher. The dispatcher, which also has access to the model, utilizes a set of heuristics to decide what to do with the lot in question (which machine to send it to) and what to do with the machine in question (which lot to load into it). Control is then passed back to the simulator and the cycle continues. The Fab-Tactical system schedules by building Gantt charts (individual machines on the Y-axis, time on the X-axis, and lots as the bars on a machine across time). With access to the same model, the scheduler uses heuristics to order the machines (according to a bottleneck index, for example), and to order the lots (according to a lateness index, for example). Working up and down these lists, the scheduler uses additional heuristics to place jobs into position on the Gantt chart.

Although both systems rely heavily on heuristics, neither can be classified as an expert system. This stems from the fact that neither system attempts to model the way in which humans schedule fabs, and from the fact that none of the staff currently performing the scheduling task consider themselves to be experts. Some of the heuristics were suggested by the scheduling staff, but others were gathered from the Operations Research literature or synthesized by the software development team. In any case, the training lessons related in the following sections are based on our interaction with the current fab scheduling decision-makers including the manufacturing management, shift managers, area supervisors, and fab floor personnel mentioned previously.

2.2. Training the Manufacturing Participants

Fortunately, the manufacturing personnel for whom the scheduler was designed are computer-literate. Training them to use the applications did not require anything out of the ordinary. One- to-one hands-on sessions supported by well-written user manuals has been adequate thus far. Unfortunately, the intended users had no previous experience with AI software. This precipitated a number of interesting issues which we have had to address with training as the projects proceeded. These centered around how to think about the software development project itself, and how to think about the results of the project. Some of the issues encountered were anticipated given our knowledge of the personnel involved (at least in a generic sense), while others came as surprises and had to be handled dynamically.

Training the participants in problem and solution definition: Given the combinatorics and dynamics involved in the fab scheduling problem, it was not surprising that the users had trouble formulating a clear definition of the problem. Much discussion was required to construct a list of the manufacturing entities and relationships which should be considered, and be sure that the members of the list formed the necessary and sufficient set. Given that no one with whom we interacted was willing to claim expert scheduler status, especially the people currently assigned to perform the scheduling task, neither was it surprising that the users also had trouble providing a clear definition of the current manual and mental solution methodology. In fact, a number of ideas were collected, but it is questionable whether they are actually used when the person who suggested them is under pressure, or whether they seemed like good ways to work if only there was enough time to employ them. Similar difficulties were expected and encountered in trying to clearly state the deficiencies in the existing solutions and the desired characteristics of the new solutions. There was a general feeling that the schedules produced by the staff could be better, but not a very clear idea of how bad they are or how much better they could be. Furthermore, since the AI approach was very new to the users, it was difficult for them to know what they could ask for in the new system. Dealing with these problems turned into training by giving examples and training by asking questions in most cases. Whether this training will carry over into the next project is currently an open question.

Training the participants in the role and capabilities of AI: One of our main surprises was that the users had read enough about AI in the popular press and trade journals to have weakly held opinions, generally negative. Some believed that AI was still a topic that was under study at universities, or, at most, was being evaluated for military applications. Others had seen exaggerated claims about AI capabilities and so, as practical engineers, felt that the technology was probably useless. Both groups were partially convinced of the feasibility of our project by descriptions of some of the AI-based systems which have been installed and proved in other industries on problems of similar difficulty to fab scheduling. They were even more convinced once a prototype was ready for demonstration.

At this point, opinions moved to the other extreme. Questions were now asked about how the AI-based scheduler could provide such good answers so quickly when the engineers involved would have to take much longer to produce a schedule of lesser quality. We believe this to be a reflection of the fact that AI programs work through inference methods and knowledge representations which users find to be foreign concepts in their experience with "normal" computer programs. For example, the users believe that they comprehend the basics of how a database management system works since they can imagine how they could do the task themselves with a piece of paper and a pencil. The computer simply does it faster, but probably works in much the same way that they do. Some of these questions have been answered by giving the users insight into how the program actually does work. We hope this training on what can realistically expected from AI applications and how they basically work will carry over into the future and will be made more concrete as our current applications go into routine use.

As the users came to realize this was different than many of the number-crunching applications which they had received in the past, they began to realize that the installation of this application might change their jobs. They recognized the AI applications were also different than some of the database applications with which they were familiar which collected data and provided reports about the way they had been doing things all along. These large-scale AI applications had the potential to change the way things would be done. And this meant that their jobs might be somehow different than they had been all along. Whether this will prove to be true, and in what ways things will change awaits the integration of the schedulers into the day to day operation of the fab. How to train the users to cope with this situation remains an open question.

Training participants in their software development role: Another surprise for the development team came when we had to train the users concerning their involvement in the AI project. In retrospect we should have anticipated this difficulty. After all, the users were familiar with the development of "normal", more algorithmic software. They we accustomed to have some brief discussions with a software team, and then at some later time having software installed and ready for their use. The fact that we spent a considerable time with them asking all sorts of questions before we started to design the system caused some surprise. The fact that we continued to interact with them during development by showing prototypes and asking for help in debugging and in assessing solution quality caused even greater surprise. The fact that they were the only ones who could maintain the heuristic knowledge (whatever that meant) contained in the system after we had installed it was a revolutionary concept. Training by discussion and experience has helped with these difficulties.

2.3. Training the Non-Users

This idea of changing the users' jobs has turned out to be the biggest surprise, or at least the farthest reaching surprise encountered in the projects so far. Changing the job of the user has an effect on the person who managers the user. It also has an effect on the personnel who the user manages. The people who supply data to and receive data from the user have been impacted in some ways. Certainly the co-workers who support the user's hardware and software have noticed the change if for no other reason than the appearance of AI workstations and programs in LISP. And soon the training staff who support the user as well as the rest of the manufacturing environment will also experience repercussions. We currently believe these to be the biggest training issue that we face in developing and deploying custom-built AI-based applications in manufacturing. We are rapidly becoming aware of the fact that if you change the job of one member of a team, you change the jobs of all of the people on the team.

One of the most urgent issues which we face is the recalibration of the expectations of the users' management. On one hand, the managers must understand that we are producing an aid for the user, not a replacement. On the other hand, the manager must realize that the aid is a powerful tool which may change the nature of the workplace. The manager must facilitate the changes and monitor them to assure that they are proceeding smoothly. Ideally this means that the manager will work proactively, but this assumes that the manager has a complete, correct set of expectations about what the changes could be and has decided among the options. Today this is simply not the case. We will have to learn from experience, and then convert this experience into training for the future. During this "learning from experience" phase, the manager will have to become able to distinguish between how well the tool is performing (to a some extent, a part of the user's old job) and how well the user is applying the tool (to some extent, a part of the user's new job). The manager will have to start to evaluate the user in some new ways. How well is the user adapting to the new way of working? Is the user making different use of time and resources? Is the user effectively assisting his subordinates to adapt?

The other urgent issue which we will soon face is the recalibration of the expectations of the users' subordinates. In the case of the scheduling applications, the subordinates will receive much more detailed work instructions in a much more timely fashion than they do currently. On one hand, they could view this as requiring them to do much less thinking and could perceive their jobs as becoming much less interesting. On the other hand, they could think of this as welcome relief from some of the drudgery of their jobs and as an opportunity to take much more interest in important topics which they have previously neglected. They might, for example, become much more proactive on quality or preventive maintenance issues, work on broadening their skill set or strengthening the team bonds, and so on. The training issue is to predispose the subordinates towards the latter set of constructive options rather than allow them to be drawn toward the former set of destructive possibilities.

As our project goes forward, others in the manufacturing environment will be impacted. The users' data sources have already been impressed by the fact that the AI-based schedulers are much less forgiving of incomplete, incorrect, or late data than were their human predecessors. The hardware and software maintenance organization which services our users is being forced to acquire new skills, or to attract new people who already have the skills. That organization has been impressed by the facts that the skills are not trivial to acquire and that the people with the skills are not easy to find. Undoubtedly, more training issues will surface with time.

3. Future Training Models

Our initial training models served us well during the initiation phases of bringing large and small AI applications to Intel. As discussed, however, the initial models are too narrow and are in need of further refinement and expansion.

3.1. Future Training for User-built Intelligent Job Aids

No change in basic methodology is foreseen, that is, future training through one-on-one help and formal classes will continue. As no IJA user skill problems were observed, the brief but personalized training given to IJA users and application trainers will continue. No refinement or expansion in content planned for this audience.

Training for experts developing IJA's: As discussed above IJA developers exhibited the need for further training in aspects of PC use, in program management and in problem solving. The PC prerequisite screening will be more detailed and include facilitated registration into a PC skills class for those with identified deficiencies. The addition of a half day class on problem definition, abstraction, and decomposition is being considered. If possible, a simple screening will be developed to identify which expert's should attend this session. The standard expert system shell training course will be essentially unmodified in content. However, we propose to change its timing be from a two-day (sixteen hour class) to a series of four hour classes across four days. The change in timing is to facilitate the learning and application process as well as to be more congenial with the daily environment in which the experts work.

Training for managers and supervisors: We are considering the significant expansion of this segment in both scope and audience. The goal of this training is to change the manufacturing infrastructure to one that fosters and promotes IJA development and use. A four to eight hour course providing a detailed description of an ideal infrastructure, its required resources, together with successful examples of how to implement the changes is proposed. The course will include problem solving sessions, using Intel's Continuous Improvement Process methodology, to help the managers identify concrete action plans for their particular situation. The course will also focus on how the development and presence of IJA's in the workplace will influence the performance review process. Performance evaluation criteria to be used in assessing the contributions of the developers and users will be suggested. These criteria are not yet finalized.

Board of Advisors: We are also creating a board of advisors composed of IJA "superusers" to assist the Knowledge Application Lab in defining and refining our support and training directions. These advisors are IJA developers and users, and are members of the various manufacturing organizations. Their perspective and first hand experience will be valuable in setting more effective tactical and strategic plans for the future.

3.2. IJA's as Trainers

We have not pursued IJA's as tools of explicit pedagogy. Nevertheless, the presence of IJA's in the workplace appears to have the potential of enhancing our training productivity for specific task training of the manufacturing staff. The IJA leverages a workers core skill set enabling them to perform beyond their normal capability. Although the IJA's are not designed as explicit intelligent training systems, we have observed, as discussed in the IJA examples above, an implicit training effect on the users of IJA's. These observations are shared by other companies as well. The disk drive repair expert system in use at IBM is said to reduce the time it takes a beginning technician to become thoroughly competent from eighteen months to about three months. The results at IBM are believed to not be due solely to the presence of an IJA but also to the management policy which tracks and rewards speed and accuracy of repair. The technicians naturally use the tool whenever it will increase their own repair speed [4] In reference to IJA use an IJA developer is quoted as saying, "A lot of the questions just aren't asked any more. The users have learned the answers. They don't use the system nearly as much as they used to" [5]. It might be said, for these examples, that instead of training users to use IJA's, the IJA's are training users to not use IJA's. We do not view the cessation of IJA use as bad, given the caveat that the systems are not allowed to atrophy but are expanded to include new situations as they are recognized. Not all IJA's at Intel fall into disuse nor are expected to. Those of larger size or those that recommend equipment adjustments based on qualitative and quantitative calculations appear to contain enough esoteric information that, without explicit training and memorization, the users have not grasped the full scope of knowledge contained in the IJA.

3.3. Knowledge Erosion: "Use It Or Lose It"

It is proper to concern ourselves with the question of knowledge erosion. Will the experts lose their abilities to solve problems in the domains where AI solutions are in use? Will the organization self sufficiency be jeopardized by the application of machine versus human intelligence? Our experience to date suggests the answer is no. We say this for several reasons. First, we observe that the tools have a measurable training effect; that is, they increase the average human knowledge within the organization. The AI solution is a convenient repository for the orderly expression of domain knowledge allowing for more efficient knowledge review. Secondly, true experts are continually called upon to solve problems which extend beyond the boundaries of the AI tool. These human supplied solutions exercise the entire domain knowledge of the expert. Finally, AI solutions allow the human to solve or manipulate problems at higher levels of abstraction. In scheduling for example, the AI tools can handle

[4] Feigenbaum, E.; preface remarks to an invited panel discussion: "Results from a Study of the First Wave of Expert System Applications to Business", AAAI-88, August 21-26, 1988, St. Paul, MN. Dr. Feigenbaum reviewed the results of surveys gathered by a team of researchers. The survey results are in press, scheduled for release in late Q3 1988.

[5] PC Week; May 17, 1988, pp C/17 and C/20.

the detailed schedule preparation freeing the human to focus on the more important issues of scheduling strategies and tradeoffs.

3.4. Training for Custom-built AI Systems

Our current development model serves as the basis for the changes in our training model which we will be testing and further refining in the future. The first step in our normal development scheme consists of spending time with the user until we believe that we understand the problem, and until the users believe that we understand the problem. We consider these two sets beliefs as equally important. The second step involves the rapid delivery of a prototype user interface. Nothing that we have found assures that we really did understand the problem as well as this prototype interface, even though it uses canned data. Neither have we found a better way to crystallize the users' expectations of the system than use of the prototype interface. Our users have been especially delighted if this prototype appears early, and returns often with thoughtful responses to their constructive criticisms. These steps position us for the most realistic way we have found to attack problems of the level of difficulty of fab scheduling. In the beginning, we put the simplest AI-based core behind the user interface developed in step two which can give useful solutions to the problem defined in step one. We listen carefully to the users' evaluation as we develop a stronger core, usually based on the simpler previous one. At the appropriate time, we install the stronger core, usually undetected by the users (since they only see the user interface) except for the production of better answers in a shorter time than before. This process terminates when we detect that we have either provided a system which completely satisfies the users, or have run out of ideas to noticeably improve the core.

Modifications to this sequence for training reasons are based on a very specific philosophical perspective. We do not believe that we can or should train the users or their associates concerning the ways that they should change their environment to gain maximum benefit from the software tools and aids which we provide. These must be their decisions, even though we are judged, to a degree, by how well they do. We do believe, however, that we should make the entire manufacturing community aware as soon as possible, and as often as possible, of the issues which might be encountered and the ways in which the issues might be handled. The modifications to our way of doing business follow from this viewpoint.

We should add a new introduction to our program, one that precedes our current first step of problem definition. This new step should address technology definition, and serve to calibrate the whole of the community concerning the realistic strengths and weaknesses, costs and benefits of current AI techniques.

In the past, we have tried formally and informally to tell people about these expectations. We now see that telling is not enough. Training is required. We should then carry on with our three step development methodology, but with a major addition. More of the people impacted by the delivery of the application should be more involved in all three steps of our development sequence, especially the users' management and subordinates. It is particularly important to involve these personnel in the discussion of the characteristics of the desired deliverables. This is the first point at which the effects on the manufacturing environment can begin to be comprehended. In fact, there may be different design and development pathways, each with different implications for the working environment. The manufacturing community should be aware of the possibilities as early as possible and carefully make their decision before the software development team produces a system which solves the problem, but doesn't fit the infrastructure. Furthermore, many of the personnel involved should be invited to comment on the prototype interfaces and cores as they are delivered. This is partly to keep them updated on progress and to let them see how their comments have been incorporated. But it is mainly to keep the infrastructure issues squarely in front of them, over and over. These difficult issues can only be successfully resolved through detailed consideration and discussion by all involved, and these efforts take time.

4. Conclusions

Intel's initial experience suggests that both large custom systems and small user-developed IJA's require the same general type of environment and training support. The majority of training needed is not in the use of the final tool. Many participants in the development process require assistance in the learning proper knowledge extraction and maintenance skills. The greatest challenges we see are not technical but rather organizational. The need for management and employee training in understanding how AI solutions will change their individual and organizational roles and responsibilities and in the setting of proper expectations for AI solutions is of great consequence. The development of an infrastructure and environment that promotes successful AI applications development and deployment requires not only formal training but also continual discussion and personalized attention. We do not believe that the trainers should dictate to the manufacturing sites what this infrastructure and environment should be. We do believe, however, that through education and teaching the trainer may facilitate the process of discovery that will lead each site to their own satisficing solution. Finally, we do not see the use of AI solutions as threatening the knowledge or skill base of the true experts; there will continue to be more than enough challenges left to hone their skills and stimulate their knowledge growth.

EXPERT SYSTEMS IN PRODUCTION AND SERVICES II
Th. Bernold and U. Hillenkamp (Editors)
Elsevier Science Publishers B.V., Amsterdam – Printed in The Netherlands

Transferring Experts Systems Technology to Business – The Use of Learning Contracts

John B. Wallace
Research and Programme Development Section
Management Development Branch
International Labour Office
Geneva, Switzerland

1. Introduction

Currently there is great interest in the business community in developing business applications of expert systems. But one of the major problems faced is the shortage of people who know how to develop and implement these systems. A company that is trying to solve this problem has several alternatives including:

- Subcontracting the whole process to specialists in AI;
- Trying to train and hire its own AI specialists.

One of the most promising approaches to this problem is the use of learning contracts. In this paper we will discuss how learning contracts can be used to transfer expert system technology to a company and give a few sample materials that can be used to start the process of using them.

1. Contractual Arrangements to Aid Technology Transfer

Technology is almost always transferred through some sort of project; a turnkey project, a build-and-operate project and so forth. The behaviour of the parties in a project closely follows the terms of the contract that binds them: cost-plus contracts, for example, often generate cost overruns, while fixed price contracts tend to result in quality compromises.

Contrary to what many people profess, technology is transferred through people. Unless the recipient can use the technology and make it work for him, there is no transfer. So when people say that they are in the technology transfer field, and all they do is construct turnkey facilities or sell equipment, it is best to take their word with caution: they may be doing nothing than building white elephants in the desert. In other words, it is an assumption of this paper that training and learning are involved in technology transfer.

In the training field typical contracts with trainers cover time and materials - the trainer are paid for preparing learning materials and for spending time in the classroom. A training institution or training department of a firm that is engaged in helping companies learn about expert system technology might hire some trainers who profess to know how to train people to develop and use expert systems. But what if these trainers failed to do their job? The clients who paid good money to send their employees on such courses would be understandable angry.

To protect its interests the training organisation must exert some sort of quality control. To protect itself against faulty preparation and delivery by the trainers, the typical training institution asks the participant how they liked the course, the instructor, the arrangements, etc. They then eliminate from future courses, the instructors who rated poorly by the participants. But this sort of quality control does almost nothing to assure that technology was transferred.

Such contractual arrangements only cover the reactions of the participants and are inadequate for controlling whether the participants actually learned anything or whether they were able to do anything with it back in their organisations. To overcome these weakness a number of organisations interested in technology transfer have developed what is called "negotiated learning contracts" which allow self-managed learning while providing a contractual backup to assure that learning occurs and is applied.

There are three parties to a typical learning contract: the learner(s), the boss and the trainer. To see why this is so, consider the relationship between a trainer who wants a time-and-materials contract and a boss who wants to make sure that his subordinates learn how to build and use expert systems. The trainer is naturally worried that the learners (selected by management) might be incapable of, or interested in learning such an arcane subject as expert systems. To lower this risk, the trainer might insist on knowing the learners before he signs a contract where his payment depends on whether they actually learn and apply what they learn. In fact in such situations it is in the trainer's interest to persuade the learners also to sign a contract stating that they would do all their power to learn about expert systems and to build and use one. But the learners might be reluctant to sign such a contract. They would want to be sure that their bosses are truly interested in the project. Otherwise, a boss might make demands on them at work that would leave no time or make it difficult for them to carry out their side of the bargain.

Thus learning contracts are based on three interlocking relationships. First, all three parties must be satisfied that learners have the intellectual capacity and the motivation to learn the required material with a reasonable chance of success. Second, the trainer and the learners must be convinced of the boss's commitment to cover the cost of the training, the time and the facilities to consolidate the learning and transfer it to business (usually through a real-life project) and the personal interest to support the learners while they carry out the projects. Third, the learners and the boss must be convinced that the trainer is capable of carrying the project to completion. When this triangular relationship exists, the transfer of the expert system technology to the company is likely.

2. A Typical Arrangement

An increasing number of companies interested in strengthening their capacity to build and apply computer-based expert systems have begun to set up learning contracts with groups specialising in these systems, such as computing departments of leading universities, especially in the United Kingdom. By treating the transfer process as a commercial contract, some such organisations have been able to demonstrate successful transfer of technology to client companies.

A typical programme begins with a traditionally taught three-day introduction to computer-based expert systems, attended by the prospective learners and their bosses. This phase consists of lectures, discussions, demonstrations and easy exercises to raise interest and give confidence. At the end of this phase, those who merely wanted to become familiar with the technology drop out. Those who remain are usually sufficiently committed to acquiring skill that they negotiate learning contracts.

Once the three parties – learners, trainer and boss – are satisfied of each other´s commitment and capability, a working and reporting schedule is drawn up that has the elements of a conventional software development contract, but with additional elements as well. For example, rather than one long contract, the project is broken up into several short contracts. The first contract might cover an in-house survey to find a suitable application and a literature review to determine how that application has been tackled elsewhere. Another contract might cover the detailed specification of the system and a third the development and testing of a prototype.

In typical contracts the learners are required to devote two days a week to the projects, until completion, usually about 10 months. In addition, learners fill in weekly time sheets which are countersigned by the boss and passed to the trainer, who is designated project manager.

At the end of each phase the learner writes a report which he presents to his boss and the trainer. The boss, in turn, must attend the milestone presentations. The trainer-project manager takes responsibility for directing the projects and uses project control charts to make sure the milestones are met.

In summary, negotiated learning contracts are a promising way of guiding the transfer of expert system technology from a specialised organisation to business application. These contracts leave no necessary elements to chance: the boss's interest and commitment, the learner's willingness and capability, and the trainer's capacity to transfer the knowledge and skill and the time and the money to carry the transfer projects to completion. Having laid out the framework for the transfer let us now turn to the types of learning materials that might be used in the first phase of such a project.

3. The Use of Case Studies to Introduce Expert Systems

Recently the author was faced with the task of designing learning materials for the first phase of a learning contract to transfer expert-system technology to several businesses. The materials were designed so that the participants could work in small "learning teams", because we had found that managers and technicians seem to learn much faster when they are given a learning task and a set of materials with which to complete the task. The materials consisted of a glossary of expert system terms, textual materials describing expert systems and a set of case problems.

One of those case problems is reproduced as annex 1 and can be used by trainers who are introducing managers to the issues they may face in introducing computer-based expert systems. The case concerns a person who must forecast the price of the shares of a company exactly two years in advance. The stakes are so high that the person is willing to spend a great deal of time and money on this one-shot task. He is surrounded by people who have some skill in building expert systems, and so he is tempted to develop an expert system for this task. But as the case unfolds it is not at all clear that this task is really one of pure forecasting. Elements of control are involved.

Consequently, whenever this case has been used a number of issues emerge about the nature of expertise, the nature of knowledge and the true domain of computer-based expert systems.

To use the case, it is suggested that the learners have at their disposal a good text on expert systems and a glossary of terms. Then the trainer may wish to follow three steps:

1. Hand out the case (annex 1) and arrange the participants in small, competitive groups. Give them 45 minutes to an hour to decide what they will recommend. Let each group present its suggestion pick the best set of solutions. This session should come up with a variety of solutions, in addition to the building of an expert system.
2. Hand out the first supplement (annex 2: "William's Crystal Ball-the meeting). Ask the participants to form groups and answer the questions before them. This session should come up with some details about how to build an expert system to help solve the problem.
3. Hand out the final piece (annex 3: William's Crystal Ball - The final meeting). This piece suggests combining an expert system with another strategy. Ask the participants to discuss this solution and critique it.

4. Annexes

4.1. Annex 1: The Case: Billy Bob's Crystal Ball

Billy Bob, a 23 year old student of Computer Science and Artificial Intelligence at Stanford University in Palo Alto, California, was shocked to learn that his beloved Grand Pa Buck had suddenly died back in his home town, Houston, Texas. Even though he and his grandfather had been very close, Billy Bob never dreamt that he would one day be the sole heir to Buck´s immense fortune - a one billion dollar oil company. Yet that was just what the will said - with one proviso: he would inherit all the assets of the company on his 28th birthday, if by his 26th birthday, he could deposit a sealed envelop with the trustees of the estate predicting the stock price of the company on his 28th birthday. In this "Grandfather clause" as Buck jokingly called it, it was explained that Buck was concerned that Billy Bob had gone away to get an education that might not prepare him to properly exercise his responsibilities. He didn´t want a "California Playboy" making crazy decisions, it said in the will.

Further, Buck had allowed for a margin of error. If the prediction was within 15% of the actual price, Billy Bob would get the whole company, if he was within 16 to 30%, he would get the half. If he missed by more than that, the company´s assets would go to The Home For Old Cowboys and Billy Bob would get an annual annuity of $ 100,000 for life.

"I'm in a one shot, hit or miss situation," Billy Bob mused. "Although I have three years to prepare, I must use my time wisely." After several days he decided to build an Expert System to help him. He could at least scrape up the cash to build a prototype. Furthermore, he was surrounded by some of the best potential knowledge engineers in the world, people who might jump at such a challenge in order to test their technology and generate publicity for their work. Third, he had learned from his professors and fellow students to distrust the farfetched, unscientific speculations of stock market analysts and economic forecasters, many of whom seemed to make self-serving forecast solely to fatten their commissions.

He began by collecting a "knowledge base" of historical data including the economic indicators of oil producing countries, past quarterly reports of Buck's company, information on the fluctuations of the prices and production figures of different types of crude oil, piles of old news letters and technical journals, and so forth. At first this "knowledge base" was physically just boxes of papers and an index on an ordinary data base on his PC clone.

An informal group of friends began to hang out with Billy (they tended to call him William now) and discuss the challenge. They began to concentrate on two knowledge domains: the company and its environment. Those who concentrated on the company looked at information such as in Figure 1.

One friend discussed the company with a stock broker and learned that he expected the stock to rise in the next three months from $ 40 a share to $ 44 a share. His reasoning was as follows:

About 6250 share holders owned 5% of the company. The typical share holder has about 200 shares of the company. In three months he expected the company's annual net income to be reported at about $ 9 million and the share holders could expect to receive about $ 3.75 per share. This should increase their value. He said that most investors felt the company to be solid and would continue its healthy growth in sales and profits. He felt confident that the shares would rise by 10% from $ 40/share to $ 44/share in the near term.

A friend majoring in finance told Billy that buying and selling are subjective and the path of public speculation was dictated by the level of trading. If a large amount of a certain stock is bought, people often assume that the "smart money" expects a larger return and they will join in purchasing that stock in order to get a piece of the expected return. This friend encouraged Billy Bob to try and control some of the volume of the trading in the company so as to influence the market price on the critical date. "Of course, that might sound like insider trading, what Ivan Bronsky is in jail for, but it seems quite common," he said.

Revenues:	in millions $	%
Sales (excluding excise taxes) and other operating revenues	107.0	
Dividends, interest and other revenues	10.0	
Total Revenues	1170.0	100
Costs and Expenses:		
Costs of products sold and operating expenses	33.0	28
Exploration expenses, including dry holes	21.0	18
Selling, general and administrative expenses	42.0	36
Interest expenses	0.5	
Depreciation	1.0	
Lease impairment	0.8	
Provision for federal and state income taxes	10.0	09
Total Costs and Expenses	108.0	92
Net Income	8.8	08
Number of publicly owned Shares	1.250.000	
Net Income per Share	7.00	
Dividends Per Share	3.75	

Figure 1. Statement of Consolidated Income in Buck´s Company (All figures in millions of US dollars expect per share data)

"I don't have the capital to follow your lead," Billy remarked. But was told he could form a syndicate of business partners to purchase the shares he needed to influence the price within some target range. He would also need to avoid getting so far in debt that the would be forced to sell company assets (That he doesn't even own yet). "Owning enough of the company to be able to influence prices would make me a "Wizard" because just like a wizard I would be casting a spell by buying or selling shares to control events," he concluded.

This role of wizard could be complemented by his computer programme which would be a kind of "fortune teller". The fortune teller and the wizard together would reinforce each other. One part of the fortune teller would be an expert system to predict, through fundamental analysis the reference price of oil per barrel. The system is illustrated in Figure 2.

The components shown in Figure 2 is connected with the "environmental knowledge domain". Those concentrating on this domain would gather data about consumption and production. They note for example that France imported 127 million tones of oil in 1977 and only 88 million in 1987. The friends also talked about the importance of going to OPEC countries and interviewing oil ministers. One said, "I could go to Nigeria, a country that currently exceeds its OPEC quota by 15% and claims that it must do so in order to service its debt. It uses the oil industry to lower unemployment - a threat to political stability. It even seems that the industry employs illegal immigrants from Cameroon."

Another friend who wanted to be a "knowledge engineer" suggested to go to countries like Iran and Iraq. He thought information concerning the price of oil after peace breaks out between them, would be vital.

As loyal as some of Billy's friends may have been, some remained critical about the use of a system as complex and as time-consuming to solve a problem like price prediction. One critic of the project was a major in organizational behavior. He argued that what was really needed was a simple P.C. into which one could program mathematical equations. The numerical values of the equations would be the subjective or objective values of various indicators. The effect of certain indicators on other indicators will be calculated and retained for future reference. His idea is illustrated in Figure 3 and 4.

Target Indicator: Texas oil price/Barrel	$ 18.00
Rule set by expert	IF: Price per barrel = $18.00 THEN: Net revenue above $ 40 million
Qualitative Transformation	$ 18/barrel = Ideal price
Expected Value of Indicator based on subjective values such as readings press releases, opinions:	between $ 18 and $ 19/barrel
Individual Indicators (each ones influence on the target indicator):	– a Mkt. price of oil – b Administrative expenses – c Operating expenses
Group indicators.(the influence of the group as a whole on the target indicator:	
Group 1 geographical	Weight attributed by expert
– a. Exploration expenses	40/100
– b. Mineral and soil content	30/100
– c. Environment protection	30/100
Group 2 economic political	
– a. Tariffs on foreign soil imports	30/100
– b. OPEC production quotas	40/100
– c. State and Fed taxes	30/100
Rule to show how an individual indicator can influence another indicator	IF: Operating Expense=$100,000 THEN: Oil price/barrel = $18.00 IF: Operating Expense = $400.000 THEN: Oil price/barrel =$19.00
Qualitative Operator: This operator associates the value of the consequence or out put, with that of the cause or input.	Consequence:oil price increase Cause:OPEC sticks to quota Operator:Cut in level of spending

Figure 2. Possible expert system to analyse oil prices.

No. of site engineers and chief executives	5000
No. of drilling sites	200
Drilling output capacity barrels/day	100'000
Current non OPEC price/barrel	$ 18
OPEC price/barrel	$ 19
Value of the Company´s total assets	$ 1 billion
No. of public share holders	6250
Share holder´s investment per person	$ 8000
% of company publicly owned %	5
Revenue from profit margin to go to share holders equity %	10

Figure 3. Some information about Buck´s company

Aim:

To get Mkt price/share over a period of time.

Given:

Current price/share	$ 40.00
% of company owned by share holders.	% 5
Engineering and Executive incentives	Increased wages
Innovation	Advanced drilling technology

Function:

1. Incentive / Innovation	=	Output.
2. Output / Oil Mkt Demand	=	Price of oil/barrel
3. Price oil X Output	=	Total Revenue
4. Total Revenue / % stock owned by S.H. Total cost	=	Perceived Mkt.Price/share.

Figure 4. A Friend´s Simple Model

Another friend who was majoring in finance suggested that Billy should not waste his time on electronic fortune tellers and wizards. "Make your best guess, put it in an envelop, relax on the beach. The best financial theorists have shown that share prices are a random walk. If that is so then an expert system that generated random numbers would be just as good as one with all the expertise in the world."

A friend majoring social psychology argued that stock markets operate on rumors. "When a company is about to announce its earnings," she said, "everybody in the market listens for hot tips and buys or sells a few days ahead of the announcement. If that is so your E.S. needs three components: the oil price forecaster, a company behavior simulator and a component to mimic the behavior of investors - it would look at oil prices and how the company is positioned, then predict the price."

4.2. Annex 2: William's Crystal Ball: The Meeting

«I have invited you all here tonight because you have all shown an interest in this project to predict the price of shares in Grand Pa Buck's company a few years from now. I have talked with many of you and found that there is a lot of agreement with the idea of brainstorming to decide on the best way to solve the problem.

I suggest that we form pairs and brainstorm in "Nominal Groups". That is each pair will come up with their best ideas quietly for a few minutes. Then we will share all the ideas and decide what to do. Let's start with some assumptions:

1. This is a task that must be done. I have to make a prediction on a certain date about a price two years later.
2. The best predictor of tomorrow's price, in the absence of any other information is probably today's price.
3. The information that we have been collecting is going on a data base and a spreadsheet. I expect also to build some simulations of the behaviour of the company, the market, etc. If we use AI techniques they should interface with keyboard input and the spreadsheet, at least.
4. We don't think there are any true experts. That is someone who routinely predicts the price of this stock, or any other stock on a certain date two years in advance and has a low error rate.
5. One way to start is to build a programme that, given past data will predict a current price. We could build a system and refine it little by little, getting it to make longer and longer predictions with a certain level of

accuracy. It doesn't even have to predict the price. It might say, "Two years from now, the price will be today's price, plus or minus a certain amount."

What questions should we try to answer tonight?

a What type of data should the system be asking for?
What is today´s date? What is the price? What date do you want the prediction for?

b. How should the system end its questioning?»

4.3. Annex 3: William's Crystal Ball - The Final Meeting

«Well it is a pleasure to meet this evening, as we have done so many times before in our effort to develop the expert system which will assist us in the pricing of Grand Pa Buck's corporate stock price on my birthday in two years. I think it is appropriate at this point to review the primary elements involved in our process to date:

Objectives and Parameters

1) In my typical think-big Texan style, I decided right from the start my objective; to obtain control of the company in its entirety, thus I required the prediction of a stock price which was within 15% of the actual value, this being in accordance with Grand Pa's rules.

2) I liked the idea of influencing the stock price as this method would provide us with a reduced probability of "prediction variance". It was necessary to set primary constraints on this option. First we will not take on any additional debt in the process, second, the disposition of assets is not an integral part of our strategy, and third, we must conduct all our business in a legal and ethical manner.

Strategy:

1) With the use of an expert system we should be able to predict the stock price to within a reasonable reality, however, we know that the volatility of the market could throw us off and exceed the boundaries of our %15 percent limit. If the expert system can put us within %35 of the actual then we will be in good position to perform the second half of our strategy.

2) With our expert system price in hand we will add ca. %25 premium to the price to determine a final stock price to seal in the envelope to be opened on my birthday in two years. Why if the expert system uses all its knowledge to predict a stock price will we exceed it by %25? Simply because my market experts have told me that if we made an offer to the shareholders to purchase the shares at a %25 premium to the market price, the shareholders will react positively and the market will adjust to reflect the new market price as put forth in the tender offer prospectus.

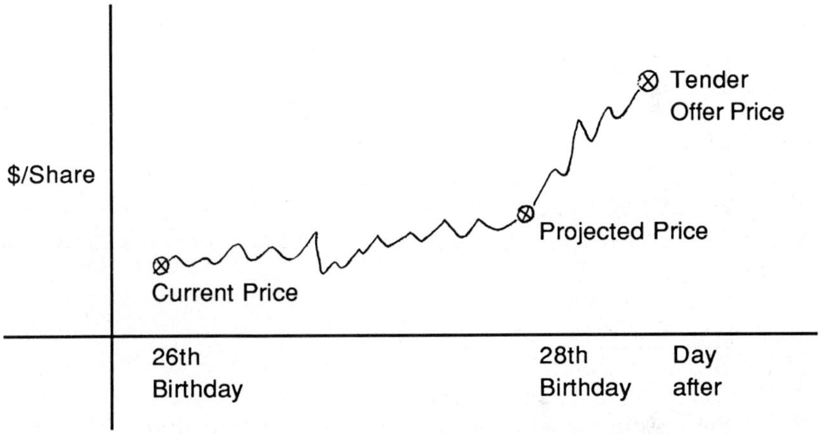

Figure 5. Estimated Share Price and Impact of Tender Offer

3) As the tender offer will be made one day before my birthday in order to allow the market enough time to react to the public news of the offer, the day of my birthday the enveloped price should equal within %0.5 of the actual price. Now I know some of you had concerns that to pay a %25 premium on the entire stock issue will cost a lot of money and will mean either debt or sale of assets. Well "don't worry, be happy" as our strategy does not end here.

4) As is typical and required of all tender offers to shareholders, there has to be a shareholders meeting where they vote "yes" or "no" to the offer price. If they vote "yes" they soon receive a check for their shares. If they vote "no" then the market will usually wait to see if a higher offer will come back. Well I have arranged with a private banker in Geneva to buy up %51 of the %5 shares that are outstanding. Why? Because in the voting meeting that will be held approximately three weeks after we

make the tender offer we will majority and will vote "no" to the offer. The result is clear: the whole tender offer falls-through with the vote but this is only after I have received full control of the company on the date of my birthday. I will then pay the Geneva banker a tidy $1,000,000 management fee, leave %5 of the stock outstanding on the market and I have control of the company in the end.

4.4. The Expert System

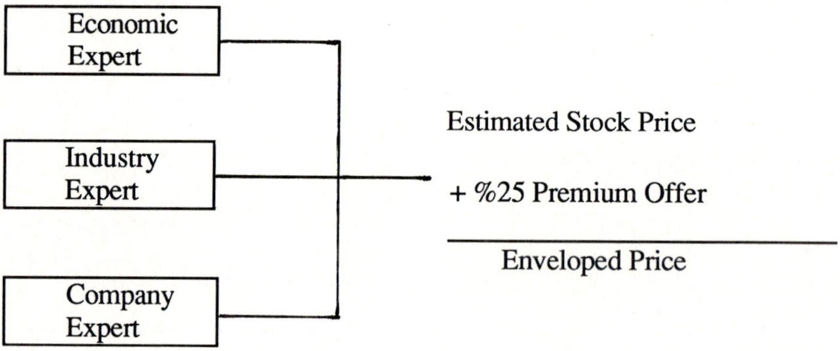

Figure 6. Expert System Framework

4.4.1. Expert System Knowledge Domains

I. Economic Environment

Knowledge Base	Knowledge Prompt
economic expansion is good for corporate profits	Is the economy in a re-cession, level, or expanding phase? For how long?
rates are major stimulus/ dampeners of the economy & stock markets.	Are interest rates increasing, decreas-ing or stable?
stock market, housing starts, consumer spending, constitution permits, etc.	What is the current trends in the leading economic indicators?
Reagan was a spender, what about Bush.	What is the attitude of the US Admini-stration?

II. Industry Environment

Knowledge Base	Knowledge Prompt
crude oil prices & retail petro-prices	What are the primary variables impacting on corporate revenues
economic output (i.e. industry demand for energy)	What impacts the demand for the industry products?
alternative energy sources (gas, nuclear, coal)	
energy conservation	
OPEC production Non-OPEC production	What impacts the supply of industry products?
drilling costs per barrel, North Sea ($17), Saudi, Arabia (3$)	What are the primary variables impacting
Northern Canada ($13), U.S. ($15)	
taxes, Royalties, government incentives	

III. Company Environment

Knowledge Base	Knowledge Prompt
develop a price-sensitivity analysis for every $1 increase in the price of oil, what is the impact on revenues. This figure determines the company risk.	What was the company's revenue at pany´s revenue at $10, $11, $12, $13 per barrel crude prices?
price earning ratio	What were the company's share prices relative to earnings at the various oil prices?
relative industry positioning and comparative analysis.	What is the industry average in terms? of the price/earnings ratio?
offers a measure of Beta, the measure of the stocks movement relative to the market as a whole. This figure will determine the relative market risk.	What was the company's coefficient correlation to the market when the Dow Jones was at 1500, 1700, 2000?
determines the estimated growth rate and future expected dividend stream.	What were the last 5 years of dividends and stock prices?

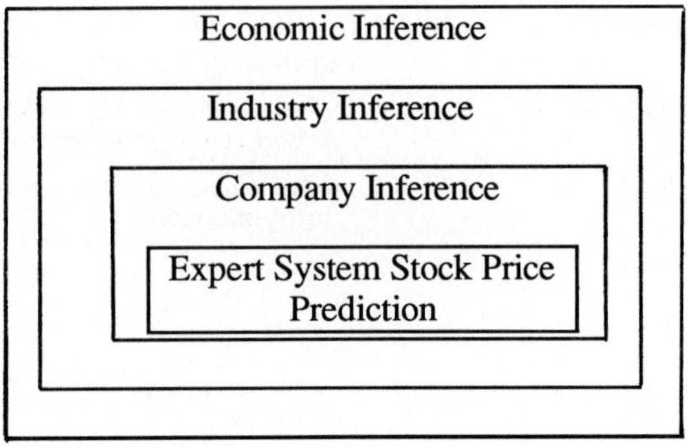

Figure 7. Inference Engine

4.5. Annex 4: Ten years later.

Well I wonder what old Grampa Buck would think of me now sitting here on the beach in California - long hair and all, living the life of a playboy? How was I to know that the Geneva banker would strike a deal with a large US merchant bank, offer a %45 premium, vote "yes" at the meeting, then subsequently do a leveraged buyout of the whole company? I did learn one thing - that expert systems can only assist in the decision making process, they do not provide direction in a world of rapidly changing environments. Well I guess Grampa would not be to upset at me sitting here on my private beach . Who would have known that I ended up selling over $1.5 billion worth of an expert system called "Grampa-Knows-Best", which is used to predict the price of petroleum stocks».

EXPERT SYSTEMS IN PRODUCTION AND SERVICES II
Th. Bernold and U. Hillenkamp (Editors)
Elsevier Science Publishers B.V., Amsterdam – Printed in The Netherlands

The Setting of Today's Education and Training with Regard to the New Technologies

Henk Koster
Consultant
OECD
Organisation for Econonomic Co–Operation and Development
Paris, France

Before introducing you to the theme 'The setting of today's education and training with regard to the new technologies' I would like to congratulate the organizers, ILO, Gottlieb Duttweiler Institute, Arthur Andersen and Office for technology assessment, on the excellent quality of this workshop and its socio-cultural context. I further wish to thank them on behalf of OECD for the invitation to disseminate the results of some of its work.

I deem it useful to inform you briefly of what OECD stands for: the organization for economic co-operation and development started its work in 1961 with the aim of, inter alia, promoting economic growth of its member countries (at present 24, i.e., the industrialized democracies, Yugoslavia having a special observer status) through discussion and co-operation on economic policy. In fact, the OECD is much older than 27 years as it forms the continuation of the organization for European economic co-operation which was in charge of implementing the post-war marshall plan aid, and it is much broader than 'European' as, in alphabetical order, Australia, Canada, Japan, New Zealand and the United Status are also full members of this organization.

Within OECD's organization you will find a directorate for manpower, social affairs and education, and closely related to that directorate is the center for educational research and innovation. This CERI is not itself a research institution but promotes and co-ordinates research. It is also in a good position to promote the dialogue between research and policy-making committees. One of CERI's projects at this time focuses on the relations between the introduction of new technologies and human resource policies (new technologies and human resources development: the service sector), in particular with respect to the consequences for education and training (1). It is not specifically es or ai oriented; in formulating our key research questions, we took as our starting point that skill profiles and skill formation are affected by a number of transformations (e.g. Internationalisation, new technologies, blurring). specific situations may therefore well be due to both technological change and particular cultural and historical conditions. In an earlier phase of this research project the focus 2 was on technological change in the automobile industry in five countries (ford, USA; Toyota, Japan; Volvo, Sweden; Volkswagen, Germany; and Renault, France (2). We changed our focus to the service sector as this is the main and fastest growing employer in OECD member countries, and some additional countries joined our project (Belgium, Italy, Netherlands, Yugoslavia). annex no. 1 might give you an idea of the service sector's growth, employing in 1985 roughly close to 60% of total civilian employment for the countries then participating in our project.

However, work is being carried out not only within CERI--nor only within the service sector--but also through much wider OECD activities related to technology and new technologies (3). In annex no. 2, OECD's programmes in relation to nt's are reproduced

Of these, apart from CERI's project, in particular those under chapter iv are of great importance to the present subject. In addition to that, OECD's ministers of labour requested the secretary-general to set up a group of distinguished experts to examine "the great potential importance of the new technologies for growth, jobs and welfare". This group, once established, was chaired by the former minister of education and former minister of industry of Finland, Ulf Sundqvist (4). I will mention later some of the major findings of a number of these activities.

In our CERI project (5), observations from the preceding research in the automobile industry have been confirmed, namely that the impact of technological change upon work content, employment and skills cannot be understood in isolation from the effects of structural changes in the division of labour between enterprises on the one hand and of changes in management styles and procedures affecting work content and functional relations inside enterprises on the other. Concepts like deregulation, blurring, externalisation and internationalisation explain the rapid expansion of the service sector and, as a consequence, strongly influenced manufacturing. increasingly, existing service functions are externalised (e.g. Specialized functions related to the use of sophisticated information technology as well as routine tasks of data processing, cleaning, etc.), And also new types of services (market research, introduction and servicing of new information systems, adaptation of work procedures and personnel management). New modes of transport and communication enforce these trends even at a global scale (6). According to the New York Times of 14

December 1986, some American firms are transferring routine data processing and other service jobs to Asia, the Caribbean, Ireland and other places where people can be hired at lower costs.

CERI's research is not done in what might be called "an ivory tower": it is done with both feet on the ground and to a great extent through case studies. our results are therefore subsequently based on daily practice. As a consequence, our results are not yet ready for generalization but seem to be already policy relevant. in our enterprise studies, some important issues were observed which deserve closer attention. Referring to all of these findings would take too much time: in order to gain time for the main subject, the key words of these findings are shown in annex no. 3.

Some of these topics are also to be found in a report by Peter Schefe, recently distributed by ILO, entitled "expert systems-present state and future trends; impact on employment and skill requirements (an assessment)". But we should be very careful in comparing nit's with es and ai. we will return later to some of the topics mentioned in annex 3.

As you will understand, all these issues will have repercussions for education and training which might be illustrated briefly with findings from the banking sector. Both in an EEC report by Rene Eksl on "employment trends within the banking sector in EEC countries" and in relation to a presentation by Mr. Rajan, as well, in the OECD publication "human resources and corporate strategy" - technological change in banks and insurance companies" (7) it is emphasized that the banking sector has a problem with the composition of its workforce in terms of skill structures in relation to management structures. where Rajan presents a rather segmented pyramidal structure, Noyelle and Bertrand discern for the purposes of new competencies upper-tier workers, middle-tier workers and lower-tier workers. In the first category there is a growing need for high-level specialists as distinct from traditional operating managers. these high-level specialists must complement operating managers. Traditional managers tended to be trained as generalists, but increasingly firms must find high levels of expertise and these new, higher-level skills must often go hand in hand with a strong capacity to interact with others as these new specialists are called upon to create and develop new products and systems meant to be responsive to the needs of their final users. Parallel to this development, operating managers are moving away from skills that once simply executed policies discussed by senior management towards competencies for setting strategic goals, sharing information with subordinates, motivating individuals, etc.

These changes met by upper-level personnel are being matched by shifts affecting middle-tier workers, in particular a shift from specialized skills for routine to less specialized and broader competencies for defining problems and finding solutions themselves instead of applying prefab-solutions to standard problems. A continued shrinking in the firm's need for low-level clerical skills characterizes the drive on lower-tier workers. These trends are reflected quantitatively in annex no. 4.

Our OECD study finally concludes that to meet these challenges for skills first of all, a much higher level of formal preparatory education is required. Secondly, skill formation should aim at expanding interactional skills to increase customer assistance and sales efforts. Further, there is a need for expanding high-level technical expertise as well as a growing need for entrepreneurship, especially among middle-level professional and managerial personnel.

It may be clear from this example that arriving at new skill competences is not only a task for initial education, nor is it exclusively a task for governments and formal education systems or is it simply an educational or economic problem. In "the economist" of 10th September, a study is mentioned ('homelessness in Chicago', by Michael Sosin, Paul Colson and Susan Grossmann, the Chicago community trust) which indicates that "homelessness stems from poverty caused by too few unskilled jobs...A lack of education...". our task, therefore, is not only an economic one, but may be also primarily a social and humanitarian one. One of the papers for OECD's intergovernmental conference on education and the economy in a changing society (Paris 16 - 18 march 1988) reads that "the state, enterprises and individuals may all share in meeting the costs of skill training and further education, and the extent of such participation determines the training facilities available to the individual. The way the costs are shared also indicates the degree to which vocational education and training is regarded either as beneficial to the community as a whole (relatively large government share), beneficial to specific groups (relatively large share borne by enterprises) or beneficial to the individual (who then also pays a relatively large share of the costs)". (8)

The required changes, therefore, do have an impact on the whole structure of education and training institutions, whether in the formal educational system or the informal. The main challenge lies on the one hand in relation to their capacity to raise the education level of young people entering the labour force and to avoid an early elimination of some of them whose basic level would be insufficient. On the other hand, they should be able to promote new attitudes such as creativeness, adaptability, capacity to adjust to a changing environment, etc. The central question in this respect is what balance should be constructed between the internal system (i.e. The in-school system providing basic knowledge and a preparedness and interest for further training) and the external system

tem (i.E. The out-of-school system providing the specific skills for the occupational role). This new equilibrium will of course be defined not only in terms of curriculum but also of resources. In other words, will companies take a greater responsibility for the development and training of their personnel by increased in-company training and how much of the necessary training will be provided by other sources? (9)

The organizers asked OECD to embark upon "today's education and training". But tomorrow has already started yesterday, whilst in educational terms today is not a fixed concept but a process of continuous change. It goes without saying that initial education and its adjustment is of great importance to the individual, to the economy and to society as a whole. But you will, I hope, not expect me to give concrete answers regarding specific changes in the curriculum. In the report by peter Schefe, which I mentioned earlier, some indications have been given in this respect. others, as well, have touched upon curriculum issues. I do not think I am in a position to be able to present to you recommendations which are highly political in nature and, moreover, have to be implemented at national level in its particular socio-cultural context. At this moment, I cannot but repeat what has been said in the previously mentioned Sundqvist report that the education system needs to provide workers with an adequate basis for the later acquisition of new skills, and to facilitate the movement of workers between industries, occupations and employers.

This implies a more flexible response by the education authorities to the changing pattern of occupational skills, but above all a higher minimum threshold of competences for all young people if they are to compete in the fast-changing labour market. These competences provide the basis for long-term flexibility and should be combined with subsequent training opportunities which facilitate transition into working life and provide an adequate supply of creative and highly qualified people. To achieve the necessary degree of responsiveness in the education system, teachers themselves have to be retrained.

Education and training systems will increasingly be required to meet the demands of modern production processes. As we have seen before, new technology tends to change work organization and job content towards greater emphasis upon qualities like teamwork, initiative, creativity, entrepreneurship, problem-solving, multi-skilling and openness to change. many of these characteristics cannot be developed at the workplace but depend on appropriate education and socialization particularly experienced in schools. (10)

We already touched upon the issue of teacher training. Here also we are confronted with a subject which can only be dealt with in a superficial and unsatisfactory way because of limited time. The new objective of training will increasingly emphasize the fostering of an enquiring approach to encourage and stimulate action and creative responses to problems. So, it is no longer a question of designing a profile of a teacher to suit a particular society, but rather of starting the teacher off on a process of constant reformulation of his functions and his skills. And, therefore, they need to be given the tools to ensure that they are able to cope with reality and with facts. (11) OECD/CERI will devote a special conference to this subject in Novisad (Yugoslavia) which might give you an idea of the importance of this issue.

There are a number of reasons justifying the focus of our attention on the further education and training of adults. Far from being exhaustive, we point to the relative aging of the population as a result of rises in life expectancy and falling fertility rates. The latter leads to a relative aging of the labour force because of a slowly growing (and sometimes decreasing) number of labour force entrants. Of course, there are, as well, political, economic, education and cultural reasons for underlining adult education, but our demographic data represent the facts and are not subject to further interpretation.

You will find these data in annex 5 and they were specially prepared for the meeting of OECD's manpower and social affairs committee at ministerial level (6 - 7 July 1988). Even if we take into account a wide margin of error regarding younger age cohorts and a decline of the relative share of education in social expenditures, it is certainly not too early to give thought to these tendencies.

So we will be confronted with at least two categories of adults:

Firstly, adults seeking to requalify themselves for entirely different occupations cannot succeed without further training and education. This requires improved cooperation between education, enterprise and the trade unions. The reforms now being contemplated in member countries should benefit from open dialogue between the educational establishment and all the parties that have a stake in educational outcomes, including the social partners as well as labour market and regional development authorities. an active society requires education and training throughout life. (12)

Secondly, there will be a growing group of incumbent adults that either should be retrained or should follow refresher courses, be it as a result of structural shifts in the occupational composition of employment or because of new production, new technologies or by changes affecting traditional sectoral divisions (blurring) and the diversification and interpenetration of formerly distinct work functions and occupations (13). In both cases, "recurrent education" seems to be the key concept. Again, you will have noted that new technologies only form one of the factors with an impact on education and training systems. Two issues should be dealt with here in more detail: The first one relates to the tendency, as indicated above, regarding the gradual distribution of organized learning opportunities in favour of adults, not only for demographic reasons, but also because more adults and, increasingly, older adults participate in formal and informal education, training and skill formation at work and in educational institutions. Annexes 6.1 - 6.5 are intended to give you an idea of the participation in adult education and training, formal and informal. What is most interesting in view of the demographic trends is the participation in relation to age cohorts. Annex 6.1 shows the age distribution of enrollments in university and non-university higher education for a number of OECD member countries, of which column "plus 30" is very relevant in this respect.

We do not have aggregate data on an international comparative basis regarding participation in adult education in toto, although we might present to you some information on individual OECD member countries. For instance, in annex 6.2, We see the proportional recruitment to adult education in percentage of age cohorts and the proportion of birth cohorts reportedly engaged in education programmes in 1968, 1974 and 1981 in Sweden.

Similar tendencies are found for France annexes 6.3 and 6.4 and for Germany (annex 6.5). Two main conclusions may be drawn from these data: firstly, there is evidence of an increased participation in adult education and training courses. secondly, this increase is particularly clear for the higher age cohorts.

Systems of formal post-compulsory and higher education might thus be called upon to contribute more actively to the extension and broadening of learning opportunities for adults - opportunities which should respond to but also transcend specific training needs defined at the level of enterprises, in particular, education institutions would have to play an important role in helping adults to understand and cope with social and cultural change, essential to their capacity to take an active part in public life as citizens, consumers and members of different interest groups, cultural associations, etc.

The second issue relates to the fact that stronger involvement of education institutions in further education and training for adults would, however, present a serious challenge to education systems. besides an extension of teaching capacity, it would imply greater responsiveness from curricula and organizational frameworks to highly divergent and changing needs for skills and competences of both individuals and enterprises. (14)

But apart from teaching capacity and responsibilities, the financial aspects may certainly not be neglected. It is sometimes mentioned that the market aspects of adult education and training are insufficiently taken into account and that traditional institutions of post-compulsory and higher education should have to compete more actively for training candidates with private schools and multiple training associations of employers, unions, etc. (15) apart from the political aspects of the development of these training markets, it is important is that the extension and development of training markets could contribute to broader educational provision beyond the specific needs of enterprises but would these training markets really be able to meet the specific skill requirements of individual industries? some indeed would favour the latter.

In order to optimize the productive potential of recent technologies and to survive in increasingly more competitive markets, enterprises depend primarily upon the skill development of their adult labour force. the review of enterprise strategies and national policies of human resources development in the framework of the CERI project shows that many enterprises, and in particular large ones, are heavily engaged in the adaptation and development of the technical skills of more qualified workers as well as the permanent upskilling and training of their management staff. such investment in human capital is, of course, not new. however, it seems to have strongly increased in recent years. estimates of enterprise expenditure and of the numbers of workers involved in both formal and informal skill development are unfortunately rare, incomplete and not comparable across countries. (16)

Existing data do not always take into account financial efforts by enterprises through taxation. in Sweden and France, for example, a certain percentage of the turnover of enterprises flows into national training funds or is directly budgeted for training purposes. strong differences are observed between the training efforts of different groups of enterprises - differences related to sectorial particularities, the size of enterprises and their labour intensity as compared to capital intensity. training tends to be provided in capital-intensive rather than in labour-intensive activities, in big rather than in small enterprises and in developing rather than in declining economic sectors. our studies showed, inter alia, that great efforts are made by the automobile and service industries to train and retrain their workforce.

The responsibilities of the economic sector towards adult education and training is therefore two fold. on the one hand there is a general responsibility shared with other institutions to provide the economy with a qualified workforce. on the other, they are confronted with an educational challenge regarding individual skill formation.

Again, our data are rare and incomplete. if, for instance, you look at annex 7.1), the training efforts of the manufacturing sector seem almost negligible, which is in sharp contrast with the more detailed data on expenditure for overall vocational training by the private sector in relation to public expenditure for Germany (annex no. 7.2) or for the us (annex no. 7.3).

Anyway, important efforts in the field of training and skill formation have already been undertaken at the company level probably because the up-leveling of qualifications in all jobs of a tertiary character and the changing qualification profiles have led to relative shortages on the labour market as their demand for precise qualifications has (still?) only partially been met by the traditional educational system. it is no wonder therefore that we found interesting data in the reports regarding the investments companies make in training their personnel. these vary from 3 per cent of the total wage costs (in the finance sector in France) to 6.50 per cent for information service companies (also in France). (17)

In 1984 in the United States (compare with annex 7.3), employers spent at least 30 billion dollars for the formal training of 15 million trainees and 180 billion dollars on informal training in the enterprise. according to a recent survey of corporate education training, more than 50 per cent of the included companies report increasing participation of employees in training over the last five years. (18) in Germany, it is estimated that more than one million adult employees take part in formal courses of continuing education every year, half of which are provided by enterprises. in japan, about 80 per cent of all firms implement vocational training and one third of all workers participate in formal enterprise training per year. in France, enterprise expenditure for continuing training in the framework of the 1972 training act amounted to 14.7 billion francs in 1982, and covered 113.5 million training hours. (19)

However, all these efforts seem to be somewhat unrepresentative, somewhat elitist. still, the provision of training facilities is directly related to the size of the company (we noted this before) and it is the predominantly better educated and better paid participating in training programmes. in Sweden, for example, the highest income groups have an attending percentage in adult education which is twice that of the lowest income groups. (20)

In France, participation rates vary between 3.8 per cent for companies with more than 2,000 employees and 1.14 per cent for those with less than 20 employees. (21)

A considerable effort still has to be made also by the social partners. fortunately, this is recognized by both partners. in a joint meeting of management and trade union experts under the OECD labour management programme, it was explicitly recognized that "initial training should be financed by the state and the training of workers by the enterprises"...but..."that no (financing) system could be regarded as a (universal) model". (22)

A final important issue was raised as well, in that one of the prerequisites for an increase in resources available for training is the understanding on the part of all enterprises that training is not merely an outlay but an investment similar to that made in equipment. the potential productivity increase that new technologies are supposed to provide will only be achieved if the labour force is adequately trained and able to make the best use of them. in this respect, worthwhile results have been arrived at with what is called "integrated innovation". this is to say that the development of a new economy can only be successful - in particular when new technologies are at stake - if all parties involved form part of a cybernetic process. this is schematized in annex 8. this model has been developed by one of our consultants, prof. ford of the university of new south wales, who formulated it principally from his experiences in japan and Sweden. with regard to the impact of these processes of change on skills and skill formation, skill formation is more than education, training, experience, knowledge and personal development; it needs to be supported by the appropriate work organization and to be an integral part of technology transfer, organizational innovation and organizational integration. (23)

It is true, as the expression goes, that "knowledge is the only property which cannot be stolen". we should probably say "it cannot be stolen as long as it is not in the form of es or ai. anyway, it is very valid for skills. but both knowledge and skills are without worth in an environment that does not appreciate, develop and apply them.

Bibliography and References

1. For detailed information on this project, reference is made to documents CERI/CD(87)12 and CERI/CW/88.01, respectively, which outline the description and guidelines for the empirical phase of this project.

2. During this project, company reports were presented and expert studies were done. These papers are as follows:

Company Reports: Expert's Studies:

Ford, CERI/CW/84.01 CERI/CW/84.02

Toyota, CERI/CW/84.03 CERI/CW/84.04

Volkswagen, CERI/CW/84.05 CERI/CW/84.06

Renault, CERI/CW/84.07 CERI/CW/84.08

Volvo, CERI/CW84.09 CERI/CW/84.10

A synthesis report, entitled "New Technology and Human Resource Development in the Automobile Industry", OECD, Paris, 1986 (General Distribution), was written based on the above studies. Following the studies, it became evident that there was a need to extend the enquiry into the tertiary sector. A study was drafted by Dr. Olivier Bertrand (CEREQ) and Dr. Thierry Noyelle (Columbia University) under the title "The Evolution of New Technology, Work and Skills in the Service Sector, OECD, Paris, 1986 (General Distribution).

3. An inventory was prepared to determine the scope of the OECD's work related to technology: "Inventory of Recent and Ongoing OECD Work Related to Technology", Document CES/87.18.

4. The report of this group has been published by OECD (1988) under the title "New Technologies in the 1990's: A Socio-economic Strategy.

5. The results of this project are contained in the following national reports on the service sector:

France, CERI/CW/87.02

Germany, CERI/CW/87.06

Japan, CERI/CW/87.04

Sweden, CERI/CW/87.05

United States, CERI/CW/87.03

A synthesis report was prepared by the Secretariat based on these reports: CERI/CW/87.07 and will be available for general distribution in December, 1988.

6. Reference is made to the papers mentioned under 1. as well as to the CERI document CERI/CD(86)13 "Changing Work Patterns and the Role of Education and Training" and document ED(86)15, lst Revision, "Education and Structural Adjustment".

7. - Employment Trends Within the Banking Sector in EEC Countries: Analyses and Comments". Report of the Working Party on Banks. Rapporteur: René Eksl. Document of the Commission of the European Communities, V/1059/87-EN (pages 103-106).

- FIET (Fédération Internationale des Employés et des Techniciens prepared a background report for a conference under the theme "Trade Unions and the Future of Financial Services" held in May 1987. The report is called "Vocational Training in Banks in Europe: A changing Workforce Requiring New Skills". In this paper (pg 4-5), reference is made to a presentation by Amin Rajan of the UK Institute of Manpower Studies which is now included in an ILO report on employment and Multi-national banking.

"Human Resources and Corporate Strategy: Technological Change in Banks and Insurance Companies", Dr. O. Bertrand and Dr. T. Noyelle, OECD, Paris, 1988 (in particular, pages 42-43).

8. Education and the Economy in a Changing Society, OECD (forthcoming).

9. CERI/CW/87.07, page 14.

10. Opt. cit., page 14.

11. CERI/TE/88.07 (pages 7-8).

12. Sundqvist Report, opt. cit., pg. 14.

13. ED(86)15, paragraphs 17-21.

14. Education and the Economy in a Changing Society, OECD (forthcoming).

15. Ibid.

16. CERI/CD(86)13, pg. 9.

17. CERI/CW/87.07, p. 15.

18. Carnevale, A. "The Learning Enterprise", Training and Development Journal, January 1986.

19. CERI/CD(86)13, opt. cit. pages 9-10.

20. Annex 6.2

21. Le Figaro, 22 August 1988.

22. "Training in and by Industry in the Context of Post-Compulsory Education and Training". Report on a joint meeting of management and trade union ex-

perts under the OECD Labour/Management Programme, October 1986 (General Distribution).

23. "Models of Adaptive, Innovative, Productive Quality Cultures - The Need for Improved Cross-cultural Learning and Transfer". Paper presented at the International Conference on Skills for Prosperity (Perth, 8 - 11 November 1987) by Prof. G.W. Ford, Program in Organizational Behavior, University of New South Wales, Australia.

Annexes

1. Civilian Employment by Sector: Average Annual Growth Rates in %. source: OECD Employment Outlook, 1986, Table B, p. 137.

2. Table of contents of the "Inventory of Recent and Ongoing OECD Work Related to Technology"; document CES/87.18.

3. Main findings of CERI project "Technological Change and Its Educational Consequences".

3A. Size and Composition of Part-time Employment, 1979-1986. Source: OECD Employment Outlook, 1987, Table 1.3, p. 29.

3B. Total Employment by Sex - average annual growth rates in %. Source: OECD Employment Outlook, 1987, p. 193.

4. Occupational Structures in Banking in "Human Resources and Corporate Strategy" by O. Bertrand and T. Noyelle, OECD, 1988.

5. Tables on demographic trends. Source: Social Expenditure Trends and Demographic Developments, OECD, 1988, General Distribution.

6.1 Age Distribution of Enrollments in University and Non-University Higher Education Enrollments. Source: OECD document SME/ET/87.5 "Education and Labour Force Preparation and Adjustment: The Role of Education in Increasing Employment and Reducing Unemployment".

6.2 Recruitment Patterns in Adult Education in "Recurrent Education and Socio-economic Success: A Theoretical and Longitudinal Analysis", p. 61, A. Tu@nman: Institute of International Education, University of Stockholm, 1986.

6.3 Age of Trainees in French Continuing Occupational Training, document CERI/CW/84.17 "The Development and Utilisation of Human Resources in the Context of Technological Change in Industrial Restructuring: Public and "Private Policies for the Development of Human Resources in France". This is the French report in a series of reports on Phase II of the CERI study regarding human resources policies. The other reports are:

CERI/CW/84.15 (USA)

CERI/CW/85.02 (Sweden)

CERI/CW/85.04 (Japan)

CERI/CW/85.06 (Germany)

6.4 Trends in Training Efforts in France, ibid.

6.5 Participation in Continuing Training courses in Germany. Document CERI/Cw/85.06, same series as under 6.3.

7.1 Composition of Non-Wage labour Costs in EC Countries, 1981. Source: OECD Employment Outlook, 1986, table 33, p. 91.

7.2 Public and Private Expenditure for Initial and Continuing Education and Training, 1970-1984 in "Recurrent Education Revisited", OECD, 1986 (General Distribution).

7.3 Costs and sources of Funds for Post-Compulsory Education and Training Programs, 1980 (USA) in "Post-Compulsory Education and Training: an Inventory of Programs and Sources of Support", Alan Wagner, "Education and Urban Society, Vol. 14, No. 3, (p. 282-283), May 1982.

8. "Models of Adaptive, Innovative, Productive Quality Cultures - The Need for Improved Cross-Cultural Learning and Transfer". See also reference no. 22 in Bibliography.

Summing Up

EXPERT SYSTEMS IN PRODUCTION AND SERVICES II
Th. Bernold and U. Hillenkamp (Editors)
Elsevier Science Publishers B.V., Amsterdam – Printed in The Netherlands

Some Implications of Expert Systems for Work

Peter Senker
Science Policy Research Unit, University of Sussex, UK

Joanna Buckingham
Center for Business Research, Brighton Polytechnic, UK

Joe Townsend
Science Policy Research Unit, University of Sussex, UK

1. Introduction

Computer control systems may be theory-based, or they may rely on heuristic methods. Only a minority of computer programs rest on mathematical control theory and on firmly established physical theories. Such programs include those that control petroleum refining plants, navigate spaceships and monitor and largely control the environments in which astronauts work, and they enjoy "the enormously important advantage that when they misbehave, their human monitors can detect that their performance does not correspond to the dictates of their theory and can diagnose the reason for the failure from the theory"[1].

Weizenbaum emphasizes that "most existing programs, and especially the largest and the most important ones, are not theory-based in this way. They are heuristic, not necessarily that they employ heuristic methods internally, but they appear to 'work' under most foreseen circumstances, and on other ad hoc mechanisms that are added to them from time to time". [2]

We shall argue that the use of Expert Systems extends the scope for the application of automation using 'heuristic' methods in the sense used by Weizenbaum. It is not, however, yet obvious that the use of Expert Systems – as opposed to other types of 'heuristic program' – necessarily has unique effects on opportunities for enhancing the quality of working life – or, alternatively, for deskilling work, if this is what managements wish to do.

This argument is based on analysis of three case studies on the impact of Expert Systems (ESs) on skill requirements and working life in relation to skilled workers and clerical personnel which we conducted in Britain in 1988 [3], and on research in relation to the implications of CNC and CAD.

The case studies presented below were undertaken on the basis of the hypothesis that the use of Expert Systems was likely to have more or less direct effects on the organization of work, training and the quality of working life. But Hartmann and others criticize writers such as Braverman[4] and Noble[5] who have suggested that new technologies are used by capitalist firms in ways which directly affect "the labour process". Hartmann and others suggest that "work-traditions in different societies will not (authors' emphasis) be changed by the incidence of microelectronics, but will be expressed in new ways, particularly as far as skills are concerned".

Two examples of studies which support this proposition are considered below – the study by Hartmann and others themselves on Computer Numerical Control (CNC) and our own work on Computer-Aided Design. We follow this by discussion of three case studies specifically on Expert Systems use carried out recently in Britain for the International Labour Office.

1.1. CNC

Hartmann and others[6] hypothesize that "The development and application of microelectronics and CNC will follow a different path in Britain and Germany" because "the integration of CNC... follows quite different logic in the two countries". By this they mean that "the conception and practice relations ...will follow quite different paths. British companies will ... train and use noticeably less skilled workers than German ones, and the difference will be particularly visible in production". They suggest that German firms are likely to use more trained labour because of the more abundant supply of trained manpower in Germany at all levels.

As they expected, they found that formal qualifications in plants using CNC were more common in both large and small plants in Germany, and that formal engineering qualifications were especially rare in small British plants. Polarization of skills was not inevitable, and German companies were more concerned to take advantage of the potential of CNC to stress the use of craft skills. [7]

1.2. CAD

Although the Computer-Aided Design technology (CAD) in most widespread use in Europe is of US design and still embodies characteristics relevant to its initial market – large drawing offices in the US – the way CAD is used in European countries often reflects the traditions of design specific to each country. For example "France, FR Germany and the UK have characteristic ways of organizing the mechanical engineering design process which are superficially similar, but differ from the US. In general, the bottom echelon of the European drawing office has a longer training than its US counterpart, and this training has a higher engineering content. Germany is the only one of the three countries where tracers are still used in substantial numbers, but their training is nonetheless two years long – as compared with three and a half years as a technische Zeichner (design draughtsperson) in FR Germany....In the UK, draughtspeople undergo a four-year engineering apprenticeship, only part of which is directly oriented towards design work ...The high engineering content of training and the relative closeness of draughtspeople to the engineering function leaves less scope in the UK, France and FR Germany than in the US for the achievement of productivity benefits designed essentially for the automation of line-drawing."

In the late 1970s and early 1980s, a principal management aim in British engineering firms was to deploy CAD so as to reduce design and drawing office employment. [8]Findings of a study which we plan to publish soon indicate that, in general, as Arnold had suggested, this aim was not realized. Instead, CAD was being used to remove the need for performing detailed drawing tasks from drafters and this was permitting them to spend more of their time considering alternative designs and using design analysis techniques such as finite element analysis to improve the quality of design – leading to both improved designs and production cost reductions.

Recently, there have been speculations about how the use of artificial intelligence, including Expert Systems, will affect the development of CAD use. Our recent study gives grounds for believing that here too, management expectations are unlikely to be realized.

Computer-based systems are currently being used for the separate design processes of geometric modelling, engineering analysis and the provision of guidance on specialized engineering design topics. Some commentators suggest that AI techniques could have potential for the integration of shape and form design with non-geometrical functional design. The information and skills from analysis, scheduling, manufacturing, marketing, etc. may be brought upstream to designers and drafters [9].

A situation could be reached in which a component will 'know' its relationship to other components within the assembly, and the assemblies within the whole product, so that if one change is made, it is reflected throughout the whole product and in every 3D view and 2D plan. The next generation of CAD systems may enable designers to draw on a variety of Expert Systems: sets of rules culled from human experts, ready to provide prompts or advice should the designer go wrong. Expert Systems hold out the promise of an 'intelligent' conceptual design tool that goes far beyond the electronic drawing board, to accommodate production and manufacturing within design.

In future, designers may have available on-line feedback concerning such parameters as the geometric and functional constraints associated with the product and its constituent parts: what nut will cope with what stress; the type and quality of material that should be used for a certain load and given tolerances; whether or not a surface is machinable given the tools available in the factory.

In contrast to some of these speculations, and in accordance with Hartmann and others' findings we suggest that the use of Expert Systems in relation to the use of CAD is likely to continue to be constrained in Britain by existing 'work conditions': in this case, lack of management knowledge and understanding of the technology.

In our recent study, we found that the use of CAD in Britain has been shaped and constrained by management unwillingness to undertake the training necessary for them to understand its implications more clearly, and by their inability or unwillingness to make organizational changes which would assist in promoting effective use of new technology.

We suggest that similar conditions could well apply to the use of Expert Systems in CAD in Britain, and that it is unlikely that Expert System programs will be used as envisaged by the speculations reported above, in the foreseeable future.

The case studies presented below provide specific support in relation to Expert Systems for Hartmann and others' hypothesis. For example, they show that concern for formal qualifications, for training and for the quality of working life is low. Such findings are typical of the situation in Britain in relation to new technologies. [10]

2. The Three UK Expert System Cases Studies [11]

2.1. Case Study Number One – Exshel

The Exshel Expert System has been installed in seven plants so far. The particular works studied is a major plant in the South East owned by Union Production. This plant was rebuilt in the early 1970s partly on the basis of supplying Commonwealth markets for chemfluor, but these countries increasingly installed their own manufacturing facilities. The plant is nearing the end of its raw material reserves. Union Production is one of the few firms which dominate British production of chemfluor. The use of chemfluor has diminished partly because, like many sectors of British manufacturing industry, it has been affected by recession. In addition, other materials are increasingly being used as substitutes. There has also been increased competition from imports.

A Director was reported as saying that "The UK trading position leaves us no choice but to reduce costs so as to maintain a viable business and to protect the jobs which remain". The company was aiming to maintain a strong technical support service but to switch emphasis from development of new technology to improving performance at the works and supporting the marketing drive. Later the same year, Union Production reported that they had spent several hundred million pounds in the previous five years modernizing their UK capacity and that they were well placed to take advantage of increases in demand. Union Production's chief executive outlined the efforts made in various plants to achieve low cost, energy efficient production. [12] He also announced their plans to achieve further increases in efficiency by adopting a new approach to work organization in all their UK works. Union Production has established new flexible working practices at two sites and is now extending this to its other plants.

In the last ten years, the UK chemfluor industry has perceived a need to reduce its manning to levels equivalent to those of its major world competitors. To meet this need, Union Production had announced plans to make substantial redundancies during 1987 and 1988.

2.1.1. The Management View

Exshel is expert system process control technology developed by Union Production in conjunction with Lilac Ltd. [13]Its development was supported by government funds. The benefits claimed for its use are financial, arising mainly from energy savings and improved product quality. Skilled process operators used to control the complex reactions which occur in the process by the use of conventional control systems. They tended to run the process a little hotter than absolutely necessary which wasted energy, adversely affected the plant and degraded the final product.

The ES aims to mimic the action of a competent process operator. While an operator using manual control might change the control parameters once every two hours, the ES control is based on controlling three variables four or five times per hour. The process can, therefore, be 'fine-tuned'. Its application in another Union Production works has achieved substantial audited cost savings, giving a payback period of less than three months. Cost savings derived mainly from fuel savings and improved product quality. [14] Lilac's managing director suggested that the number of practical Expert Systems in every day use is still small, and that, unlike Exshel, most of the others are consultative advisory systems for off-line use.

Operators were heavily involved in the development of the rule blocks. Program development is carried out by personnel on the site.

Before the introduction of the ES, the operators (OPs) used to vary fuel, air and raw material feedrates in response to indications from a panel of instruments in the control room. No formal qualifications were required to operate the system or to do the OP job. It took about four to six weeks for the OP to learn the basics of operating the system. But it took about one year's experience to be able to run the system and to be competent to intervene to correct any problems which might arise. OPs, as they gained experience, developed and adopted their own 'rules of thumb' and succeeded in maintaining steady conditions in the process.

Video cameras were used to record conditions in parts of the process, and before the ES was installed, management used to change target settings on the basis of the video camera's view of the inside of the process, to the distress of the OPs who believed that management were interfering in their jobs on the basis of inaccurate information: the operators did not always agree with the management's interpretation of process conditions.

Exshel (the ES) is used to run the process for most of the time, except for the 10% of time (plus breakdown time) during which the system is not in operation. In practice, the ES is working for between 80% and 85% of the time. The original concept was 'sold' to the management and operators as an autopilot: like an airline pilot, the operator "takes the system up" (sets up the process) and then the system follows a preset "route" automatically. The operator then "brings the system down to land".

The process engineer – a graduate in chemical engineering – changes the parameters of the ES when changes in the operating conditions require. The operators then make changes in line with the process engineer's new targets. If minor changes in the program are called for, he can do this himself;if they are major, he has the opportunity of calling in outside experts.

Before the ES was installed, the OPs operated the process, overseen by the process engineer. The process engineer had difficulty in maintaining detailed knowledge of the state of the process because of the long time constants involved and because he was only present for a small part of the full three shift working of the process (168 hours per week). Now the OPs are more confined to changing a range of set points and variables within given parameters, while the process engineer has wider discretion (see above).

Initially, the operators did not believe that the ES could to their job. The OPs tried to compete with the system to show that they could do better. From the management point of view, the ES soon established its superiority: management believe that it is more expert than the operators because it combines the knowledge of the operators, the process engineers and R&D personnel. In addition, the improvements made to the process by the use of the ES were augmented by the use of a new sensor which the operators had difficulty in interpreting.

The operators resigned themselves to the system when once it became obvious that it was there to stay. In addition, a recent process change made the process more difficult to control. A process engineer commented that the ES resulted in an apparent loss of status to the OPs: previously, their work was a 'black art'. With the installation of the ES, their work was formalized and to some extent demystified.

While the OPs accepted that the plant was not necessarily working as efficiently as it might have done, they resented the implication that somebody from R&D could tell them how to do their jobs better.

It took only six to eight weeks to get the control strategy right and about a further three to six months for it to be fully accepted.

When the ES was introduced initially, all personnel were briefed about the project. Operators and process engineers were given only limited training initially due to the need to concentrate on how to control the process. Subsequently, formal off-site training was introduced for the process engineers, and a briefing on-site was given to all personnel involved. OP training was carried out through hands-on training during the first weeks of the system being on-site. The operators regarded this as perfectly adequate. Formal off-site training was regarded as unnecessary for the OPs and therefore was not carried out.

However process engineers were trained. Maintenance personnel also need to be trained, and training will be initiated shortly. Special circumstances prevented the management from spending as much time on training as they felt desirable.

Reorganization is now being proposed by management with the aim of making significant reductions in manning levels. Management proposes that there should be shift teams with collective responsibility for the process. It is proposed to diffuse responsibility amongst shift teams, but specific plans are not yet fully developed. These changes are now being challenged by the trade unions.

2.1.2. The Operators' Views (Based on interviews with two operators (OP1 and OP2).)

Both operators had worked for the company for a long time (OP1 nine years, OP2 16 years). OP1 had been an operator for two and a half years and OP2 for 14 years. Neither of them had any previous experience with computers. As far as both are concerned, the ES is just a computer or a 'black box' – they do not distinguish between the ES and computing in general, as they have no other computing experience to form a basis for such comparisons. Neither had been trained as craftsmen. Management did not consult with them about its introduction.

The ES program was based on how the operators did the job, based on three years of records of manual operation. "We didn't believe that the system could do it, we hoped that it would go wrong. After six months, we got used to it, but (it) still can't start the process. " (OP1)

No OP used to control the process in the same way. For example, one kept a book in which he recorded the readings from his previous shifts and changed his readings back to where they were. Others were more inclined to let the process continue on the settings found when they arrived at work.

"We knew it (the ES) had to come. Some said we'd lose our jobs, but we knew we wouldn't, because the company couldn't shut down or start the process, so we knew there would always be a job. " (OP2)

The ES is in use throughout the shift, with the exception of when the process is being started up or closed down, or when it breaks down. The two operators agreed that it was very easy to learn to use. "You give it the information and it makes up its own mind what is the best action to take. " (OP1)While OP1 thought that it took only five minutes to become proficient in its use, OP2 suggested two to three weeks. "From the outside, it looks as if anyone could do the job, a child of five, or you (the interviewer). But when the computer goes down, then we really have to know what to do. " (referring to the need to run the system manually when it is "unsettled")

"It's boring now. Before (the ES was introduced) it was quite boring. Once you'd got the process going OK, you just made a few adjustments. Now (the ES) does it. You can get on a shift now with the process running and there's nothing to do all shift – nothing happens ... (the job is) more routine. We're still responsible for the process working correctly, we can't make excuses, the responsibility still comes down to us ... (the ES) does what you want it to." (OP1)

"It's a boring job. We used to decide what to adjust and we'd adjust it, but probably too much. Now the machine does it. We just watch. The job's boring – you can go for a walk to look at the plant, but that's all. The machine does everything – what we could do with around here is a TV[15] the job is more routine. I don't worry too much about the pressure – that can make you ill. One (of us) does worry – he blames the computer for everything[16] the computer only controls what you (the OP) put into it. It can't do some jobs like starting up the process ... (the ES) has enabled management to have tighter control over the job ... we have gained no extra skills. "

There are occasional failures. "When there are failures, we switch off (the ES) and get on (manually). I look forward to that – unless it's the end of the shift. " (OP2)

OP2 said at one stage that he could not really call himself a process operator any more, because the system enabled management to have tighter control over the job. Management thought they could run the process as well as any operator and OP2 resented this.

Before the introduction of the ES they had had to discuss how the process had been, what adjustments they had made, etc. , in order to "get a feel" for how the process was working. OP2 complained that the use of the ES had lessened communication: OPs hardly talked to each other now as they changed shifts. The same applied to communications with management. "They used to come in to see how things were going. Now they just say 'Is the system on?'. If it is, they go away, if not, they ask 'why not?' – and that's it. "

2.2. Case Study Number Two – Tefad Fault Diagnosis

2.2.1. The Management View

Eletel devices are used for commercial and industrial purposes. In effect, they are complicated electronic devices which incorporate a printed circuit board (pcb). When these devices develop a fault, they are sent to one of Eletel's Regional Repair Centers (RRC), where it has been normal for them to be repaired by apprentice craftsmen as part of their training. But they had to be instructed and supervised by experts, and this is time consuming. Each Regional Repair Center serves a large area, and over 20,000 Eletels are in use in the area in which the Tefad Fault Diagnosis System has been piloted.

Eletel laboratories had developed an Expert System shell and were looking for ways of using it. The Bornham RRC had heard of the Expert System work being done by the Eletel Laboratories and saw possibilities of using it. The Eletel Laboratories have been promoting the use of the ES amongst the RRCs. The system is now in use at three or four RRCs. The system operates on an IBM PC (or compatible) and by no means all the RRCs are yet equipped with PCs and this is a factor inhibiting their use. RRC managers are generally relatively easy to convince of its benefits, but persuading senior managers to the point where they are prepared to authorize the necessary expenditure (of the order of #3,000) is not always easy.

In the case reported below, the ES is enabling an operator to repair the pcbs without having to trouble the experts for assistance. It is reported to have located faults successfully that had not been explicitly entered into the system. Benefits claimed include reduced costs in terms of man-hours and components needed to effect repairs.

2.2.2. The Operator's Views

The operator, in his mid-thirties, had been trained as a (craft) electrician in the local technical college. This involved learning to use a soldering iron, test meter and oscilloscope, which are the principal skills necessary for doing the diagnosis and repair work involved. The operator had worked previously on outdoor repairing and installing work for ten years. He had had no involvement with the Eletel equipment and very limited experience with computers. On medical advice, he was transferred to indoor work – with the prototype ES.

The operator received less than a day's training in the use of the ES, and this enabled him to spend his time diagnosing and repairing faults. The system was easy to learn. Within two weeks he attained the productivity of the apprentices who previously did this work – i. e. 17 to 20 repairs per day. The ES was easy to get into and allowed you to get quicker and more sure as he got to know it. The way in which it operated seemed like "common sense".

As this work was entirely different from the outdoor work he did previously, the operator could make no direct comparison. His work was more routine than his previous work, but he was working under less pressure. He felt that the ES was "a good thing" in that it allowed him to know what was happening in each instance and he felt fully in control. His own work situation was much improved. The system allowed him to use conventional repairing techniques under guidance from the program. He became very familiar with the pcbs and found that some faults were more common than others. The present ES applies only to Eletel systems, but he was eager to get to grips with other ES programs which enabled people who were not experts to deal with faults in much more sophisticated and complex electronic equipment. He had pointed out to the supervisor how the system could be improved: there had been some minor errors and omissions in the program, and these errors and omissions have now been dealt with. "The system does not let me down these days. I do not need any assistance at all now ...I like this job, it allows me to work unsupervised, it's a fair living and I will probably work here for some time. "

"We all work in this big workshop. We know who to ask if there are problems. Mr X is in charge here and we would work through him if there are any new developments or changes made (to the ES). "

2.3. Case Study Number Three – Lansure Insurance Company

Insurance was one of the first service industries to be automated because of the enormous volume of routine information it has to process. Insurance companies are centralized and were in a position to use early generations of mainframe computers in batch mode to enjoy economies of scale in handling vast and increasing volumes of business. By the mid 1970s, many companies were experimenting with on-line systems, and the transition to on-line systems led to a change in the attitudes of users to computers. The centralized batch processing mainframe computer was regarded as "a remote authority which made unreasonable demands on the staff, particularly in the branches, but which contributed relatively little in return". In contrast, on-line systems "could be regarded as a valuable aid to the users, which could enhance the service which they gave to their customers. "[17]

This appears to be an appropriate context in which to place the Expert System considered in this case. Nevertheless, it has to be appreciated that this case study appears to be very untypical of insurance companies' experience of Expert Systems in the UK so far. A recent survey of financial services companies in Britain found that none of them were yet using Expert Systems commercially, and only 6% of firms were experimenting with them. The majority of firms surveyed were not using ES and had no plans to do so. [18]

2.3.1. The Management View

Prior to the implementation of the ES, there were areas of the business which could only be underwritten by the experts at the Head Office. This resulted in a bottleneck: every customer requiring this service had to be referred to Head Office.

The ES was introduced to try to deal with a situation in which two experts had been trying to deal with 3,500 enquiries per year. The experts could only make themselves available on the telephone to transact business for two hours per day, as they needed the rest of the time to process enquiries, deal with queries, etc. The company perceived that they were losing business and wasting experts' knowledge on trivial questions, as well as wasting time on communications between the branches and Head Office. The ES saves the company money because it permits the right decisions about risk to be made consistently. The ES alerts the user to wrong decisions, to particular relevant facts. Less mistakes are made now because workers are not so rushed.

The role of the promoters of the system within the company is to develop systems and 'sell' them to the company: initially, they just wanted to "dabble with the (ES) technology". When once the system was developed, it was demonstrated at the Head Office. The departmental managers responsible for the work of the experts decided to go ahead and the regions were instructed to install it. The insurance company is constantly losing staff, in particular underwriting experts. The promoters were able to convince management that the ES could make a contribution to the solution of that problem.

It took about one and a half to two years between starting to examine the potential of ES and the implementation of the system.

The aims of the ES were not to replace experts' knowledge, but to spread it further. The system enhances decision making. It gives a consistent approach which is important in some areas. The company was quoting too high or too low, too many excesses etc. This can result in expensive mistakes.

An ES 'shell' was used, and the reasoning is shown, which is an essential feature in their application to avoid the need for constant reference back to Head Office. The explanations also afford an aid to training. The ES is an excellent training tool, especially as the experts were under such pressure that they never had the time to train – they only had time to tell the user the answer.

The expert's name is given in the front of the system. The Systems Manager thinks that this is important because it acknowledges the contribution made by the expert.

Updates to the system are made on request by the Computer Department when requested to do so. The Computer Department telephone all the regions at least once a fortnight so as to ensure that the system is in use, to monitor progress and to collect comments. Updates and minor improvements to the system have been suggested by users. The process of telephoning for comments is regarded as essential to the future of the system to reassure users. It is envisaged that this will continue for another six to nine months.

Users of the ES are underwriters and clerks, with no specific required level of qualification. A selected user from each region was given one day's training at Head Office. These people were carefully chosen. The courses explained the basics of using a Personal Computer and then took the trainees through the "HELP" screens. These trainees then went back to their regions and trained other users.

The system was 'sold' to the experts on the basis that it would enable them to rid themselves of the routine 90% of their work, enabling them to concentrate on the interesting work. The regions were happy about the introduction of the ES because they can now deal with questions which they had to refer to Head Office previously.

Immediately before implementation, two potential users were given the system to see that it was working satisfactorily. There were no serious problems: 50 to 60 clerks in 10 centers are now using the system. The users' jobs are more interesting because there is an increase in the range and variety of the work they can handle. The ES enables unskilled clerks to do an expert's job: it allows lower qualified staff to handle complete risk cases which they would be unable to do without the use of the ES. Although the ES is relatively slow to use because it requires users to answer a large number of questions, it enables people who have never had experience of underwriting to become good, productive underwriters.

Users are favorably disposed to the color screen VDUs which they are now using. Within three months of starting to use the ES, they no longer need to refer to the "HELP" screens constantly. However, the users are accustomed to using a mainframe computer, and there have been small problems getting used to the Personal Computers, e. g. learning to use diskettes.

Section heads are responsible for training new users. They like the ES because it enables new users to be trained using the "HELP" screens without having to go through the manual.

Previously, information was available only at Head Office. The regions now have more information and there is less communication between the Head Office and the regions.

2.3.2. The Operators' Views(Based on comments contributed to the Computer Department's surveys of user reactions to the ES.)

Generally, the system was very easy to operate. But users in some regions felt that it had not been programmed in a way to make it sensitive enough to the differing conditions in various regions of the country. Other users felt that it reacted too conservatively to the information given to it, and disagreed with the parameters on which the program was operating. Management was prepared to examine the basis for these complaints and was considering what action to take.

There were several comments about people using the system as a training aid. Two new members of staff commented that, when using these systems as a training aid, they liked the "HELP" screens especially.

3. Discussion

It is apparent from the case studies that the implications of Expert Systems can vary considerably, depending both on the specific application in which the Expert System is used – and on how and to whom tasks are allocated when implemented.

The principal motivations for installing all the case study Expert Systems were economic, but in detail the motivation varied between the cases.

In the case of Union Production, cost savings were sought, initially mainly in terms of energy savings and product quality, and, in these respects, it has been very successful. Currently, labour-saving reorganization is being undertaken. This is largely in compliance with the company's central plan to reorganize all their chemfluor plants. The specific contribution of the ES in facilitating labour cost reduction is incidental. In the Tefad case, the economic motivation was mainly labour-saving. Lansure's principal motivation was to remove bottlenecks which had been inhibiting the growth of some parts of the business.

The Exshel case is one involving on-line process control. In the first instance, the jobs mainly affected were those of the operators whose responsibility was originally to start the process, control its operation and shut it down. The Expert System is used to control the process automatically ('automatic pilot') after it has been started up manually by the operators – who are (at present) the same people who used to control the whole process manually. The ES embodies the operators' expertise, and their jobs have been deskilled by the requirement that they use the Expert System during routine running (using the Expert System as an 'automatic pilot'). Operators feel aggrieved that their expertise has been used to deskill their work and make it (even) more boring. The Expert System has conveyed to management more control in the way the plant is operated.

Automating the control of a process which had been controlled manually involves the operators in spending most of their time watching instruments, and more rarely intervening to change settings, whether or not an ES is involved or not. If it had been possible to achieve an understanding of the chemfluor process in sufficient depth, the process could have been modelled and automated on the basis of a scientific understanding of the process, rather than on the basis of the operators' expertise. Indeed, this had been attempted. If it had been successful, the changes to the work of controlling the process would have been very similar to the changes actually experienced by the operators in changing from manual control to ES control: i. e. the change would have been from manual control to computer (or 'black box') control. The work would still have changed from manual control to control by 'automatic pilot'. The nature of the computer software controlling the process would appear to have little effect on the work of those called on to monitor the operations of the automatic pilot. The Exshel case is one in which it was impossible to devise a theory-based control system and so one based on a "heuristic" approach (in Weizenbaum's sense) was developed. There is no reason to believe that the type of program used had any direct effect on operators' work.

Accordingly, it is possible that the results of previous studies of the implications of computerized process control for process operators' jobs would apply also to cases where Expert Systems come into use. For example, Blauner[19] discusses "the work of operating the automatic equipment which exemplifies the distinctive technology of continuous-process production". He found that "Workers ...felt jobs were becoming too easy ...the chemical operator's most standardized operation is his periodic round of readings". But he went on to suggest that there was "considerable variety ...even in the most routine of the chemical operator's job tasks ...chemical workers are able to control the quality of their production ...Putting out a good quality product is one of the most important sources of satisfaction and accomplishment for the operators interviewed. "

When once the process has been started up, it is a continuous process and the work of controlling the chemfluor process is analogous to that which Blauner discusses. Nevertheless, in the works we studied, the operators' work, even before it was further automated by the use of the ES, appeared not to offer as much variety as in the cases studied by Blauner. The OPs may have derived some satisfaction from ensuring product quality prior to the installation of the ES, but any involvement in quality control was virtually destroyed by the use of the ES.

The picture of chemical process operation presented by Braverman conforms more to our findings: "because of the nature of the continuous process employed and the possibility of moving the entire product-in-preparation within enclosed vessels and piping ... the automation of processes places them under the control of management engineers and destroys the need for knowledge or training". [20]

In relation to process control applications, the availability of ES technology extends the range of applications of computerized control to applications in which it is not (yet) possible to analyze the production process to the extent necessary to develop a scientific model of the process capable of forming the basis for control using more conventional software. The essence of this application from the point of view of training and quality of working life is that it is a further application of automation to what is already a substantially automated and virtually continuous process.

In contrast, Tefad is an off-line system for diagnosing and guiding the repair of faults. The expertise embodied derives from a very experienced expert: the worker who operates the ES was previously doing entirely different work outdoors. For medical reasons, he needed to transfer to an indoor job, and is very happy with his new job, for which he required very little training to perform satisfactorily. Prior to the installation of the ES, this work was performed by apprentices, who required considerable training and guidance from supervisors. So the work has been deskilled. But, as a new worker – whose previous training and experience was not related to his new work – was employed to use the ES, he does not feel aggrieved as, in no sense has his work been deskilled. And, in this particular case, the transfer to working indoors using the ES was seen as beneficial by the worker concerned, for medical reasons.

In the Tefad case, the Expert System made it possible to 'automate' to a very considerable extent the work of detailed fault diagnosis and repair on modules which had been identified as faulty on site. This amounts to further automation in the 'maintenance chain' of automated diagnosis of faults in modules on site, followed by detailed diagnosis and repair in a central workshop which is envisaged as a growing pattern of maintenance activities in the computer industry as well as in telecommunications. [21]

Prediction of the implications of Expert Systems for skills and working life in relation to fault diagnosis and repair applications can only be carried out realistically in the light of data on the likely developments in technology, work organization and skills in the 'maintenance chain' as a whole.

Some relevant data is available from our previous research: in relation to computer maintenance, we found that technological developments in products and components had led to some deskilling of the work of field engineers, when dealing with relatively simple terminals, peripherals and small microcomputers. These equipments each contain relatively few circuit boards. In many cases, automatic diagnosis has made it possible for the field engineer to identify which circuit board is at fault, and simply exchange it for a new circuit board, sending the faulty circuit board back to a workshop for repair (or for discard if it is of low value). This is resulting in a transfer of skills away from the field engineers to the workshop, and this in turn is resulting in the need for electronics organizations to employ extra engineers in workshops with in-depth knowledge of electronics to conduct bench diagnosis and repair. [22]

The Lansure insurance case is very different. The ES was introduced to try to deal with a situation in which two experts had been overloaded by enquiries. The aims of the ES were not to replace experts' knowledge, but to spread it further and to reduce the possibility of mistakes. The experts were unable to concentrate on the high level work for which they were trained, because they had to spend a considerable amount of their time answering routine queries which did not demand their high level of expertise. As a result of the experts' inability to cope with the large number of enquiries, the company lost business.

The ES enabled clerks to deal with enquiries from potential customers which, in its absence, had had to be referred to the experts. Thus, the company was able to handle far more business with the ES in operation than it could have done without it. Operation of the ES was added to the roles of the clerks who had previously been forced to refer it to the experts at Head Office. Thus, use of the ES expanded the range and interest of the clerks' work: as in the Tefad case, the expertise embodied in the system is that of an expert and not that of the people who are now using the ES. An important feature of the ES in this application was its ability to show the reasoning on which its advice was based.

50 to 60 clerks in 10 centers are now using the system. The users' jobs are more interesting because there is an increase in the range and variety of the work they can handle. The ES enables unskilled clerks to do an expert's job: although the ES is relatively slow to use because it requires users to answer a large number of questions, it enables people who have never had experience of underwriting to become good, productive underwriters. Users are favorably disposed towards the ES, and have only experienced small problems in learning to use it. This was the one case in which formal training was used.

4. Conclusions

Those who may be tempted to look to case-study research to provide readily generalizable findings are liable to be very disappointed. For such research to make its potential contribution to policy, its objectives need to be very carefully specified.

The authors of a recent report suggest that Expert Systems could have "a variety of seemingly contradictory effects in terms of skill implications, from polarization effects, i. e. a widening of the gap between skilled and unskilled sections of the workforce, to deskilling, reskilling and even multiskilling effects, the precise combination being dependent on factors other than any inherent tendency of the technology to produce rigid, deterministic changes". [23]This paper confirms the soundness of this suggestion.

There are a wide range of ES applications in the UK alone. [24] To conduct useful research on the broad implications of Expert Systems for work would demand enormous resources.

We suggest that approaching the problem in this way would not be cost-effective. It may often be more valuable to use research to examine technological change in general in carefully defined individual broad sectors in depth as a basis for establishing training policy, or policy in relation to the quality of working life, rather than to concentrate on examining the implications of one technology such as Expert Systems programs in a wide variety of industries.

It is apparent that the use of Expert Systems extends the scope for the application of automation. But their use instead of other programs – whether theory-based or based on heuristics – may not have unique effects for training needs or for the quality of working life.

The case-study material we have presented and discussed makes it clear that the implications of Expert Systems depend on many contextual factors such as management objectives, the nature of the process in which they are incorporated (process control of a chemical plant, fault-diagnosis, insurance, CAD, etc.); the country in which the process is installed and its traditions of education and training (formation) and work organization.

Acknowledgements

We are most grateful to the managers, systems designers, engineers and operators for their cooperation in the preparation of the case studies.

We wish to express our gratitude to the International Labour Office for sponsoring the case studies. Except where specifically attributed, the views and opinions expressed are those of the authors alone and do not necessarily reflect the views or policies of the ILO.

Notes and References

1. Weizenbaum, J. (1984), Computer Power and Human Reason. From Judgement to Calculation, Pelican Books, p. 207.

2. Weizenbaum, J. , op. cit. , p. 232.

3. Senker, P. , Buckingham, J. and Townsend, J. (1988), Expert Systems – Present state and future trends: Impact on employment and skill requirements (Three case studies), ILO/FRG Project on Expert Systems and Qualification Changes (INT/86/MO3/FRG).

4. Braverman, H. (1974), Labor and Monopoly Capital: The Degradation of Work in the Twentieth Century, Monthly Review Press.

5. Noble, D. F. (1979), "Social Choice in Machine Design: The Case of Automatically Controlled Machine Tools", in Zimbalist, A. (ed.), Case Studies on the Labor Process, Monthly Review Press, pp. 18-50.

6. Hartmann, G. , Nicholas, I. J. , Sorge, A. and Warner, M. (1984), "Consequence of CNC Technology: a study of British and West German manufacturing firms", in Warner, M. (ed.), Microprocessors, Manpower and Society, Gower, pp. 311-24.

7. Hartmann, G. et al. , op. cit.

8. See Arnold, E. and Senker, P. (1982), Designing the Future: the implications of CAD interactive graphics for employment and skills in the British engineering industry, Engineering Industry TrainingBoard Occasional Paper No. 9, Watford.

9. There is relatively little concern in British industrial firms about formal qualifications, and firms often make no clear distinction between designers and drafters. Some non-graduate drafters continue to progress into design roles, although the proportion of designers who are graduates is probably increasing.

10. e. g. see Senker, P. (1986), Towards the Automatic Factory?The Need for Training, IFS.

11. Senker, P. , Buckingham, J. and Townsend, J. (1988), Expert Systems-Present state and future trends: Impact on employment and skill requirements (Three case studies), ILO/FRG Project on Expert Systems and Qualification Changes (INT/86/M03/FRG).

12. We were informed that energy costs represent about a third of the total variable cost of chemfluor manufacture.

13. Lilac Ltd is an independent technology center supplying R & D,technical services and engineered equipment.

14. It is expected that further cost savings will arise from reduction of employment and reduced downtime. But it is likely that some (perhaps most) of the staff reductions anticipated will be the result of work reorganization being undertaken at all Union Production plants in Britain.

15. He was suggesting that the operators had so little to do that a television set should be provided by management for operators to watch to give them something to do.

16. The OP referred to was the one who had turned the ES off when it was first introduced.

17. Barras, R. and Swann, J. (1983), The adoption and impact of information in the UK Insurance Industry, The Technical Change Centre, pp. 13-6.

18. Stevenson, H. (forthcoming), 'Expert Systems in the UK Financial Services Sector: A symbolic analysis of the hype', in Doukidis, G. , Miller, G. and Land, F. (eds), Knowledge Based Management Support Systems, Ellis Horwood, London.

19. Blauner, R. (1964), Alienation and Freedom: the Factory Worker and His Industry, University of Chicago Press. The analysis presented here draws on the process control case studies considered by Blauner and Braverman. It is not concerned with their general theoretical formulations.

20. Braverman, H. , op. cit. , pp. 224-5.

21. Brady, T. and Senker, P. (1986), Economic Incentives and Training: Changing Skill Requirements in Computer Maintenance, Manpower Services Commission.

22. Brady, T. and Senker, P. , op. cit. , pp. 20-1.

23. Jahoda, M. , Guy, K. and Evans, B. (1988), The Market Place for Expert Systems, Report to the ILO, p. 33.

24. Jahoda, M. et al. , op. cit. , p. 29: "The UK has many small scale projects in many organizations, including defence, aerospace, electronics,

telecommunications and computing. Use is increasing in public sector bodies and utilities and in the financial sector. "

EXPERT SYSTEMS IN PRODUCTION AND SERVICES II
Th. Bernold and U. Hillenkamp (Editors)
Elsevier Science Publishers B.V., Amsterdam – Printed in The Netherlands

Some Thoughts on the Impacts of AI-Systems on Current and Future Workers

Dennis Chamot
Associate Director
Department for Professional Employees, AFL-CIO
Washington, D.C. 20006, USA

Artificial intelligence systems are, of course, but one small part of much broader movement toward the development of many kinds of computer systems for use in a wide variety of workplaces. These systems are either permitting or directly causing changes in job definitions, skill requirements, work organization, work location, monitoring practices, product as well as process designs, the relationships between labor and management, and even the relationship between different kinds of non-managerial employees.

In retrospect, some of these developments might give the impression of inevitability, but it is important to note that there is no «technological imperative». Any applied technology is the result of many choices, and computer technologies in particular are extremely flexible and adaptable. Hence, one must investigate the nature of the choices to be made, and the reasons for the decisions that are adopted, in order to understand the particular systems put in place. Such an exercise is also necessary if there is to be any attempt to direct these developments so that employee needs are taken into account as much as are business goals.

It is also necessary to differentiate between the levels of employee positions, because the personnel effects of the introduction or expansion of computer systems will depend upon the level of control exercised by the employee before the changes were instituted. Many computer technologies can be applied so that the jobs that are performed while using them can be either enhanced or simplified, depending upon how the applications are designed. When the result is simplification, at whatever level, the job is often downgraded. At the lowest levels, the result is no job at all – full automation.

All of this applies to expert systems as well. The name itself implies that the systems contain some expertise otherwise not as readily available to the user. In application, this may take many forms, including, for example, programs to assist doctors in diagnosing illnesses and choosing proper therapies. At the other end of the scale, they can be used to remove the last elements of judgment from clerical or low level manufacturing jobs. Somewhere in between, they can be used to make high level expertise available to lesser skilled (and lower paid) personnel. As with most computer applications, the particular features of jobs involving the use of expert systems depend very much upon design decisions which are often made under managerial and perceived economic constraints. Enormous variety is possible.

The purpose of all the foregoing is to demonstrate that it is difficult to speak of "expert systems" or the role of apprentices or future workers in overly general terms. One must be more specific.

I would like to explore in this paper some thoughts on the effects of expert systems on new entrants into various levels of employment, as well as on existing employees faced with the introduction of new systems. I will begin with what in the United States are referred to as professional employees. These people usually have university degrees and advanced training, and their jobs are fairly specialized but not managerial. Some examples are engineers, doctors, economists, analysts, and the like. In each case, the nature of the job demands knowledge of, and access to, vast amounts of information, as well as the ability to deal with new situations by making decisions based upon professional criteria and experience. Even at the level of professional employees, however, a good deal of the time on the job may be spent on fairly routine tasks, such as collecting data, performing calculations or standard analyses, or even such mundane tasks as filing or retrieving information.

AI systems can be used in professional areas in two fundamentally different ways. One is tp use them strictly as tools, providing easier and more thorough access to stored information. As such, they can be valuable additions to the collection of professional "tricks of the trade". A program that helps a design engineer choose efficient paths for laying out and connecting components in an electronic device is an example of such a useful tool; learning how to use it would become an essential part of the training of electronic engineers.

Another approach can be taken. Expert systems can be designed in such a way that they attempt to incorporate more of the essence of the job itself, including that ability to choose among the more routing possible outcomes for a given situation. This second approach may be used by those who seek to downgrade the job (or large parts of it), reserving only those things that are truly non-routine for the few remaining professional employees. In that case, the goal is to have the downgraded work done by people with less training who would be paid at lower rates.

In this light, some expert systems can be used in either of the ways I just described, depending on the intent of the implementing authorities.

Let us take as an example an expert system that assists in choosing drug therapies for treating infections. As the number of drugs currently available is quite large and growing, it is difficult for a doctor to have at his or her fingertips the name of every drug, its indications, contraindications, and side effects, as well as to know exactly which drug is best for a particular infection under every conceivable situation encountered in daily practice. A doctor may choose to use such a program to make sure that nothing is overlooked when performing a particular treatment. The program would also be quite useful in the training of new doctors. In these areas, the expert system is a valuable tool that may improve the quality of service.

A very different scenario with the same AI system may be suggested. Reacting primarily to pressures to reduce costs, administrative authorities may seek to have medical expert systems used by lesser trained personnel, on the theory that the requisite expertise is contained in the computer, and it is only necessary for the operator to enter symptomatic data according to prompts provided by the program. In fact, such a system may work fairly well in the hands of a trained nurse or technician in routine cases. The salary costs would be much lower.

However, it is precisely in those cases which are unpredictably non-routine, or when there are conflicting symptoms or more than one illness is present, that the presence of the doctor is most necessary. If the lesser trained computer operator relies too heavily on the machine (an inevitable result of training and experience below that of a physician) then patient care, on average, will drop. In the long run, the cost to society may very well exceed the short term cost reduction to the medical organizations.

Let me turn next to managerial employees. Especially at lower and middle levels, these jobs involve such tasks as monitoring work flow, gathering data, preparing reports, and occasionally making decisions for subordinates who lack authority to do so themselves. These are all tasks that lend themselves readily to computerization, especially with the addition of AI.

Computers are becoming indispensable tools for managers, but as the software become more sophisticated and the communications technologies continue to improve, the demand for human supervisors and middle managers will inevitably drop.

A similar situation exists in the treatment of some blue collar jobs. One can argue that the early approaches of NC technology in manufacturing were designed to try to incorporate into the machines the skills of machinists and other factory workers, analogous to the attempt to capture the essence of professional knowledge into an expert system. This often led to problems which have required the practical knowledge of living craftsmen to correct.

In each of these very different kinds of work – professional, managerial, and skilled craftsman – a major problem emerges that goes beyond even the concern for the effects on individual employees. There is a danger that a heavy and continuing reliance on expert systems may actually weaken an organization's ability to grow, to change, and to deal with new developments. This will be true especially in those organizations that seek to cut costs by using lesser trained personnel.

Expert systems, after all, are only programs. They cannot think or reason, or create. They are limited entirely by the assumptions of the programmers, the rules of the programs, and the specifics of the data base. Errors contained in any of these areas, or erroneous results generated by the proper application of erroneous procedures, or errors generated by missing data, can only be recognized by experts. If we develop a world where these systems are widespread (particularly in an attempt to become economically "more competitive"), then would we not also de discouraging innovation, as this would require expert knowledge applied to new problems? What would provide the training ground, and who would be trained, as the new "hands on" experts who would be needed to generate the next generation of software?

Let us move on for a moment to factory workers and clerical employees. They perform work of a different character than that described thus far. Many of the tasks are routine, with the worker having little control over the details of the work or the design of the job. AI might be used to help automate some of these jobs, thus removing human workers from repetitive and boring work. However, boring jobs are preferable to no jobs at all and, besides, designers ought to be thinking about how to use AI to enhance, rather than eliminate, such jobs.

Job security is a real concern for employees faced with the introduction of computerized systems in general. Indeed, if one looks at a longer flow of history, new technologies have had a major impact on employment patterns, particularly in the developed countries.

For example, workforce composition in the United States has shifted in the direction of an increasing proportion of white collar workers (professional and technical employees, clericals, managers, and sales workers), a decline in the fraction of blue collar workers (machine operators, craftsmen, laborers), and a decline in direct agricultural labor to only about three percent. White collar workers now account for well over half of all people working in that country (see Figure 1).

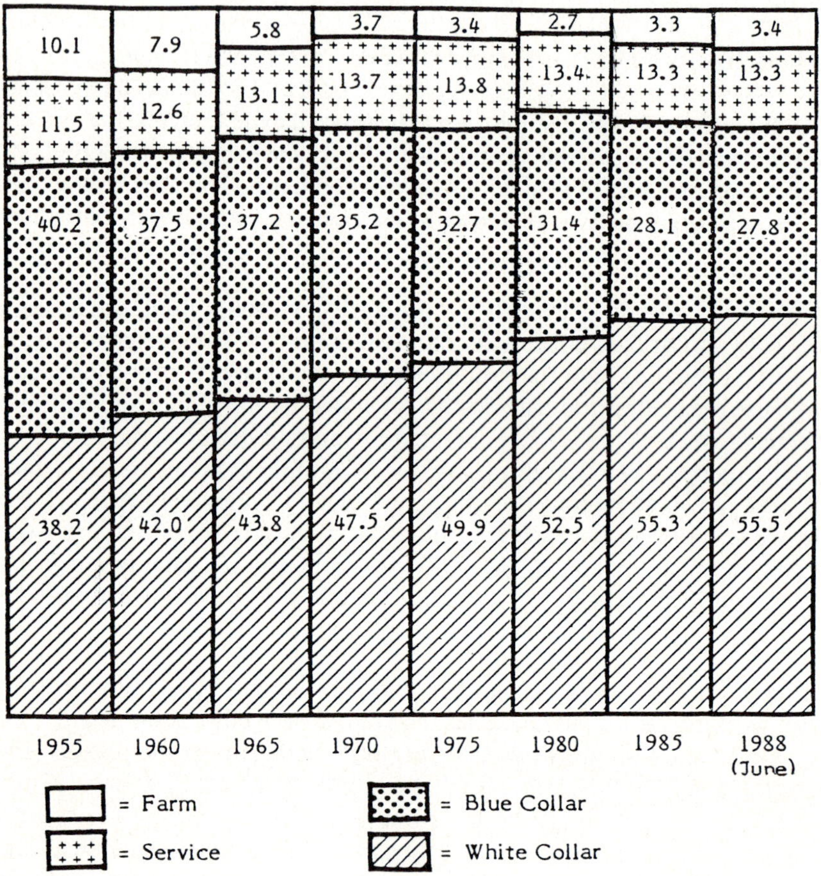

Figure 1 Composition of U.S. Workforce (in %)

Source:
Handbook of labor Statistics, The Employment Situation: September 1985, U.S. Department of Labor, Bureau of Labor Statistics, 85-416, October 4, 1985; Employment and Earnings, July 1988, U.S. Department of Labor, Bureau of Labor Statistics, Table A-22, p. 30.

Technology has been a major factor in this transformation. There are so few farm workers because agricultural enterprises have become more and more productive through the development of various kinds of machines, chemical fertilizers, new varieties of grains – and computer programs tailored to the needs of farmers.

Some have argued that the reduction in farmworkers was offset by growth in other areas of the economy relating to food processing and restaurants, for example. Indeed, restaurant employment soared as farmworkers declined. However, examination of the data in Figure 2 reveals that employment in all food related areas – direct agricultural work; food processing; wholesaling and retailing; restaurant jobs; hauling and delivery; and so forth – rose by only one-tenth while the population as a whole nearly tripled.

	1900		1982	
Total U.S. Population	76,000,000		213,500,000	
	Number (Millions)	% of Workforce	Number (Millions)	% of Workforce
Farm Workers	10,9	14,3	2,7	1,2
Nonfarm food related employees:				
– Food processing	0,1		1,6	
– Food wholesaling	0,3		0,8	
– Food retailing	0,4		2,5	
– Eating & drinking establ.	0,1		4,8	
Total nonfarm food related	0,9	1,2	9,7	4,2
Support activities (farm equipment, fertilizer, hauling, and delivery)	0,2	0,3	0,9	0,4
Total food related workforce	12,0	15,8	13,3	5,8

Figure 2 Employment in Food Related Industries

Source:
Adapted from Robert S. Levi, Manufacturing Productivity Frontiers, July 1984, p. 22.

Clearly, technological developments were having a negative effect on employment throughout this sector, first in drastically reducing direct agricultural labor, and then by increasing productivity in the other "downstream" and support industries.

During the late nineteenth and early twentieth centuries, manufacturing and construction were growth areas. However, in recent decades, while production levels and the value of finished goods have increased, employment in manufacturing has been fairly stagnant (see Figure 3). While one could argue that in recent years a flood of imported goods into the United States has kept employment levels lower than would otherwise be the case, over the longer period a key factor has been productivity increases aided by technological development, including more recently computers and chip-controlled machines.

Year*	All Employees	Production Workers
1960	16,883,000	12,659,000
1970	19,603,000	14,246,000
1980	20,146,000	14,047,000
1988	19,651,000	13,424,000

* = Data for June of each year.

Figure 3 U.S. Manufacturing Employment 1960 - 1988

Source:
Bureau of Labor Statistics, U.S. Department of Labor, Washington, D.C.

Much of the job growth in recent years has been in the service sector of the U.S. economy, and this will continue to be the trend for years to come. However, while the number of jobs has been increasing, the kinds of jobs have been changing.

There has been growth in the "contingent" workforce – part time, temporary, and leased employees – and this segment now accounts for one quarter of the American workforce. This is particularly serious in the U.S. because important fringe benefits such as health insurance and pensions are often tied to full time employment.

Furthermore, the U.S. Bureau of Labor Statistics forecasts that clerical jobs will increase to the year 2000 at a rate almost one half that for employment as a whole, and blue collar jobs will grow even more slowly ("A Look at Occupational Employment Trends to the Year 2000", G.T. Silvestri and J.M. Lukasiewicz, Monthly Labor Review, U.S. Department of Labor, Washington, D.C., September 1987, p. 46). Clearly, computer technologies and the work redesign they will permit will be major factors in slowing down job growth in these areas. The development and widespread introduction of sophisticated AI systems will undoubtedly have a retarding effect on managerial employment, as well, and may affect professional and para-professional employees, also.

Fortunately, these ominous trends are merely forecasts, and not predictions. The future is not predetermined. The structure of jobs and the level of employment in the year 2000 will depend upon decisions taken today, and every day until we reach that time.

How should current employees react to all of this, in particular, to ongoing developments in artificial intelligence? Several general points need to be discussed. The first, and perhaps most important, is the need to include employee representatives in the design of expert systems and their specific applications, at all levels within the organization. Specific employee concerns about job security, work pace and stress, challenge and variety, and possibilities for advancement all need to be dealt with explicitly. Potential problems may be avoided if employee representatives are active participants during the entire process, from design through implementation.

There is also the specific question of appropriate training. Ideally, expert systems should be designed so that the human operator is in control, or at least a partner rather than a passive follower. This necessitates the development of good training programs, both for current employees whose work will be changed, as well as for new employees who may have contact with the systems for the first time.

Even highly sophisticated specialists can sometimes be misled by computer output. The old adage, "Garbage In, Garbage Out", is just as true today as when it was first stated. The problems get magnified as the programs become more complex. Chances for error increase as AI programs make decisions rather than simply produce numbers or charts, particularly as the experience base of the user may be very limited.

In spite of this, or perhaps specifically because of it, there must be ways for employees at various levels to question the outcomes presented by AI systems. This is a difficult area, because the response to this problem involves both technical issues and questions of organizational design and power relationships. In part, this is a matter of training. The operators of the system, at whatever levels in the organization they work, need to be able to recognize that something is wrong. Again, this is a particularly serious problem for users who have inadequate "hands on" experience. Furthermore, after a problem is identified, the system operator must have a ready means for overriding the computer.

In this context, it is important to note explicitly that the vast bulk of people who will use expert systems in the future, including professional and managerial employees, will not be computer experts or programmers. Their training in the use of these new tools must include extensive discussion of the limitations of the systems, as well as their benefits. Ideally, no one should be permitted to use an expert system who does not also have training in the subject upon which the system is based.

A worst case scenario would have expert systems widely applied primarily to substitute cheaper, lesser skilled labor for more expensive, more highly trained and experienced experts. Such an approach can only lead do disaster in the long run, as all of the problems outlined above come to pass.

As the systems move beyond the exploratory and experimental stages, and become more widely used, they will have a profound effect upon the nature of the jobs of which they will be a part. This brings us right back to the comments made at the very beginning of this paper. There is no such thing as a "technological imperative". AI systems can be used to more narrowly control employees and strictly define their work, or they can be designed to support the human workers and expand the jobs to take better advantage of precisely those characteristics that make them human.

Artificial intelligence systems offer great promise. It is our responsibility to see that they fulfill that promise.

EXPERT SYSTEMS IN PRODUCTION AND SERVICES II
Th. Bernold and U. Hillenkamp (Editors)
Elsevier Science Publishers B.V., Amsterdam – Printed in The Netherlands

Prospect

Ulrich Hillenkamp
International Labour Office
Geneva, Switzerland

The project of the International Labour Office in Geneva on the impact of Expert Systems in production and services on qualifications of skilled workers and clerks is coming to an end in mid-1989.

The two international workshops, the results being published in this book and in its predecessor, Volume 1 (Bernold, Hillenkamp, 1988) contributed substantially to the research work. They were held on the basis of an intensive literature review, of numerous interviews carried out in the five countries of the study (Federal Republic of Germany, France, Japan, United Kingdom and United States of America) and of an evaluation of conferences and tutorials. Case studies and expert's opinions were used to study practical experiences on the shop floor and in offices to deal with important issues in more depth.

The main findings of the research project will be summarised in a report of the International Labour Office. This paper will become available during 1989. A draft of the report was presented to a small international group during the third and final workshop, March 1989. The group helped considerably in establishing the results.

Though much remains uncertain and speculative due to the early stage of the application and diffusion of this technology, statements can be made which might promote the commercial use of Expert Systems in a human centered way. It is likewise important to look at this technology in the context of the on-going rationalisation and automation of the industrial production and services procedures. There is a wide range of options and not yet a predetermination by technology. Expert Systems will probably be best suited to serve as job-aids and programmable working tools supporting but not replacing human experts, skilled workers and clerks in their daily work. They will influence many jobs but should rather reinforce than weaken the importance of a good general and vocational training of the workforce.

As the field is moving rapidly, the experiences made within the research project should be re-examined in the years to come when more Expert Systems have been applied on the shop-floor and in offices, so that the influence of this technology on industrial production and on office procedures can clearer be marked.

Reference

Bernold T., Hillenkamp U.(Editors), 1988, Expert Systems in Production and Services – Impact on Qualifications and Working Life, Elsevier Science Publishers B.V. (North Holland)